MW01029043

Creation Myths

A C. G. JUNG FOUNDATION BOOK

The C. G. Jung Foundation for Analytical Psychology is dedicated to helping men and women to grow in conscious awareness of the psychological realities in themselves and society, find healing and meaning in their lives and greater depth in their relationships, and to live in response to their discovered sense of purpose. It welcomes the public to attend its lectures, seminars, films, symposia, and workshops and offers a wide selection of books for sale through its bookstore. The Foundation also publishes *Quadrant,* a semiannual journal, and books on Analytical Psychology and related subjects. For information about Foundation programs or membership, please write to the C. G. Jung Foundation, 28 East 39th Street, New York, NY 10016.

CREATION MYTHS

REVISED EDITION

Marie-Louise von Franz

SHAMBHALA • *Boston & London* • *1995*

Shambhala Publications, Inc.
Horticultural Hall
300 Massachusetts Avenue
Boston, Massachusetts 02115

9 8 7 6 5 4 3 2 1

First Edition
Printed in the United States of America on acid-free paper ∞
Distributed in the United States by Random House, Inc.,
and in Canada by Random House of Canada Ltd

Library of Congress Cataloging-in-Publication Data

Franz, Marie-Luise von, 1915–
    Creation myths / Marie-Louise von Franz.—Rev. ed.
        p.   cm.
    Rev. ed. of: Patterns of creativity mirrored in creation myths.
    Includes index.
    ISBN 0-87773-528-X
    I. Franz, Marie-Luise von, 1915– Patterns of creativity mirrored
in creation myths. II. Title.
BL226.F73   1995
291.2′4—dc20   94-45173
                                                              CIP

Contents

Preface

The text in this volume derives from lectures presented at the C. G. Jung Institute, winter semester 1961–62, as transcribed by Una Thomas. Andrea Dykes prepared an index, which was revised for this edition by Austin Delaney.

For helping in the revision of this edition, I want to thank Dr. Vivenne Mackrell for her great support and Mrs. Allison Kappes, who did the comparison with the German edition and the typing. I also want to thank Kendra Crossen of Shambhala Publications for her patient cooperation.

My thanks also go to Princeton University Press for quotations from the *Collected Works* of C. G. Jung (Bollingen Series XX), translated by R. F. C. Hull and edited by H. Read, M. Fordham, G. Adler, and William McGuire, and for quotations from *Aurora Consurgens; A Document Attributed to Thomas Aquinas on the Problem of Opposites in Alchemy* by Marie-Louise von Franz, translated by R. F. C. Hull and A. S. B. Glover; to Pantheon Books of New York for quotations from Mircea Eliade's *The Myth of the Eternal Return* (Bollingen Series XLVI), 1954; to the Museum of Navajo Ceremonial Art of Santa Fe, New Mexico, for quotations from *Navajo Creation Myth* by Hasteen Khah as recorded by Mary C. Wheelwright; to John Murray of London for quotations from Sir Arthur Grimble's *A Pattern of Islands,* 1952; to H. Schuman of New York for quotations from Post

Wheeler's *The Sacred Scriptures of the Japanese,* 1952; and to Doubleday for quotations from Isobel Hutchinson's translation of *Festens Gave (The Eagle's Gift)* by Knud Rasmussen, 1932.

The Creation Myth

1

In this book I shall try to interpret motifs that occur frequently in creation myths. Creation myths are of a different class from other myths— hero myths or fairy tales, for instance—for when they are told there is always a certain *solemnity* that gives them a central importance; they convey a mood which implies that what is said will concern the basic patterns of existence, something more than is contained in other myths. Therefore, one may say that as far as the feeling and emotional mood which accompany them are concerned, creation myths are the deepest and most important of all myths. In many primitive religions the telling of the creation myth forms an essential teaching in the *ritual of initiation*. They are told to the young initiates as the most important part of the tribal tradition. In many other ways also, as we shall see later, they refer to the most basic problems of human life, for they are concerned with the ultimate meaning, not only of *our* existence, but of the existence of the whole cosmos.

Because the origin of nature and of human existence is a complete mystery to us, the unconscious has produced many models of this event. The same thing happens wherever the human mind touches the borders of the unknown. If, for example, you look at maps of antiquity, Greece is shown more or less in the center of the map, but on the borderline things become a bit distorted and unknown; the upper part of Yugoslavia tends toward the upper part of Italy, and then at the end of a known area there is simply a drawing of the uroboros, the snake which eats its own tail, which on old maps also represents the ocean. As decoration, at the corners of the maps, there are pictures of animals or monsters, or of the four winds. In the Middle Ages the area of the known world was always shown in the center surrounded by all-embracing symbols and sometimes even demonic figures: the four winds blowing toward the center, heads with blowing mouths, or something similar. These maps demonstrate *ad oculos* that wherever known reality stops, where we touch the unknown, there we project an archetypal image.

The same applies in the case of medieval astronomical charts. In the Middle Ages they drew all the constellations they knew, and outside them the cosmos was surrounded by the Zodiac snake, the snake on which were all the signs of the Zodiac; beyond that lay the unknown. There again the snake which bites its own tail, the uroboros motif, comes up where man reaches the end of his conscious knowledge. In late antiquity, the beginnings of chemistry show that people also had certain knowledge of the elements and some technical knowledge, but when it came to the end of known facts, they again projected this archetypal image, the symbol of the uroboros, to characterize the mystery of unknown matter. In alchemy it was the symbol of the *prima materia*, of the original matter of the world.

Most of the questions as to the origin and substance of our cosmos have not been resolved for us; in spite of the increase of technical instruments, unknown factors still remain. There are archetypal models and projections of modern science which I shall discuss later, but we are still confronted with completely puzzling facts and with contradictory theories. Other civilizations have not been less naive than we, for they too fell into this hole of the unknown, and when confronted with a mystery, they projected mythological symbols out of which, among other things, the creation myths arose.

In order to explain what projection means, I would like to call your attention to Jung's definition of projection. One sees again and again that projection has not been really understood, but always gives rise to all sorts of misinterpretation. Jung says in his definitions at the end of *Psychological Types:*

> Projection means the expulsion of a subjective content into an object; it is the opposite of *introjection*. Accordingly it is a process of *dissimilation* (v. *assimilation*), by which a subjective content becomes alienated from the subject and is, so to speak, embodied in the object. The subject gets rid of painful, incompatible contents by projecting them, as also of positive values which, for one reason or another—self-depreciation, for instance—are inaccessible to him. [Now comes the sentence which is important for us:] *Projection results from the archaic identity of subject and object, but is properly so called*

only when the need to dissolve the identity with the object has already arisen. This need arises when the identity becomes a disturbing factor, i.e., when the absence of the projected content is a hindrance to adaptation and its withdrawal into the subject has become desirable.[1]

We sometimes use the term *projection* in talking about primitive societies, saying that their myths and gods are projections of archetypal images. This leads to confusion, because in the society within which those Gods are still psychologically alive, the necessity has not yet arisen for the withdrawal of the projection. So there you really still have a state of archaic identity. It is only because *we* do not believe, say, in the Gods of the Shilluk of the Upper Nile that we may now speak of projection, but that is an indirect application of the term. We often clash with ethnologists, who say that it is not *only* a projection, that they have lived with such primitive people, and for them the Gods are a living reality, that you cannot just call them "only a projection." Such scientists have simply misunderstood how we use the word *projection*.

There is another reason why I would like to comment on this, but first I want to go on to the term *archaic identity,* which Jung uses and defines in the same book:

I use the term *identity* to denote a psychological conformity. It is always an unconscious phenomenon since a conscious conformity would necessarily involve a consciousness of two dissimilar things, and, consequently, a separation of subject and object, in which case the identity would already have been abolished. Psychological identity presupposes that it is unconscious. It is a characteristic of the primitive mentality and the real foundation of *participation mystique,* which is nothing but a relic of the original non-differentiation of subject and object, and hence of the primordial unconscious state. It is also a characteristic of the mental state of early infancy, and, finally, of the unconscious of the civilized adult, which, in so far as it has not become a content of consciousness, remains in a permanent state of identity with objects. . . . It is not an *equation,* but an *a priori likeness* which was never the object of consciousness.[2]

Thus we must assume that in relatively early stages of our development there was no difference between our unconscious psyche and the outer world; they were in a state of *complete equality,* that is, archaic identity. Then certain mysterious psychic processes, mutations, took place which disturbed the peace of this identity and forced us to withdraw certain representations and see that they were inner not outer facts. We then always replace the idea about the outer facts with a new "projection," of which we do not yet see its subjective aspect.

As you will see when we study several creation myths, it is sometimes revealed very clearly to us that they represent unconscious and preconscious processes which describe not the origin of our cosmos, but *the origin of man's conscious awareness of the world.* This means that before I become consciously aware of the world as a whole, or of a part of my surroundings, a lot happens in my unconscious. The preconscious processes that take place in a human being before this awareness befalls him can be observed in dreams and in unconscious material: as an analyst you can sometimes see a fortnight ahead, or even longer, that now a new form of consciousness is approaching, but the dreamer has not as yet any realization of it. It is like a annunciation of a process in consciousness which appears in the dream but has not yet taken place within reality. A fortnight later the dreamer will come and say: "Now I understand, now I have realized something," but you saw in the dream that this new understanding, this sudden realization, was prepared some time ago in preconscious processes. I give this now as an *a priori* statement but hope to demonstrate it in a convincing way when we look at the creation myths.

What we cannot any longer see is that such processes also should mirror the origin of our outer cosmic world. This is because the old identity has been disturbed and other new projections have been produced—projections which seem to *us* to represent "objective" scientific models of the outer world. These new models have pushed away the old ones, and thus we see the old ones as projections. If I may use a drawing, the process of projection is very much as in the diagram shown here.

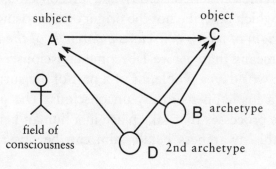

A, the human being or the ego in the center of his field of consciousness, looks at an object, he being the subject. When there is an original projection, it means that an archetype has been constellated in the unconscious, B. The subject stares at the object, C, and can make no sense of it, but wonders what the hell it is! Then he gets an idea and conceives of the object as being so-and-so, but he is not aware of the fact that the archetype, B, has been constellated in his unconscious and has conveyed to him the model of the idea from which he recognizes C; he sees only that the object coincides with his idea. This is what constitutes the cognition process as a whole.

Now, this mode of apperception is all right as long as it works. If, for instance, I say that Mr. X seems to me to be a genius, and if he continually behaves as if he were one and never does anything to contradict my opinion, then nobody will ever convince me that he is not a genius. But if one day he behaves like a complete idiot (that is the factor of the disturbance), then I will say: "Now, why and how did I ever get the idea that this man was a genius?" But only when there is a disturbance, a not-coinciding, do I begin to realize that something has happened which must have disturbed my idea. This is the case which Jung mentions: the projection does not fit anymore. For instance, I want to be convinced that an object is like this or that, but my idea does not fit; there are a lot of factors which, as one says in modern natural science, do not converge, there is no convergence of results. If in Edwin Hubble's idea of the expanding universe, some other results of atomic investigation do not coincide and you have no convergence of results, you begin to wonder if this is not just a speculative idea or, in our language, a projection of Hubble's. But as long as the results seem to converge in the same direction, as long as the object seems really to behave in accordance with my mental model, I have no reason to withdraw the projection. I will be naively convinced that I know the quality of the object itself.

So one reason for withdrawing a projection is that the idea of the object does not fit the facts, that something limps somewhere and does not coincide with the facts. The other, very frequent possibility is that another archetype (D) constellates: a second archetype pushes itself forward in the unconscious and puts another model, or idea, into the subject's mind, and another projection onto the object. The subject then jumps to this new idea, claiming that *this* is the truth and the former idea was an error, an illusion—a projection. Looking back, one calls it a projection, but as long as one is caught in it, as long as the archetype is validly constellated in one's unconscious and conscious, one will never call it a projection but will consider it to be true cognition. The subject then feels that he is talking about true facts as honestly as he can. This shifting of archetypes naturally generally coincides with outer changes in conditions so that certain theories do not fit them any longer. As long as we feel subjectively that we are not talking about projections but about the true quality of the object—a special aspect of our Western mentality—then we call it the scientific truth.

Easterners are so introverted that even when they

feel convinced, they yet have a certain doubt and are capable of putting a question mark against their "true convictions," but we are sure we are talking about the outer object so long as our projections seem to fit them. We are now under the domination of a new archetypal constellation which for the moment is working and with which all the objective qualities seem to fit. Where there is what Bavink called convergence of scientific results, where everything seems to fit into the picture and one cannot think of any facts which contradict the model we have in mind, this is, for the time being, our truth. Being less critical as a whole, and having only a fragmentary knowledge of outer facts, or only a partial knowledge compared to ours, the primitives have produced cosmogonic explanations of the origin of existence which to us are absolutely transparent projections. We have to keep this fact in mind, because we cannot understand these myths if we simply call them projections of preconscious processes without understanding "projection" accurately in the sense I have tried to describe.

Before trying to understand the creation myths, we have also to remember another fact, namely that *we cannot speak about any kind of reality except in its form as a content of our consciousness.* As Jung has pointed out, the only reality we can talk about is the reality of which we are aware.[3] If it is difficult for you to understand this, then imagine that you had a dream at night and do not recall it in the morning. If there was no observer proving that you dreamt, then the dream has no existence. You can *assume* that it existed, or that it did not, you can say anything you like arbitrarily about it, but, scientifically speaking, you cannot say that it existed or that it did not. All of this means that no factor which has not somewhere entered the field of conscious awareness of some human subject can be talked about as being real. The only facts we can talk about as real are those which have somehow, somewhere entered the field of awareness of a human being. All the rest is arbitrary speculation. Naturally in the morning one can *assume* one has had a dream and forgotten it, but it cannot be talked about as a *fact*.

In practical terms we may say, therefore, that the only reality we can talk about, or with which we are really concerned, is the *image* of reality in our field of consciousness. The spontaneous argument of the extravert, who is by temperament terribly object bound, will be to say, "Yes, but there *is* a reality, only we cannot talk about it." There we can only say that if he likes to assume it, he may, but it is a sheer subjective assumption. If you take a stand and say, "I believe that there is a reality beyond my field of consciousness," that is a belief which springs from certain temperamental needs, and if somebody else prefers not to believe it, you have no right to cut his head off. Therefore, if the Indians prefer to say that there is no reality beyond what enters the field of their consciousness, we have no right to say that they are fools. We can simply say that that does not suit our temperamental disposition, that we prefer to deal with things as if we believed there is a reality which is transcendent to our consciousness, though we cannot deal with it directly. Here we enter the field of metaphysical and religious beliefs and assumptions where everyone is free to make his own assumptions; but we have left the field of discussable scientific fact. It is therefore understandable that stories which are supposed to describe the origin of the real world are completely intertwined and mixed up with factors which we would rather call *stories of the preconscious processes about the origin of human consciousness.*[4]

Here we arrive at a further important question: how do these obviously vital mythical ideas of reality differ from wishful thinking? Most people would say, "It's all just a fairy tale." But this is inaccurate. If we observe ourselves psychologically over a longer period of time, we are soon able to differentiate and say "it" is thinking in us; that is, certain contents present themselves to us, and we act upon them because they make sense to us and because we feel better if we think in this manner. Despite the fact that we all know that the question of life after death, or of the origin and meaning of life, can never be answered rationally with any final certainty, according to Jung it is of tremendous importance, if not absolutely essential, that we try to form some idea about it. If a person has no myth about such questions, he is psychically dried up and impoverished and is likely to suffer from a neurosis. Jung, for example, suggested to all the elderly people around him to give thought to the question whether there is life after death and to the meaning death had for them. One of Jung's students asked him, "I am now seventy and you are eighty years old. Won't you tell me what your thoughts are on life after death?" Jung's answer was, "It won't help you when you are lying on your deathbed to recall, 'Jung said this or that.' You must have your own ideas about it. You have to have your own myth. To have your own myth means to have suffered and struggled with a question until an answer has come to you from the depths of your soul. That does not imply that this is the definitive truth, but rather that this truth which has come is relevant for oneself as one now is, and believing in this truth helps one to feel well."

So we see that there are myths which are of vital importance. We can say there exists a similar phenomenon on the physiological level. For example, all peoples of the world knew about the vital importance of salt. As is well known, people migrated and, in some circumstances, even gave away all their treasures and possessions for a handful of salt. Just twenty to thirty years ago it was not known why this was the case. Today, it is a well-known fact that salt plays a great role in human physiology. But this "it" in us, which was mentioned above, has always known this fact. In earlier times one explained the importance of salt mythologically. One searched for ideas to explain why it is so vital to man. All of this was based upon vital, instinctive knowledge. Myths, therefore, express vital, instinctive knowledge, and when one trusts in this knowledge, then one is healthy. This has nothing at all to do with wishful thinking or some kind of fantasy.

Up until the present day, there are still some primitive tribes left, even if they sadly number but a few, who strongly refuse to tell their secret myths to white people. They realize that these myths embody their own vital and life-saving knowledge. If a white person were to come in and interfere in a disrespectful and hurtful manner by saying, "I don't believe this. It is nothing but a fairy tale," he would seriously and deeply hurt the soul of these primitive people. One can only say that a person who has no myth or solid idea about the meaning of life, or simply believes what he reads in the newspapers, is neurotic and is to be pitied, for he is caught in believing in only ideological half-truths. We must bear in mind that when we try to interpret creation myths as projections of inner, psychological processes, then we are always doing so from the standpoint of a white mid-European population. This standpoint would be inappropriate if I were dealing with myths from the religious beliefs of Eskimos or some other ethnic group. With understanding for who they are, I would say, "Yes. I, too, believe that the world was created in this way," and it would not even be a lie of diplomacy, because for them the world was created in this manner, and this belief reflects their consciousness about the world.

Where do we see creation myths nowadays, or elements, or typical motifs of creation myths in our practical analytical work and in dreams? The most visible form of it can be observed in *schizophrenic material,* where a schizophrenic episode is often prepared by dreams of world destruction. In modern terms it is generally an atomic explosion, or the end of the world, the stars fall down—absolutely apocalyptic images; or one wakes up and everybody is dead, one's surroundings are going to pieces, the surface of the world splits open, and so on. This generally announces that the consciousness of this human being is in a state of explosion or is going to explode, and his reality awareness will soon disappear; his subjective world will actually go to pieces. But very often when a schizophrenic episode begins to fade, or to pass out of its acute phase, then in fantasies and dreams the motifs of creation myths come up and the world is re-created from a very small germ, just as it is in creation myths. Reality is rebuilt. From my practical experience, if you understand these rebuilding symbols, if you understand what is going on when such symbols come up after an episode, and as a therapist can support them adequately and join in with them and deal with them properly, you can sometimes help in the rebuilding of a new conscious personality that the return of the tide will not smash up again.

I remember a case where this took place, though it was not quite so bad; it was not a clinical schizophrenia. It was a borderline situation, a woman who, in complete animus possession, had smashed up her relationship with a man to whom she had a terrific transference. She was a walking animus and had nothing but her animus to live on. Complete destruction of her feminine personality had gone on for many years (a schizophrenic disposition), and she was within an ace of going off her head. A colleague who treated her with me proposed hospitalization, considering that she would either commit suicide or do something crazy, like murder the man who had seemingly disappointed her so badly. Before agreeing to it, I wanted to see her myself, and when I did, I realized at once that I could no longer make any contact. She stared past me with glaring eyes, and I could not reach her emotionally. I had the feeling she did not hear me, which was later confirmed when she told me that she had not heard a word of what I said. She was in such a state that her awareness, her consciousness, was completely gone. In my despair I finally said to her, "No dreams, no dreams in such a desperate situation?" She said: "Just a fragment: I saw an egg and a voice said, 'the mother and the daughter.'" I was as happy as could be and went off telling her all the creation myths and of how the world is reborn from a world egg. I said that this showed the germ of a new possibility of life and that all would come right, that we had only to wait until everything came out of the egg, and so on. I talked myself into a terrific enthusiasm, saying that "the mother and the daughter" naturally referred to the Eleusinian mysteries, and I told her about this and of the rebirth of the feminine world where the new consciousness would be a feminine consciousness, and so on. I saw that while I was talking she became quite quiet; finally I put my hand on her arm and said, "Do you feel any better?" She smiled at me for the first time and said she did. I asked her if she thought she could go to bed and not do anything silly, and she said, yes, she thought she could! And so it proved, and the difficult episode was bridged. Later she told me that she was in such a black hole and her consciousness was so far gone that she didn't understand a word of what I had said. She only realized that *I* understood her dream motif and understood it positively and so, on the way home, she said to herself, "Well, it *can* be understood, and it seems to be O.K." So you see I had understood what was going on. I couldn't convey it to her, her ego complex was already too far gone, but even the fact that she felt that somebody understood was sufficient to bridge an exceedingly dangerous situation. There you see how important it is to know about these preconscious archetypal processes.

I have had the experience that generally you cannot convey the meaning of such creation myths to people when they are right in the darkness, because the material describes processes which are very remote from consciousness. In contrast to other mythologies, the themes do not give you that intimate reaction of understanding something and being able to apply it to your own case, which you have when you listen to interpretations of fairy tales or hero myths, where you have an emotional and feeling bridge with the material. The motifs of creation myths seem weird and extremely abstract, and are therefore very difficult to bring up into consciousness. Because the meaning is so remote, when you try to convey it to other people, it is difficult to give them the feeling that they have understood.

What you can observe in borderline cases, namely the destruction of consciousness and of the awareness of reality and the rebuilding of a new consciousness, is only the extreme case, the exaggeration of something which you can also find in normal situations. You find creation myth motifs *whenever the unconscious is preparing a basically important progress in consciousness.* The psychological development of a human being seems to follow the pattern of the physical growth of children, who do not grow continuously but in fits and starts. The growth of consciousness also tends to make sudden jumps forward: there are periods where the field of awareness enlarges suddenly to a great extent. Whenever the enlargement of consciousness or the rebuilding of consciousness is very sudden, people speak of getting an "illumination" or revelation. When it is more continuous, they do not notice it so much and have only an agreeable feeling that they are growing, that they are moving in the flow of life and that life is interesting, but they do not have this feeling of sudden illumination or awakening. Whenever the progress of consciousness takes a big jump forward, there are preparatory dreams, generally with creation myth motifs in them.

Last but not least, one has to know the motifs of creation myths if one ever analyzes a *creative personality*. To analyze creative people is a great problem because often such people think they are neurotic or in a neurotic crisis, and show every sign of this, but when you look at their dream material, it shows that they are neurotic not because of a maladjustment to the outer or inner facts of life, but because they are haunted by a creative idea and should do something creative. They are haunted by a creative task; outwardly they behave exactly as other neurotic people do, and very often diagnose themselves as neurotic on account of it. Now, the difficulty is that you cannot make the invention for the other! Let us say that a physicist who should invent something comes to you; his unconscious wants that of him. You cannot do it for him! For one thing, you probably do not know enough about physics, and besides, it would then be your invention, and *invenere* means to step into something, to discover something new, and you cannot do that for another person. Thank God, for you would steal the most valuable experience of his life if you did. So you have to accompany the other on his painful way. He says, "Yes, but *what* have I to find out?" Well, I don't know either, but he has to find out something! But he says that if I can't tell him what it is, that does not help him. But you must have enough scientific material on hand to be able to show him that now a creative act is taking place, that a new world is about to be born, that something new wants to enter consciousness. There are certain preparatory processes which must be understood, because from them you can at least derive some indications as to the direction the invention will take and can spare your analysand a painful waste of time. You can serve him like a dog who sniffs and says, "Not there, not that track, but rather over there!" Thus you can circumscribe intuitively the direction in which his creative inner process is moving, so that he need not waste his time for years in chasing wrong tracks but can sooner come close to the original world-creating event which has constellated in his psyche.

This is tremendously important if you think how widespread is the belief that psychoanalysis, and Jungian analysis too, is destructive to the creative personality. A number of artists and creative scientists avoid contact with us because they believe that we, in a reductive analytical way, are going to destroy their creativity. Rilke said, when he was pressed to go in for a Freudian analysis, that he was afraid that by driving out his devils, his angels would be driven out as well, and therefore he refused analysis. I would say that this fear of the creative personality to go into analytical treatment, or to be interested in analysis, is justified to the extent that not enough analysts know about the creative process in the psyche and, misunderstanding it, use reductive neurosis-cure methods when they should rather take the attitude of supporting a new birth of consciousness. The creative personality, when weighed down and depressed by a creative task, *does* very often behave like an awful neurotic, in a maladjusted and impossible way. To correct a little, or to cut off neurotic behavior a little, and at the same time not to destroy the creative kernel of the process is a very delicate task. There it is very important to know the material so that one can recognize the processes. You will see that the creation myths will help us to find such material.

Sometimes you can say that the creative part is 80 percent of the problem, and readjustment 20 percent; sometimes it is the other way around. Some of it is always there, and that is one of the subtleties in analysis. It depends very much on the feeling relationship between analyst and analysand, for if there is too much countertransference, the analyst tends not to be sufficiently reductive, and if the analyst has a secret depreciation of the analysand, he might do him harm by being too reductive and thus destroy his creative possibilities. That is a very delicate situation in which one has sometimes also to rely on one's own dreams. It is like a gardener who has to make up his mind what he is going to weed out and what he is going to support in its growth. But one might have too strong a transference, of thinking that everybody's kernel of creativity is the main thing and whatever nonsense comes out is creative and therefore must be nurtured. An overmaternal analyst, who sits on a lot of phoenix eggs, hatches "phony" eggs!

On the other hand, I think the creative instinct is so strong that if the analyst tries to destroy it, the analysand will leave him and analysis. One cannot destroy it. If the analyst has made a wrong attempt to squash it, it causes ill-feeling and a hatred of psychology. It will create bitterness, but the dynamic strength of a creative disposition will never be suppressed. One can say that there are also human individuals who have no strong creativeness but have some minor amount of creative fantasy which could enlarge their horizon and make their life more meaningful, so why not let them live! Because, after all, one does feel better if one does not squash the impulse. If every time you want to play with something that is amusing, you think that it is childish, then you dry up. It is not a catastrophe, but I think it is a pity to squash minor creative impulses which could be quite an embellishment to life. Generally, thank God, the dreams get wild about it if one wrongly squashes something.

On reading Eliade, you will find that creation myths in many civilizations have been repeated under specific conditions. Cosmogonic myths and mythology, in India for instance, are used every time a new house is built. Eliade gives an example:

"The astrologer shows in what spot in the foundation is exactly above the head of the snake [that is a star constellation] that supports the world. The mason fashions a little wooden peg from the wood of the Khadira tree, and with a coconut drives the peg into the ground at this particular spot, in such a way as to peg the head of the snake securely down. . . . A foundation stone is placed above the peg. The cornerstone is thus situated exactly at the 'center of the world.' But the act of foundation at the same time repeats the cosmogonic act, for to 'secure' the snake's head, to drive the peg into it, is to imitate the primordial gesture of Soma (*Rgveda,* II, 12, 1) or of Indra when the latter 'smote the serpent in his lair' (VI, 17, 9). . . . The serpent symbolizes chaos, the formless and nonmanifested. Indra comes upon Vrtra (IV, 19, 3) undivided *(aparvan),* unawakened *(abudhyam). . . .*"5

At the moment one lays the foundation of a house, one (as it were) re-creates the whole world once again. In the early Middle Ages when the Vikings or the Anglo-Saxons first set foot in a new country, they built an altar and repeated the creation myth, meaning that this country had not formerly existed, and only now that they were there and it had entered their field of consciousness and they had set a conscious order in it, did they create it by coming into it and settling it. What it felt like to the conquered people was not considered. The same repetition of the creation myth is to be found also in many civilizations whenever a town is founded: every town which is founded repeats, so to speak, the cosmogony; a center is established which is the navel of the world and around which everything is concentrated, and the town is a new order, a new cosmos established from this center. So the creation myth is either partially enacted once more in ritual or solemnly retold. Another use of the creation myth, where it is still alive within a religion, is to retell it at every New Year festival. I mention the New Year festival not only in our sense of the word, but whenever a new year in any sense begins. Whenever this new time begins, then a creation myth is solemnly retold, which means that now the world begins again and therefore one has to bring back into one's consciousness everything which happened *in illo tempore,* as Eliade calls it.

Another situation in which the creation myth finds expression is among the Fijians. These islanders repeat it not only at each enthronement of a new king, but also whenever the crops are bad: "Each time that life is threatened and the cosmos, in their eyes, is exhausted and empty, the Fijians feel the need for a return *in principio;* in other words, they expect the regeneration of cosmic life not from its restoration but from its re-creation. Hence the essential importance, in rituals and myths, of anything which can signify the 'beginning,' the original, the primordial. . . ."[6] There you see confirmed what we can observe whenever a new conscious attitude, a new readjustment to reality from a very basic depth, is needed. If as a conqueror, for instance, you enter an unknown country, you are in a psychologically and physically dangerous situation; it is a tremendous risk, you have lost your roots, you are not adapted, and therefore you are threatened by physical death and psychological dissociation. Therefore in a new country the conqueror establishes a new cosmos. The New Year ceremonial shows that our conscious awareness of reality and our adjustment to it tends to fade, to become sloppy and a half-unconscious habit instead of a conscious effort, and it ages just as the king symbol ages, as the symbols of religion age. What was once perhaps in one's youth a fervent prayer, said with all one's heart, becomes a mechanical "blah-blah" in later time. This constant threat of relapse into repetition and mechanical continuation and of gliding off into unconsciousness, so that the feeling of aliveness fades out of it, has to be fought by this re-creation of the whole reality, by going back to the source of consciousness. The Fijians have a less mechanical way of doing the same thing—they don't do it only every New Year, but whenever they feel suddenly that there is an urgent threat to life. Whenever they are threatened by dissociation and panic and social disorder, they try to restore the creation and the whole cosmos by retelling the creation myth.

They create again, as it were, the conscious order of things and then await the corresponding effect upon their souls, which would mean that they once again feel themselves to be in order. For the aboriginal inhabitants of this area, this can go so far that, for example, when the rice crop is not growing well for some reason, then the medicine man will circle the field, citing all the while a creation myth of how rice came into being. Thereafter, it is as if the rice were able to say, "So now I know once again how I am to be," and it is able to grow again in ample quantity. This is, of course, a projection onto the rice which hardly has any influence upon it. But it makes a great impression upon *us*. When we know again the reason for which we were born, and what is, in fact, our task upon this earth, and when we know again what the real meaning of our lives is, then we can once more get on with living our lives. This is why Jung said that he had never treated a patient who was in the second half of life without arriving at the question as to the meaning of this person's life. It made no difference which everyday problem had led to the commencement of treatment; it always came down to this final question. For if one knows that one's life does have a meaning, then one is able to endure it. Man is able to endure almost anything provided that he sees some meaning in it.

Finally, we can still see that when the individual is threatened physically or by complete dissociation, as in the example I gave earlier, the creation myth is retold by the unconscious. The unconscious retells parts of the creation myth to restore conscious life and the conscious awareness of reality again. There will be one more element in this, namely the analogy of the creation myth to the symbolism of the process of individuation, which is seen most clearly in alchemical material; this I will mention later.

I shall discuss the creation myths as follows: First I will tell a myth that shows more clearly than others how creation is an awakening toward consciousness: where we can catch *in flagrante* how awakening toward consciousness is identical with the creation of the world. Then I will bring a few examples of the birth of the cosmos through *accidental action*. Third,

I will go on to the type where creation is represented as a *movement from above to below*—where spiritual beings in the Beyond create by coming down or throwing things down. Then I will turn to creation through a *movement from below to above,* such as we find in emergence myths, where everything comes out of a hole in the earth. Then I will take up the motif of the two creators, such as the *two animals,* or the *twin creators.* The motif of the *Deus faber,* the Godhead which manufactures the world, as in our biblical creation myth, will occupy us next. Afterward I shall take the motif of the *first victim.* Then I will briefly describe the *subjective moods of the creating Being:* for instance, creation by laughing, by fear, by crying, and all those creations through a feeling of longing, of yielding, and of love. Then I will discuss briefly a few of the *basic primordial motifs,* namely the *world egg,* the *primordial man* through whose decay the whole cosmos is built, the libido concept by a *creative fire,* a *mana,* a *world energy* from which everything springs. Then I shall briefly discuss why so many creation myths contain innumerable *chains of generations.* These are mostly in the Polynesian and Hawaiian creation myths, but also in the Japanese, and again in the Gnostic creation myths, where God produces twin pairs such as life and truth or Logos and Word, and so on, chains and chains of generations of either Gods or spirits or other beings, till reality is born. Then there is the motif of the particles, the *seeds of the world.* Then finally, the *subjective reproduction of creation in meditation* as practiced in alchemy, where making the philosopher's stone was looked on as reproducing the creation of the world on a subjective level.

A great problem in this book on creation myths is that they are the most basic myths in every civilization and therefore the essence of humanity; that does not mean that they are easy to understand. On the other hand, it seems to me that creation myths are not especially interesting in those languages in which I have a philological understanding, for example in Greek and in Latin. Many creation myths are very abstract and based on weird ideas and seemingly weird concepts. In order to lecture appropriately on them, one ought to know Hebrew, Sanskrit, Babylonian, Sumerian, and all the primitive languages as well. Of that I am not capable. Therefore I am forced to rely on translations. I have tried to get good ones, but cannot guarantee that every nuance and every word in each myth is completely appropriately translated. Because of this, I have planned to put my main emphasis and attention on certain similarities of motif and types of motif and not to go so much into the nuances of a single myth.

I am also fully aware that many readers might be shocked at reading such a hodgepodge of myth from different civilizations, some Greek and other highly differentiated varying cultural groups. I do not try to elucidate the cultural differences. Ethnologists and historians of religion are much better equipped to do that. The aim of my survey is to show that there are archetypal basic structures shining through the variety of motifs and that these structures among other functions are manifestations of the mystery of creativity in the unconscious human psyche. By trying to interpret some of the motifs, we reach this creative factor, which manifests itself symbolically. I will try to provide for the reader a tool for understanding creative processes in the depths of the human psyche.

The Cosmogonic Awakening

 I shall begin by taking up a myth that describes the creation of the world as an awakening to consciousness. This myth is reported by Knud Rasmussen in his book *The Eagle's Gift*, where he reproduces a collection of Eskimo myths. One myth is told by Apatac of the Noatak River, whom Rasmussen asked how the world was created. He answered:

> People do not like to think. They do not like to work with the things which are difficult to grasp, and that is perhaps the reason why we know so little about Heaven and Earth and the origin of men and animals. Perhaps, and perhaps not. It is very difficult to understand how we came into existence and where we go when we die. Darkness lies over the beginning and over the end. How could one know more about the most numinous which surrounds us and which keeps us alive, about that which we call air and Heaven and sea, and what we call the human and all his dwelling places and the animals and the fishes and the seas and the lakes? Nobody can know anything for sure about the beginning of life. But whoever opens his eyes and his ears and tries to remember what the old people said, *might fill the emptiness of his thought* by this or that knowledge. [There you see how the projection is really described—we fill the emptiness of our thought, we project into the gap.]

That is why we like to listen to those people who bring us information from the experience of dead generations, because all the old myths which our forefathers tell are what the dead people tell us. We can still talk to all the many people who were wise a long time ago, but we know so few like to listen. My grandmother knew a lot of surprising things about old facts, and from her I know what I am going to tell you now.

Heaven came into existence before the Earth, but it was not older because when it came into existence the Earth was also already forming. It had already a firm crust before there was any land and before there was also the first living being about whom we know anything. This being we called Tulungersaq, or Father Raven, because he created all life on earth and in human beings and is the origin of everything. He was not an ordinary bird but a holy life-power which was in everything which existed in this world in which we now live. [There you have the energy concept.] But he, too, began in the shape of a human being (so don't think of Father Raven as a raven, he only became a raven) and was groping in the dark, and all his deeds were completely casual until it became manifest to him who he was and what he should do.

He sat crouching in the darkness when he suddenly awoke to consciousness and discovered himself. He did not know where he was or how he had come into being, but he breathed and had life, he lived. Everything around him was in darkness and he could not see anything. With his hands he groped around, touching objects, and his fingers touched clay wherever he expanded them. The earth was clay and everything around him was dead clay. He let his fingers pass over the clay, and then he found his face and he felt that he had a nose and eyes and a mouth and also that he had arms and legs, as we have. He was a human being, a man. Above his forehead he felt a hard little knot but did not know why it was there, he had no idea that he would once become a raven and that this little knot would grow and become his beak. He sank into meditation. Now he suddenly understood that he was a free being, something independent which was not connected with all his surroundings. He crept over the clay, slowly and carefully. He wanted to find out where he was. Suddenly his hands met an empty space ahead of him and he knew he should not go further. Then he broke off a bit of the clay and threw it into the depths. He listened because he wanted to hear when it reached the bottom, but he heard nothing, so he moved away from the abyss and found a hard object which he buried in the clay. He did not know why he did this, but he did it, and then again sat in meditation and wondered what could be in all this deep darkness which surrounded him. Then he heard a whirring in the air and a very small, light creature alighted on his hand. With the other hand he touched it and felt that it had a beak and wings, and warm, soft feathers on its body and tiny little naked feet. It was a little sparrow, and he realised that this sparrow had been there before he had and had come towards him in the darkness and had hopped around him and that he had not noticed it before he touched it.

As this man liked social contact, he became bolder and crept more courageously over the earth and approached a place where he had buried something before and it had made roots and had become alive: a bush had grown and the earth was no longer sterile, for the naked clay was now covered with bushes; it also had grass. But the man still felt lonely, and so he formed from clay a figure which resembled his own and then he again sat crouching and waiting. As soon as the new human being became alive, it started to dig the earth with its hands. It had no peace, but restlessly, constantly dug in the earth around, and he discovered that this other human being had a different psychological makeup from himself, and that it had a hot, quick temper and a violent attitude. He did not like it and therefore took it and dragged it to the abyss and threw it in. This being, it is said, later became Tornaq, the evil spirit, from whom all the evil spirits on earth stem. Then the man crept back to the tree which he had planted, and behold there were other trees there, tree after tree. It had become a forest with rich soil, and plants had grown there. He touched them all with his hands and felt their form and smelt them, but he could not see them. So he felt impelled to know more about the earth which he had himself found and he crept around with the little sparrow which always flew over his head. He could not see it, but always heard its wings, and sometimes it alighted on his head or on his hand. But the man crept about because he did not dare to walk upright in the dark, and everywhere he found water and so discovered that he was on an island. Now he wanted to know what was below in the abyss, and he asked the little sparrow to go down and find out. At this the sparrow flew away and stayed away for a long time, and when it came back it said that far below in the abyss there was land, new land which had just started to crust over. The man decided to go down and asked the sparrow to sit on his knees. Then he found out how it was made, and he tried to discover how the sparrow could by its wings keep suspended in the air. He took twigs in the forest which looked like wings and put them on his shoulders, and the twigs were transformed into real wings, and he himself grew feathers which covered his body, and the knot in his forehead began to grow and form a beak. Now the man realised that he could fly like the little sparrow, and together they flew off. The man said: "Gowk! Gowk!" and he had become a big black bird and called himself Raven.

The land from which they came he called Heaven. It was as far as nowadays Heaven is from the Earth, so that when they arrived at the bottom they were completely exhausted. Here everything was deserted and sterile, and he again planted the land as he had done in Heaven and he flew about and called this new land Earth. Then, in order to populate the Earth, he created human beings. Some say he made them out of clay in the same way as he had made the first being in Heaven, but others say that he created man by chance, which would be even stranger than if he had created him by will power and intention.

Father Raven went about and planted herbs and flowers. He discovered some pods, and he looked at them and opened one, and a human being popped out of it—beautiful and completely grown, and the Raven was so bewildered that he threw his bird mask back, and through his bewilderment he became a human being again himself. He went laughing to the newborn man and said: "Who are you and where do you come from?" The man said: "I came out of this pod," and showed the hole from which he had come. "I did not want to lie there anymore, so I pushed with my feet against the hole and then sprang out." Then Father Raven laughed heartily and said: "Well, well, you are an odd creature! I never saw anything like you!" Then he laughed again and added: "I, myself, planted this pod, but I did not know what would come out of it. But the earth on which we are walking is not yet finished. Do you not feel how it shakes? We should go higher where the crust is harder." And so the first man came into being, and later Father Raven created all other beings.[7]

I shall skip the rest of the story, which tells how the bears and foxes and all the birds, and so forth, were made and how, always with the help of the little sparrow, Father Raven could take a step further. He teaches the human beings to build houses and kayaks, how to catch fish, and so on. One day an enormous black mass came out of the sea, and Father Raven helped the human beings to kill it—it was a sea monster. They cut it into bits, which they threw around, and from them came all the large islands. So, slowly, the earth grew and became a dwelling place for people and creatures.

The story ends by saying that when the earth had become what it should be, the Raven assembled all the human beings and said, "I am your Father and to me you owe the land you have and your being, and you must never forget me." Then he flew away from the Earth and up to Heaven where it was still dark, but he had picked up some fire stones on the earth and with these he created the stars. What he had left he threw out in Heaven, and from that there came a great fire which poured light over the Earth, and so Heaven and Earth were created. That is the way the Earth and human beings and all the animals we catch came into existence, but before them all was the Raven, and even before him there was the little sparrow.

This is a beautiful story which shows that the mood of the awakening to a realization of reality is something like coming out of an unconscious state. That is projected onto Father Raven, who, as it were, slowly

becomes conscious, and in the light of this consciousness reality simultaneously comes into existence.

There are a few motifs here which I will not go into
but will come back to in a later connection. One is
that of two original beings: Father Raven and the little sparrow. We will see later that this is a very widespread motif, namely that in the beginning there is
one relatively more active creator, a protagonist God
of creation; he has an accompanying shadow figure
who is passive and like the little sparrow, who is only
there but does practically nothing except exist, yet is
absolutely necessary as a counterpart. According to
this story, he is even older than the active protagonist.
We see here also the motif of the human form of the
first creative being, an anthropos figure whom you
will find is another very widespread archetypal motif
in creation myths. The creation begins in the shape of
man; only afterward do all the other forms appear.

In our myth we see the picture of an unconscious
creator, who creates the world in an in-between way,
by discovering it, by becoming conscious of it, and
partly by accidental actions like throwing down clay,
listening, and then planting a seed and later finding a
bush and then planting the pod. But, as he confesses,
he himself never knew what would come of it and was
absolutely astounded when a human being appeared.
He had not intended to create a human being. Yet this
creator is not as unconscious and animal-like as some
other creators of primitive myths, for it is said that
he sometimes sat back and sank into meditation. The
German word is that he sinks into "thought." That
means that every time he makes a step toward cre-

ation, he reflects and wonders about it. There is also a certain degree of planning, as when he wants to know what is in the abyss. He also tries to imitate the sparrow, who has wings, when he wants to get down into the abyss below.

This awakening toward consciousness is also to be found in the Winnebago creation myth published by Paul Radin. There, at the very beginning it is said: "In the beginning the Earth Maker [i.e., the creator, who is a parallel figure to Father Raven] was sitting in space when he came to consciousness and there was nothing elsewhere."[8] Here is the same motif that first there is a completely unconscious being, of human form, and his first step is the awakening to an awareness of the outer world. If this does not prove that the story of the origin of the world, and the origin of awareness of the world, are absolutely coinciding factors, I do not know what can prove it.

Creation by accidental action is a highly important fact when we try to arrive at an understanding of the creative process in the unconscious. You know that if you try to draw or paint, it often happens that, by mistake, you make a spot—the brush goes off on its own and there is a bad spot. Often, if you allow for such accidents, you will suddenly see a face in it, or you make a figure to cover up the spot, and so the picture changes. Such accidents are one of the most constellating factors in unconscious fantasy. In modern art they play a great role; certain artists even cultivate this form of creation where spots, holes, and objects found by accident at a certain moment are fitted into the picture. They try to get close to the creative process by picking up those accidental things which offer themselves. This is why when we let an analysand do active imagination and he is a painter, we generally advise him not to paint but to write, and if he is a writer then to paint, because where one is incapable and therefore helpless, and therefore unconscious, it is much more likely that such accidents happen. If you cannot paint, it happens that the unconscious constellates much more in the act of painting, while if you know a craft, you are too skillful and therefore are able to exclude such disturbing accidental interferences of the unconscious; you know how to handle the brush and can prevent the spot, but if you are helpless you become unhappy when you have made a blob in painting and you get an affect, for you have worked three hours and the wretched thing has now got smudged, so you fall into an affect and then the unconscious shows itself! You suddenly have a fantasy about the spot which tells you something, like a Rorschach spot; then it is really a picture that comes from the unconscious; you feel it is something spontaneous that appeared just when you got angry and wanted to tear up the whole thing. It helps, therefore, to get into the mood of Father Raven, of groping in the dark and feeling lost; then the creative process of the unconscious is constellated. This is why it is important in active imagination to use a medium in which you are not skilled, where you have no technique by which you can exclude the interference of the unconscious.

In the history of the inventions of civilization there are many which were discovered by accident, through someone playing with an object and then suddenly getting an idea. Schiller even says that man is at his highest level only when he plays, when he has no conscious purpose. Creativity through play is such a well-known and essential factor that one does not need to point it out, but we see again and again that if we try to induce our analysands to do active imagination, all the skeptical rationalism pops out—that it is a waste of time, that one cannot do it, that one does not know how to draw, that one has no time today, or tomorrow, that one is not inspired—and whatever other blocking resistances of consciousness there may be. But every new beginning of consciousness, every essential process of consciousness, must first arise from such a state; only then is the human being open-minded enough to let the new element in and let things happen. Many creative people start their creativity with terrific depression. They have such a well-constructed and strong ego consciousness that the unconscious must use very strong means—send them a hellish depression—before they can loosen up enough to let things happen. I have noticed that people who tend to have those creative depressions, if they can anticipate them by playing, need not have the depression, and whenever one can induce a person in such a heavy depression to start playing in some way, the state of depression is lifted at once, for the secret final intention of that kind of depression is, as the word says, to depress, to lower the level of consciousness so that these processes can come into action. So this darkness, this nigredo in which the highest divine Being of this Eskimo tale sits, is a symbol for something that occurs again and again wherever an essential creative impulse of consciousness appears.

Creation from Above, Creation from Below

3

 I want now to proceed to the next important motif, creation from above downward, and from below upward. In the example I shall quote in some detail, both motifs occur in the same story. I intend always to give one creation myth in more detail, as representing a whole type of myth, and the others only in part, because I think we will get a better feeling of the myth this way than if I race through a number of single motifs. The one I am going to tell is taken from the Iroquois tribe of the North American Indians.[9]

According to this myth there were on the "other" side of heaven, which is turned away from us, beings who were called Ongwe. In the notes it is said that the word *Ongwe* means man-being and stands for the *images* of all things which later existed on earth, i.e., an image of the houses, an image of the trees, and of all the animals.[10] These archetypes—I cannot avoid the expression—of all earthly things were called the Ongwe, and they lived on that side of the heavens which is turned away from us. Heaven was seen as a kind of cupola over our earth, beyond which the

Ongwe lived. We shall see later that some of these Ongwe are identified with constellations of the fixed stars. They lived in houses, the same as those in which the Iroquois lived. Generally they went hunting in the morning and in the evening returned home. So the Ongwe really lived a life similar to that which the Iroquois lived later.

> In one place there were two Ongwe, a man and a woman, people of high rank who lived a very religious, retired life. One day the woman went over to the place where the man lived. She had a comb, and she told him to get up, as she wanted to comb his hair. He got up and she combed his hair. The same thing happened every day. But soon the woman's relatives began to whisper together because she was changed, and from day to day it became clearer that she was going to have a child. Her old mother noticed it and asked what man she had slept with, but the girl did not answer. At the same time the man fell ill and the old mother went to him and asked him if he felt ill. He answered: "Oh, Mother, I have to tell you that I am going to die." The mother said: "To die! What does that mean?" For those people who lived in heaven did not know what dying meant; so far none of the Ongwe had ever died. The man continued: "When I die, the following things will happen: life will leave my body, which will turn completely cold. Oh, Mother, then you must do the following: you must touch me with your hands on both my sides, and you must look fixedly at me when you see that I am dying. When you see that my breath is getting weaker and weaker you will know that I am dying, and then you must put your hands on my eyes. I will tell you something more: you must make a coffin and put my body into it as for a tomb, and then place the

coffin on a high place." The woman did as she was told and everything happened as predicted. They put him in a coffin and placed that on a high place. Then the old woman asked the young woman again who was the father of her child, but again she got no answer.

The child, a girl, was born and developed quickly and was soon running about. But then she started crying, nobody knew why, and she cried for five days. The grandmother then said that they should show her the coffin, and they took the child and lifted her up. When she saw her father's corpse she stopped crying, but as soon as they put her down she cried again. That happened for days, and they always had to bring her back to see the dead man. One day the child brought back a ring which the dead man had worn and they scolded her and asked her why she had taken the ring. The child said that the man had told her to take it because he was truly her father, and after that nobody said any more about it. After a time the father called to the girl from his coffin and said that now the time had come for her to marry and that she should get up very early the next morning and go to a very faraway place he would show her, where she would find a chief of good repute whose name was Hoohwengdschiawoogi, which means "He who holds up the Earth," and he was the man she should marry.

So the girl got ready and left the next morning [I will skip the details of the journey about which her dead father had told her], but she has to cross a river where there is a dragon and the dragon is the Milky Way. She has to pass a lot of dangerous constellations as well as to withstand the attacks of the storm dragon and other dangers. Finally she arrives at this chief's hut, beside which there is an Onodscha tree whose flowers emanate light, the light which we see on earth and which also gave light to the Ongwe. She goes into the hut, puts down her basket, and says: "You and I are going to marry." The chief makes no reply but spreads out a carpet on which she may lie down and tells her she can stay there the whole night. The next morning he tells her to get up and work, as was usual for a woman. She is to cook maize, but while doing this she suffers great pain because he has ordered her to be naked while cooking it, and her body is burnt by the hot maize mash which spurts. But she grits her teeth and stands the pain. Each time, after she has gone through this suffering, he heals her body with oil. They are together two more nights. On the fourth day the chief tells her she can go back home; he just sends her away again and tells her he will send her the maize as a reward for what she has done.

So the woman goes back the dangerous way she came [I am again omitting some of the details of the journey], but when she gets back to her parents she is homesick for her husband and returns to him. She makes this journey three times. The chief is very much surprised to see her again, but he notices one day that she is pregnant. Day by day and night after night he thinks about this and cannot understand how she became pregnant, since he has never touched her physically. He is astonished. He thinks it must have happened by their breath uniting when they talked to each other. But it is quite obvious that she will give life to a child. The chief gets upset and asks her who can have made her pregnant, but she does not understand. Then this chief who "holds up the earth" becomes very ill and feels that he is going to die. He tells his wife that it is now quite certain that an Ongwe girl will be born and says that she should feed and nurse this girl who will grow up and must be called Gaengsdesok—"Warm Whirling Wind." The wife does not understand what he tells her, but after a time gives birth to a girl, and after ten days she takes her away. Slowly the chief's suffering gets worse and worse. So he says that the tree Onodscha, the tree of light which stands beside his hut, must be pulled up by the roots; then the earth [which is really the cupola of the heavens] will have a hole in it, and beside that hole he is to be placed with his wife sitting near him. This is done, and as soon as the woman sits near the hole with him, he says that they should look down together and that she should take Gaengsdesok on her back and wrap her up carefully in her clothes. He gives her some food and tells her to sit beside him with her legs hanging down through the hole. He tells her to look down, and while she is looking down he catches hold of her and pushes her down the hole. As soon as she starts to fall through the hole, the chief gets up and feels much better. He says that now he is again the Old One, that he feels all right again, and that the tree Onodscha should be erected again. He was jealous of the Northern Lights and the Fire Dragon with his white body—one of the dragons she had walked past; that was why he had become ill, for he had thought that perhaps one of them was the father of the child, and because of his jealousy he had pushed her through the hole.

The woman who had been pushed through the hole in heaven sinks down through the deep darkness. Everything around her is a dark blue color; she can see nothing and does not know what will happen to her as she sinks further and further down. Sometimes she sees something but does not know what it is. It is the surface of a great water with a lot of water birds swimming about on it. One of the birds suddenly calls out and says that a human being, a woman, is coming up out of the water—he is looking into the water and sees the mirage—but another bird says that she is not coming up out of the water but falling down from heaven. [There you see the two movements.] The birds consult together as to what they can do to save the woman. They all fly up together, and when they reach the woman, they take her on their backs and slowly come down with her. Meanwhile a big tortoise comes up to the surface of the water, and the birds deposit her on its big back. Then [and this is a famous motif which is to be found in many North American creation myths] a number of birds try to dive for earth, and in the end one of them succeeds in bringing some up. They spread it on the back of the tortoise, and when they do this, the earth remains there and spreads and becomes the whole earthy surface of our world.

In the meantime the woman again becomes pregnant because [and this is just remarked in an aside, but you should remember it] during the fall the child has reentered her womb. The birth which had already taken place in heaven becomes regressive, as it were; when the woman arrives on the back of the tortoise on earth, she is again pregnant with the girl and again gives birth to Warm Whirling Wind. The mother and daughter then stay together, and the girl grows up amazingly quickly. Again this girl finds an unknown man. The same theme repeats three times. In a mysterious way, she becomes pregnant. Her husband is a man who looks like an Indian; he has an arrow and later it is said that he is the spirit of the big tortoise on earth. The girl then gives birth to twins, one a positive savior type of twin who creates the world and mankind, and one a negative, devilish being who creates all the destructive things such as mosquitoes and bad animals [i.e., the unpleasant aspects of creation. As we have another chapter reserved for the twin motif, I do not wish to give this in detail now; it is rather bewildering].

According to certain commentators, the first pregnancy of the first Ongwe woman comes from the fact that she combed her husband's hair and probably, the commentator thinks, swallowed one of the lice. We know that among some primitives it is a friendly gesture to comb each other's hair, and some not only crush the lice between their nails but eat them. It is a famous mythological motif that a supernatural pregnancy can come through fleas or other such insects. The louse in symbolism usually carries the meaning of a completely autonomous thought; something that sticks in your mind, though you don't want it, and sucks your blood. It is a beautiful symbol for thought obsession: an idea that stays in your mind, obsesses all your other thoughts, and at the same time sucks your blood, takes away your psychic energy.

I was very much impressed to find how alive this louse symbolism is when in America I visited one of the big institutions near San Francisco, the Napa Valley State Hospital. One of the doctors introduced me to a Polish woman of very simple origins who, according to his diagnosis, was schizophrenic. She was a very communicative type who lived in a delusionary state which she seemed rather to enjoy. She worked in the hospital and was not unhappy in her delusions. When the doctor asked her to tell me some of her ideas about the system of the world, she poured out a quantity of mythological material: that she had seen God, what he looked like, how the world had been created, and so on. And then in the middle of a long story she said that on the moon all the Indians and crazy people lived—the "lunatics"—and the people who went crazy were those who constantly forgot to pick the lice from their heads, those who did not crush the lice on their heads! There you can still see the original symbolism in a beautiful illustration, for those who do not criticize and continually fight obsessional ideas—pick their lice and say, "Now, what is that? What am I thinking? Is that true?"—are those who go to the moon, to the lunatics and the Indians; they regress to a primitive state. I was impressed to find the symbolism of the louse in this modern form.

In many mythologies, divinities or earth demons steal human beings in order to catch their lice. There is the famous motif in Eskimo mythology of the Goddess Sedna, who lives under the sea and is responsible for attending to all the sea creatures, the seals, whales, and fishes, for the Eskimos. But when there are no seals or other creatures to catch, it is a sign that Sedna's head is full of lice and dirt. When this happens, a shaman has to dive under the sea and meet Sedna, who would then be in a very bad mood, and therefore very dangerous to approach, for she would try to kill anybody who did so. The shaman has to go to her and comb her hair and clean her head and catch the lice on it, after which she will thank him very warmly and will again send up the animals to the Eskimos. This must be done every now and again. There is a constant growth of autonomous contents in the unconscious, which can become destructive if man does not concern himself with them.

I am dwelling on this motif because it is a variation on the motif that creation begins by a completely accidental little event—a woman combs her husband's hair and perhaps has eaten a louse. It is even a conjecture, and not contained in the text, but from it comes a chain of events which to me seem extremely meaningful: this tiny little beginning points to the phenomenon of an autonomous thought coming up somewhere in the unconscious and later having enormous consequences.

The motif of the father falling ill as soon as the mother becomes pregnant is repeated twice. In the first case he dies and in the second would have died if he had not pushed his wife down onto the earth. The motif of "the first being to die" will come into some other cosmogonies. I just want now to point it out; we will deal with it later in connection with the twin motif and the idea that if one thing comes into reality, something else has to disappear beyond the threshold to the other side. One could say that in the unconscious everything is and is not. When it becomes conscious, it "is," and therefore the aspect "it is not" also becomes manifest. One could also say that in the unconscious everything is everything, there is complete contamination of contents, but as soon as a content comes over the threshold of consciousness, it becomes definite and therefore detaches itself from its surroundings; that it goes back and is dead, or becomes the shadow aspect of the thing. That creation is essentially connected with something dying or being destroyed will come up in many other tales. I want first to give a survey of different variations of the same motif before we go more closely into its interpretation. In this story I am mainly keeping to the motif of falling downward from above and the mirror image of the woman coming upward.

On the motif of the Ongwe, namely that in heaven there once were all the archetypal images of those things which later came into being on earth, there is not much to say. From the Jungian standpoint, it is a confirmation of what we have discovered from a completely different angle, namely of the archetypes. The Ongwe one could call the archetypal images in the collective unconscious. There was a similar motif in our first creation myth. Father Raven first creates everything in heaven and then flies down into the abyss and re-creates everything in the same way on earth; everything is created first in heaven and a replica is created afterward on earth. This is not confined to the North American Indian and Alaskan primitives, but is to be found everywhere, and I would refer to a collection of such motifs in Eliade's *The Myth of the Eternal Return*. He says in his section "Celestial Archetypes of Territories, Temples and Cities":

> According to Mesopotamian beliefs, the Tigris has its model in the star Anunit and the Euphrates in the star of the Swallow. A Sumerian text tells of the "place of the creation of the gods," where "the [divinity of] the flocks and grains" is to be found. For the Ural-Altaic peoples the mountains, in the same way, have an ideal prototype in the sky. In Egypt, places and homes were named after the celestial "fields": first the celestial fields were known, then they were identified in terrestial geography.
>
> In Iranian cosmology of the Zarvanitic tradition, "every terrestrial phenomenon, whether abstract or con-

crete, corresponds to a celestial, transcendent invisible
term, to an 'idea' in the Platonic sense. Each thing, each
notion presents itself under a double aspect: that of
mēnōk and that of *gētīk*. There is a visible sky: hence
there is also a *mēnōk* sky which is invisible. . . ."[11]

There are hosts of similar examples where one can
see that this idea of everything having a replica, or
rather a model image in the sky, is to be found in
many civilizations and, last but not least, also in Platonic philosophy, though there it has become slightly
abstract. More primitive beliefs, of civilizations that
have progressed less in a collective conscious tradition, have the same notion, but then the model images
are not in the sky but on earth. For instance, the
Naskapi Indians, a very primitive tribe who live on
the Labrador peninsula, and some African tribes say
that every species of animal has one doctor-king animal which is responsible for the life of all the others.
Let us say among the wapiti—there are hundreds and
thousands of them in the woods—there is one ghost,
or super-wapiti which you must never kill or hurt or
annoy. You cannot really kill it, but if you shoot at
this super-wapiti, this "idea" wapiti, then all the others will disappear from the woods and not one will be
found; he is responsible for the fact that there are wa-
pitis and is the one principle behind the manifoldness
of the others. Therefore a hunter who meets this archetypal animal must show it due respect and never
hurt or try to shoot or kill it because by doing so he
will destroy all his chances in hunting. This is the
same idea as in the cosmogonies, but the archetypal
animal here, this super-wapiti, lives here on earth

among the others and not away in the sky. There one can see what we would today describe as the collective unconscious and the psychic processes still completely intertwined with outer reality, so much so that they exist in the same sphere.

In the Ongwe myth there is a more developed state of affairs: the idea of the archetypal tree and the archetypal animal and so on are not here on earth but live somewhere beyond Heaven. This corresponds to an experience which occurs over and over again. I stumbled across it in my own life four years ago when I built a holiday resort, a little house to which I gave a rather symbolic shape. Naturally, as building is a very exciting business, I got completely lost in it and was daily covered with cement dust. I watched every step of the building with great delight and apparently, according to the unconscious, I got a bit too carried away because I had a dream that there was an exact replica of the house I was building in the Beyond and I should not forget about that. I was much impressed by this and told Jung, who roared with laughter and said, "Isn't that funny, I had the same experience!" He had never told me of that before, I had my dream quite independently, but then he told me that when he built his tower in Bollingen—which is very symbolic, he began it on a mandala scheme—he too had a dream that in the Beyond there was that same Bollingen, a replica of it, and he got the feeling that one should not forget if one did something creative in reality that it was only the replica, the second model, of something whose reality was in the Beyond and remained there. That is only four years ago, but since then I have had three more dreams in which I dreamt about such a Beyond house which appears exactly the same but has a kind of magical atmosphere. Every time I dream about it in the Beyond, a very essential and important event always happens there. Here you see a modern example; one can imagine how such beliefs probably originated, because if I wished to make a belief from my dream, I would know now that my house is only a replica of an Ongwe house in the Beyond, which I have felt the urge to repeat here on earth. Completely autonomously this idea has come up again, and probably such dream experiences have also induced the Indians to build up such a tradition. The Beyond house of which I dreamt was naturally eternal, a house that could not be destroyed by fire or water, where one can dwell after one's death; the house here will naturally suffer the fate which befalls every house on earth.

Creation is a sudden autonomous event which, from a psychological angle, we could say takes place in the collective unconscious for no outer reason. Here you can see, in a projected mythological form, a confirmation of the Jungian hypothesis of the autonomous creativity of the unconscious. In the Freudian view the unconscious is only—put rather crudely—a dustbin into which the cast-away contents of consciousness and personal experience are repressed or suppressed, with also some archaic remnants, though these are rather vague in the Freudian definition. But if anything happens in a dream there is always a tendency to trace it back to some outer concrete event, either to a childhood trauma or a conscious representation, or some other outer events. Jung, however, by watching his cases, came more and more to the conclusion that the unconscious is not only a response system, a reactive system which reacts to outer situations, such as conscious thoughts or conscious representations, but that it can, of itself, and for no outer or biographical reason, produce something new. In other words, it is creative in the essential sense of the word. This means that you can, for instance, live an uneventful life where everything seems all right, but suddenly something starts in your unconscious and you get one upsetting dream after another and slowly you get the feeling that something has been stirred up underneath, you don't know why. This movement slowly comes up to consciousness, either as a demand for a change of attitude or a widening of consciousness or as a creative impulse. Naturally, you can still conclude that there must have been some necessity for compensation. We do not know, for instance, if the Iroquois in the moment when this cosmogonic myth appeared were not in a specific situation which demanded the compensation supplied by this myth. One could say that it must be a reaction to some situation, but we cannot trace it; we must stick to the fact that the myth points out that something happens autonomously in the unconscious, of itself and for no further reason. There are many creation myths where it happens that suddenly a God feels lonely and wants a partner, or suddenly Father Raven awakens to consciousness, or a woman becomes pregnant among the archetypal beings, after which a long chain of reactions in the creative process begins. I am personally inclined to believe that we do not always have to look for outer reasons, but that actually the human unconscious psyche is capable of a *creatio ex nihilo;* the unconscious can suddenly produce a new impulse, and we cannot explain it as a reaction to anything—except perhaps to boredom! If everything is peaceful there is perhaps a slight accumulation, an amassing of energy somewhere, which falls back into the unconscious and produces such a reaction. But against this theory is the fact that I have often seen people haunted by a new creative impulse just at a moment when they were exceedingly exhausted and occupied in outward life, and not at all bored but had a reaction of: "My God, now! Just now! I don't want to do anything creative just now! I can't, there is so much else to do!" So it does not seem to me that a saving of energy in the outer world could account for such a fact; it is more as if there is really a *spiritus creator* in the unconscious which manifests in this form and stirs up new possibilities.

If we look at the "geography" in this Iroquoian myth, we have first the Heaven where the Ongwe live with the tree. Then the chief makes a hole in it, and the woman falls down. Below is a water surface, though how that came into being nobody knows, and there the water birds are swimming about, which also already existed; they appear to be coeternal with the Ongwe. On the surface of the water is the tortoise. The woman lands on it and on its back the world slowly expands: first the birds fish up the earth, and then growth begins by itself until slowly there is the surface of the earth swimming on the ocean with the tortoise as its supporting center. The woman lands and gives birth to her child, and from then on earthly events continue to come into existence.

ONGWE HEAVEN
hole
woman falling
tortoise
reflection of woman

One of the most interesting facts in this story is the small detail of the birds seeing the reflection of the falling woman; one bird calls out that a woman is coming down from heaven, while the other bird, looking at the surface of the water, says that she is coming up from below. They see it in a mirrored image, as though she came from above and below. The mirage motif would not be so important if we did not know that in some other creation myths the whole process of creation starts under the earth and is a slow process of coming up to the surface.

The type of creation myth where the whole process begins below and slowly moves upward can be found in one of its most detailed accounts in *The Navajo Creation Myth* by Mary Wheelwright, with the subtitle "The Story of Emergence." I am not going to give all the details, for the text is laden with Indian names with very difficult definitions. It is a typically primitive myth, very complicated and subtle with a lot of figures and nuances in it, but for our purposes this makes it rather difficult to report. It starts with the story of the emergence. There are different worlds which emerge one from another. The first world is the lowest.

> The story starts in the Running-Pitch Place or Jahdo-konth-Hashjeshjin. The son of the Fire, whose mother is a Comet, and Etsay-Hasteen, the first man, who is the son of Night and whose father is Nah-doklizh, which is the blue above the place where the Sun has set, were there, also Estsa-assun, the first woman, and so on. Her name has to do with the Daybreak. The earth-God is Begochiddy; he is the real creator God. He is the great God whose mother is a Ray of Sunlight and whose father is the Daylight. This earth God "built in the east a white mountain, in the south a blue mountain" and so on. First he creates below, under the earth, a sort of cosmos which is surrounded by four mountains in the four directions of the horizon. He also creates four types of ants and some bugs. In the East mountain he plants some bamboo and other things. Then, after some time, when the bamboo has grown upward, they all climbed out on it; and "Begochiddy pulled the bamboo up into the second world and Hashjeshjin blew into the hole four times which made the hole close up and the first world burned up and is still burning." This first world, created near the center of the earth, was only a temporary world and all its inhabitants, animals and gods, climbed up out of it and destroyed it after them.

The fire world underground accounts for present-day volcanoes.

Now these first beings come into the second world: "Begochiddy took the earth brought from the first world and created mountains in the East, South, West and North, and plants similar to those in the first world, and he planted white cotton in the East, blue cotton in the South" and so on. [I am again skipping much because I am only following a certain line.] Then they climb up into the third world, and there again six gods create all living things. Then they come to the fourth world; there the locust comes up through the crust which covered the third world into the fourth world which is covered with water. With the help of the locust, the people come up and settle in the fourth world.[12]

Afterward in a long, complicated process the tribal organization and tribal ceremonies take place. In Navajo sand painting the center of the painting—the center of the mandala—is always the spot that stands for this place of creation. In all the sand paintings made by the medicine man for healing sickness, the center is the place of emergence; it is where creation took place and where all those worlds came up in four steps.

Among the Hopi Indians there is a similar myth.[13] In the time of origins, people lived far under the earth. They had certain reasons for coming up—there were too many of them, they were too crowded and quarreled too much—so some of the chiefs thought something must be done. By sending birds to explore, they managed to discover an upper world. They climbed up on a fir tree, in contrast to the bamboo of the Navajos, and reached another layer. After a time they had the same trouble in the second world; the situation becomes intolerable and they have to go up another step. This continues until they reach the present surface of the earth.

Probably those myths are influenced by each other because the tribes had certain connections with each other. In the Hopi myth, there is a minor motif of the descent which is important: it is said at the end of the report that they reached the place where the sun rises before the other tribes came up and that as soon as the first group of people reached the present-day surface of the earth, a number of stars fell from heaven. "Ah!" said the people who were just emerging, "somebody is already here," and they settled where they were. Here the main movement is represented as a coming up in steps, but at the end when they reach the surface the stars fall down, so that the counter-movement is also contained in the myth, but only as a side motif, in the image of the falling stars.

In the Navajo creation myth the Gods who were in the first world at the beginning of creation were divine beings whose names all refer to celestial phenomena: the yellow light after the setting of the sun, the blue light, the dawn, all the different gradations of light that one sees in the sky. So in spite of being deep under the earth, geographically speaking, they really are sky Gods, while as you remember, the Ongwe of the Iroquois are connected with star constellations. So the creative Gods of the Navajo too have some relationship with celestial appearances, even though they come from below. In the Hopi myth, emergence is described as a coming up of chiefs and human beings, while stars fall onto the earth, so again there is a secret connection with celestial constellations, and, in a bewildering way, what is above is below—but that is putting it too strongly: there are allusions as though what was below had connections with what was above and vice versa.

The surface of the earth which is reached, or created, as an end result of a long falling or emerging process, is what we, in psychological language, would call the field of consciousness. Jung represents human consciousness as something like a field, a magnetic field, so to speak. As soon as a content enters the field of consciousness, it falls into a web of associations. If I know something, then it is associated with the ego complex, and through the ego complex it is connected with all other momentary conscious contents of my consciousness. Therefore, if one wants to imagine consciousness in a scheme, one could say that it is a field of awareness with the ego complex as the regulating center. As soon as I say, "*I* know," something has entered the field of my consciousness. There are naturally vague borders where I know and I don't know. Sometimes I know and sometimes I do not, depending on the intensity with which something enters into the awareness of the ego. The same thing occurs in sense perception: if you listen, you hear a very high-pitched note, but if you think of something else, then suddenly you do not hear it anymore, or sometimes you hear it without realizing what you hear. If you put on the radio in your room rather softly, you would notice the same thing: there would be moments when you listened and noticed the music, but as soon as your thoughts wandered to something else, you might not even know whether the radio was on or not. So there is in our field of awareness generally a center onto which the light of the ego consciousness is focused, and around there are dim and also completely unconscious areas, where you could only say that what is there is unconscious, since it does not enter the field of consciousness.

At the beginning I tried to illustrate the idea that what we like to think of as "being in reality" is the content of our consciousness. Reality beyond the content of consciousness is and remains something indescribable, something about which we cannot make statements. So we can say that the surface of the real world coincides with what we would call the field of consciousness, of conscious awareness, and that is only created slowly through all the preconscious events which are represented as a falling-down and a coming-up movement.

Already in Greek philosophy and again in Gnosticism and in medieval tradition, the human psyche has been attributed a middle place between the opposites. For instance, the psyche was looked upon as an intermediary phenomenon between spirit and body, between heaven and earth. Jung has used this scheme to illustrate the role of consciousness and the role of the psyche in his essay entitled "On the Nature of the Psyche."[14] I must point out here that we absolutely agree that the psyche is a completely unknown factor which, as in the case of matter, we can only describe as a substance, without any decision as to what it is.

The psychic phenomenon in a human being Jung says we could liken to the spectrum of light which contains all the colors of the rainbow. On the one side we see that the psychic phenomenon fades away slowly into the physical processes, into the body and its material processes. Psychosomatic medicine is now concentrating all its investigations on this mysterious borderline sphere. We know more and more that there is some connection and that there are interactions between physical and psychic processes, that a psychic reaction can influence a physical one and a physical reaction a psychic condition. That does not need any profound medical knowledge, for if you drink a quantity of alcohol you will soon notice that it influences your psychic condition, though it is quite obvious that your psyche has been influenced by something material. But there is also the opposite fact, which some people deny but which is equally obvious. If you get a letter telling you that your best friend has died, you may faint or turn quite white, because your arteries contract from this shock. It is not the letter but its contents which have affected you physically; it is what the letter conveys that has brought about the physical reaction; it is not the ink or the paper that makes you faint, but the meaning of the message.

So there is an interaction, the laws and conditions of which we do not yet know, but as a whole we can say that there is a kind of gradual transition of physical into psychic conditions, and vice versa. Much more investigation would be required before one could say how the connection takes place. Naturally this is a simile, but at the one end of the scale would be the infrared end where the psychic phenomena slowly go over into physical phenomena. At this pole there is also the phenomenon of instinct, which seems to be very closely connected with our bodily structure like animals, we have instinctual reactions which to a great extent express themselves in immediate physical reactions. If, for instance, I make a movement as though to strike you, you recoil without reflection; your body instinctively reacts at once. With Jung, we define instinct as an inborn disposition to typical physical reactions; such instinctive reactions humanity shares with all the animal world, for the animals also have instinctual structures which in specific situations always react in the same way to an outer stimulus. But we can react instinctually without any conscious psychic process. If a car comes toward you, you will jump out of its way, and only a minute afterward will you realize what happened and why you did that. Naturally you can at the same time have a feeling of awareness, but that is not absolutely necessary; you can react physically via the body, or via the unconscious.

At the opposite pole Jung puts the world of archetypes, which in itself is as mysterious and unknown as the chemistry of the body is in its ultimate setup. When he puts the archetypes at this end, he is referring to them as a psychoid factor.[15] Jung ascribes to the archetype a psychoid aspect, which means that there are traces which point to the fact that it is not "only" psychic in the narrow sense of the word, but that in certain of its aspects it transcends the field which we call psychic. For instance, when the archetype appears within a synchronistic phenomenon, then we can conclude that its nature is psychoid. The archetype constellated in a synchronistic phenomenon has the aspect of being able to appear as an arrangement of outer material facts. The psychoid nature of the archetypes is a great problem to us just now.

The bewildering fact is that there is a strong suspicion that those two poles really are secretly connected, that what we polarize into two aspects on the borderlines of the psyche are really only two aspects of a unified living phenomenon—an X which we cannot define and which we must call, for instance, the living mystery of a human being. But if we observe psychic phenomena carefully, we see that there is a certain polarization. Let us say that a medieval monk has a vision of the Virgin Mary and gets very ecstatic about it, and afterward writes a paper on Mariology and the meaning of the Mother of God. Then he is experiencing the archetype of the mother at its spiritual end, as an archetype which conveys emotional and spiritual experience and gives a certain meaning to his life. If that same monk meets a fat, motherly woman and falls into her lap and sits there for the rest of his life, then he experiences the mother archetype at the instinctual end. Then it is rather an instinct; we could say he fell into the mother-child instinctual pattern. I have taken such an extreme case to illustrate that there is a certain contrast, an age-old contrast, which has been described in philosophy as the opposition of spirit and body, of spirit and instinctual drive.

In his essay, Jung again takes up an old concept of
Pierre Janet's, that of a superior and inferior aspect of
a psychic function, which would imply that all our
psychological functions have, so to speak, an infrared
end, which is the inferior aspect of the function and
which ends up in the somatic processes, and a superior end, which more or less enters the field of consciousness. Let us take, for example, such a reaction
as love: the inferior end would be the sexual physical
impulses, and the superior end would be all the feeling and fantasies which someone in love normally
has. The upper part has a lower tail, as it were, in the
physical end. The more we approach the inferior part
of a function, its infrared end, the more we enter a
field where variation and a certain freedom of reaction—i.e., the capability of stopping in the middle of
a reaction—can no longer be realized. That is why in
the instinctual sphere we have what the zoologists call
the "all or none" reaction. In zoology it is well known
that if an animal starts an instinctual activity, it often
cannot break off in the middle; it is like a mechanism
which, once started, has to be gone through, and that
is what one calls the "all or none" reaction. If from
outside you interrupt an "activated" animal in such a
reaction, then there is the so-called displaced reaction,
for in some way the accumulated energy has to be
abreacted. If you stop, say, two animals in the middle
of a fight—before a natural decision has taken place,
the victory or defeat of one or the other—then the
animal will eat furiously, or scratch furiously, or do
anything which expresses a displaced reaction. The
same thing occurs if you interrupt mating or eating; it

is as though a mechanical process had begun which, if interrupted, has to be abreacted in another form. This means that the animal has, more or less, to go through with it to the end, even if in the middle it seems to have become meaningless.

Konrad Lorenz once gave a wonderful example of two male birds who wanted to fight, but both had as much fear as aggression. Both were driven by aggression to fight, and both were equally big and so could not fight because each feared the other equally. If they are absolutely equal, then there is an arrested reaction, there is a complete balance which neither would-be fighter can break. Do you know what they did? They stared at each other, and then both put their heads under their wings and slept! There was a kind of suspense between the two, and they came to no decision. In such a case there is a displaced reaction instead. So if you start from outside, or if there is a balance of two instincts, the thing cannot go on because there are two equally strong reactions, and this results in a displaced reaction. Something has to happen, and a third instinctual pattern then jumps in. So the two enemies slept facing each other.

Formerly, in the studies of animal behavior it was thought that the lower you went down the scale of animal life, the more you met the completely mechanical "all or none" reaction. But recent studies of insects have shown that even on the level of wasps and ants there is already not only the "all or none" reaction but a certain amount of free variation. From studies of animal instinct, as far as I know, this idea that the lower animals are like machines, engines

which just go off on their instinctual pattern, and that
the higher we go, the more there is a certain amount
of variety, seems not to be true, for the beginning of a
certain freedom is set on a very low level. But, compared with human reactions, we can say that all animal reactions are relatively "all or none" reactions
and that it is only due to a strong increase of will-
power in the ego complex that humans can assume a
certain amount of free reaction. Freedom is here
meant as a subjective phenomenon or an experience:
one feels free to decide. Philosophically you can never
prove a free reaction, and you cannot prove the contrary either, but subjectively one feels that one would
like to eat the beefsteak but will not, for this or that
reason. One feels as if one had made a free decision,
even if a philosopher afterward says that one's reaction was also conditioned by something else.

Jung says that he has not found one archetype
which does not have a corresponding instinct. That
would lend confirmation to the suspicion of a secret
connection between the two. If you move toward the
spiritual end, you experience archetypal images, the
emotional meaning of those images, and become enriched by inner representations; if you move to the
other end, then you move into action, instinctual activity, into carrying out some action in physical reality. It is not necessarily such an extreme case, for usually human consciousness shifts. You could compare
the human ego to a ray of light that moves along a
scale, sometimes approaching more one end, sometimes more the other end, and sometimes remaining
more in the middle of the spectrum. To use an exam-

ple I mentioned before: when I was building my house, the impulse to build came from the archetypal idea I had in my head, but in the activity of building I sank too much onto the opposite layer and became absolutely like an animal building its nest, lost in the "madness" of building, and then I had a correcting dream to remind me of the other end, of the eternal house in the Beyond. With my ego consciousness I had been moving too much toward the instinctual end of the scale and for reasons unknown to me was not allowed to do so. Why this is not allowed, nobody knows, for I have seen many people happily going into these physical activities and forgetting the other end without any warning dreams. So what the regulating factor is which forces one to stay more on this end or to go more to the other belongs to the mysteries of the process of individuation. One has a certain structure to realize and may not transcend the inner law.

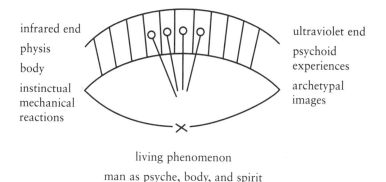

infrared end
physis
body
instinctual
mechanical
reactions

ultraviolet end
psychoid
experiences
archetypal
images

living phenomenon
man as psyche, body, and spirit

If you remember this sketch of the psyche, you will understand better why, according to creation myths, human reality—that is, the reality of human consciousness—is in creation myths described as a middle phenomenon between two poles. Obviously the psychoid archetypes correspond to the Ongwe in our first myth. They are the eternal images, the eternal constellations, and they fall down onto the human earth; in the emergence myth those images come from the opposite end. If we want to know the difference between the two ends, we have to amplify mythologically, which means *qualitatively,* what the difference is between them. You have also seen the secret identity of the two, because in the center of the earth Gods there are really sky Gods who have a strange earthly component. So, in a way, on the one side there are the semimaterial Gods, and the others are really rather spiritual. There you see the union of opposites, or the relative interchangeability of the extremes, which we know is typical of all psychic phenomena; as soon as a psychic phenomenon touches one extreme, it begins, in a hidden way, and then increasingly, to manifest its opposite quality. Thus we speak of the phenomenon of enantiodromia, where one thing falls into its opposite.

In our Iroquois myth, the tortoise comes from below: in Iroquois mythology the tortoise is the spirit of the earth; the tortoise carries the earth. It has the same role in the mythology of India. That there are animals and water below, and star constellations and human beings above, corresponds very well with these two poles of psychic phenomena.

It is important to know the qualitative difference between a creation starting from below and one starting from above. If in dreams you meet a creation motif coming from below, you have to expect something different than if the creation is described as coming from above. I remember the dream of a man: a spaceship landed and a beautiful woman came out and wanted to induce him to do certain things. That would be a modern travesty of the old theme that an Ongwe has come down to him. Modern dreams often use spaceships for this purpose. In such a case you can expect with relative certainty (at least I have not found any exceptions as yet) that when this experience lands in consciousness (when this man had the dream, nothing much was happening in his conscious life) it will take the form of an emotionally laden idea, something which will be described as a sudden illumination, a sudden awakening, a new awareness, and so on. It will take mainly what we could call an emotional mental form; whereas if a creative process is described in a dream as coming from below, then it might easily happen that the first landing in consciousness will be that the dreamer will carry out something in reality, an action whose symbolic meaning he will only understand after the event. He will suddenly be induced to buy a boat and go rowing, or to build a house, or have an instinctual urge to act in some way, and then, perhaps even much later, when he has already carried out all this activity, he will find it interesting and speculate on the symbolic meaning. But the first urge will be to carry out something in physical reality.

A creation which sinks from above has its origins in archetypal images which then descend and enter into the realm of realization. In psychological terms, if one were to apply this to a creative process, it would be as if an artist has an archetypal intuition, an intuitive idea, but of course this does not yet mean it has been realized. Anyone who has tried to paint will have experienced what I call creative disappointment. Within oneself, one has a perfect image of something, and therefore one picks up the paintbrush or pencil with great enthusiasm. What one then ends up with on paper is a very sad, imperfect, and awkward copy, most disappointing when one compares it with the inner image that one set out to portray. According to my own experience, I become completely preoccupied with these inner images, and I seem to be able to see them on the paper in front of me. It is only the next morning when I look soberly at what I have done that I see the reality, and then it seems to me to be a poor sort of scribble indeed. It only takes this extreme form, of course, for someone who is not an artist. But many artists to whom I have spoken have assured me that what they have created on canvas, when compared with their inner image, is never satisfactory and therefore always generates some kind of disappointment. A real descent from above to below is always accompanied by disappointment. One can readily understand this, for, in the world of archetypes, one is inflated, as one is dealing with the gods. But this inflation is necessary because one cannot be creative without a certain enthusiasm. One needs this intensity and momentum, and it comes from God. The difficulty lies in the realization of the task. This is also evident in the history of science when dealing with the great discoveries. For a scientist to transfer his vision onto paper in a manner which enables him to present it to his colleagues as a new theory is an immense achievement. This is also why there are so many "would-be" geniuses on this earth. These are mostly people who do indeed have certain creative intuitions, but who are much too lazy to undertake the great difficulties and trouble which would be necessary to bring such a vision down to earth.

This is, so to speak, creation from above. It means the realization of archetypal ideas originating in the unconscious and then being born into reality through consciousness. This is a kind of descent, for, seen from a feeling nuance standpoint, it is like a darkening, a deterioration of the original inner vision.

When viewing creation from below, one could say that creativity is situated in the body. Such people suffer from psychosomatic symptoms which mostly affect those functions which are controlled by the sympathetic nervous system, for example the abdominal area: they suffer from stomachache, stomach cramps, and so on. Such people find it helpful if one encourages them to work with their bodies with no conscious intent, for example to work with clay, or to take a pencil or brush and to let it move across the paper, or simply to move it in a rhythmical way as a child would do. One might also suggest that they make movements as the impulse takes them to do so.

All creative impulses originate in the unconscious, and it is more of a qualitative difference as to whether they come from above or below. If an impulse comes from above, people experience it as an idea or an inspiration, and it pops into their minds as an image or idea. Then they are confronted with the problem of realization. If it comes from below, it is like a calling from the depths of their body, from the unknown, and is very often accompanied by psychosomatic symptoms.

It is important to know the qualitative difference of the two forms of creation. For instance, if your patient has dreams from below, you must call attention to the fact that if some sudden instinctual urge should come up to do something, he should not repress it, and should not, for instance, retire into introverted reflection and say that it is nothing but symbolic, that he knows what it means and need not carry it out. Sometimes for the purpose of creativity it is absolutely essential first to carry out something physically and then only afterward to get to the symbolic meaning. If one skips this stage by introjecting too soon, by saying one knows what the thing means, that it is *only* symbolically this and that, one misses the whole emotional impact of the new content and will not get it really into consciousness. Therefore, if there are creation motifs coming from below, one should not repress the irrational, physical urge to carry out some action, unless of course it's too dangerous or too expensive. There are, naturally, reasonable limitations. But with experiences from above one has rather to warn the analysand sometimes not to be carried away too much by an inflation—that now he has had a great illumination about which he must tell the world and so on—but he must be open to some new insight which will come from above toward him and *dawn*—a wonderful word!—upon him.

Why a creative new content from the unconscious comes in sometimes by one door and sometimes by the other, we do not know. I have only one hint as to the possible reason. I once found a North American Indian myth where the great God wants to teach his people the knowledge of secret medicine, but cannot make himself heard by them, cannot convey his secret knowledge to them, so he teaches the fish otter and gives him the secret of the medicine bag and all the secrets of the medicine ritual and the medicine lodge, and then it is the otter who teaches the human beings.[16] Now here you have an interesting hint. The highest God—Mennebosh—tries to convey something to the human being but unsuccessfully, for there is a blockage. The myth does not explain what it is, whether the people are too stupid, or what; so he teaches an instinct, an animal, because he cannot get it in the other way, and then the animal gets it in. So the reason why sometimes the new knowledge comes in from one door might be that the other end is obstructed. The obstruction of the spiritual end occurs mostly through dogmatism—religious or scientific or *weltanschauliche* dogmatism of some kind. I am speaking of dogmatism in the negative sense of the word, of being dogmatically sure that something means exactly so and so, without any discussion about it. As soon as human consciousness takes on an absolutely dogmatic form of conviction against the mystery of the surrounding world and the psyche, then naturally one end of the pole is blocked. Under

these circumstances I have often seen that an archetype which wants to be observed has to go via the
fish otter. Thus an archetypal constellation can cause
physical symptoms, for there is not enough open-
mindedness to say, "Yes! Why not?" A certain elastic
open-mindedness is needed to receive a revelation
from the spiritual unconscious, but if the way is
blocked by dogmatism and there is a strong constellation in the background, then the archetype may use
Mennebosh's fish otter and affect the body in some
way. You cannot swallow, or you get some other disagreeable symptom. That means that your body, your
animal, starts to try to convey the meaning.

I am now speaking of abnormal reactions; for instance, the washing obsession, washing forty times a
day, or something like that. Obviously people who
have such an obsession should wash, not the dirt on
their hands, but their psychic shadow. There is generally, very obviously, an urgent need to wash off such
dirt. I had a patient, an introvert, a weak-willed man
who got himself pulled into his wife's extraversion
and her extraverted surroundings, and he got the obsessional idea that every time he wanted to go out he
had to outline his shoes with his finger. He would sit
there putting on his shoes and drawing his finger
along the edge of the shoe. Clearly that meant that he
should clarify his standpoint. He should say, "This is
my standpoint, and this yours," and point out that he
had a different standpoint. That was exactly what he
could never do, but being an intuitive feeling type, he
got pulled into every situation and then afterward re-
gretted it bitterly. The obsession showed exactly what

he should have done, not physically by outlining his shoes, but by doing the same thing on a psychic level. Sometimes a new realization, if it is a very essential and important one, comes from within *and* without. Let us say there is a young man who is still in an adolescent bisexual constellation and rather homosexual, but without any experience. I have often seen that such a young man would have dreams showing the anima experience coming toward him from within, with all sorts of inner realizations of the anima, while on the outside he would fall in love for the first time. Thus he met the anima at both ends, in projection onto an outside woman, as an outer physical encounter, and at the same time as the first inner realization of the feminine principle. This is not only true for this specific situation, for I have often seen that if an essential new realization is constellated, it tends to come from outside and inside and is what one then calls synchronicity. Thus a new realization of inner facts coincides with meeting new outer factors for the first time.

Now I want to touch upon a motif which appears in the Iroquois story, namely that it is a woman who is the main figure of the creative process, or rather a number of women. The myth begins with a woman becoming pregnant in heaven; then another girl becomes pregnant, and she falls down. Again a girl is born; and only then does it become a male process of creation, for only in the third generation does the woman give birth to twins, who then become the Creator and the Anti-Creator, the positive and the negative creative powers. But there is a long series of female figures before there is a male. Also unusual, if we compare it with creation myths of our civilization, is the fact that the figure which comes from heaven is feminine and not masculine.

If we cast a look at many other creation myths we see that both types do exist in different variations. We cannot say that one is the primary type and the other a deviation. The more fruitful question would be: "Is there a qualitative and a psychological difference between these two types?" Can we find in such civilizations other hints which explain or clarify the fact that the feminine is the Sky God and the masculine the Earth God (which *we* always tend to imagine the other way round)?

A famous parallel (and we can be relatively safe in assuming that there has been no influence between it and our Iroquois myth) is to be found in Egyptian mythology, where the Sky Goddess, the Great Mother Goddess, Nut, represents the whole cupola of the sky. She covers the whole earth, a huge cow on whose belly all the stars are constellated, or a female figure towering over and bending across the earth. The earth is a male God, Geb, who is her mate.[17]

The question of why the representative of the earth is here a male divinity, and why what we tend to look upon as male, the Sky God, is a female divinity, is difficult to explain. I think if we look at Egyptian civilization as a whole, one of its most striking characteristics is something which I would call a concreteness of ideas. Most primitive, semiprimitive, and even highly developed civilizations, with a few exceptions, believe in a life after death in some form, but only the

Egyptians have taken the trouble to ensure immortality by mummification of the body and by building
those enormous funeral chambers in which they portray every step of the dead person's passage through
the underworld. The idea of the immortality of the
individual has not only been conceived and taught in
a religious manner, but has been acted out in matter.

Most civilizations know that a God, even if he
dwells in a statue or a fetish, has to be kept alive by
human participation, either by the blood of human or
animal sacrifices, or by daily prayers. But no other
civilization has gone as far as the Egyptians, who
tended the statues of their Gods to an extraordinary
extent. There is a *levée du roi* in the morning, the statues of the Gods are woken up, bathed and anointed,
and then carried to the Nile and washed and then
anointed again and brought back to the temple,
where food is set before them, and so on and on. The
concreteness of the religious idea goes much further
here than in any other civilization of which I know.

To give you a feeling of how concrete Egyptian
teaching was, there is a text, a fragment of a papyrus,
which describes the chemical processes of embalming.
You know that first the intestines and the brain were
removed and then the corpse was put into a natrium
and salt solution for many days. This had a preserva-
tive quality, and after that the corpse was anointed
with certain oils and wrapped in mummy bands. In a
papyrus now preserved in Cairo but which comes
from Thebes, as well as in another papyrus now in
the Louvre, we have a text which gives the practical
instructions as to how to mummify a body. The be-

ginning part is lost, but what we have says: "First anoint the head twice with a good oil [of a specified plant] and then say: 'Oh, Osiris [here follows the name of the deceased], this oil has come to you from Punt in order that your odor may be beautified by the odor of the divinity, that some flow from the Sun God Re may come to you, that your soul may ascend to the divine realm. Horus comes to meet you through this oil.' " Afterward the ears and the nose are oiled, and then the instructions continue, saying that the viscera should be taken and put in the four canopic jars and afterward into the earthenware jars, and then the inside of the mummy should be oiled. While this is being done, a text should be read (this text has now been lost). Then the corpse must be turned over and the back oiled, care being taken that it does not fall back into the coffin, for the head and belly are filled with herbs and oil, and the Gods in the coffin must not be disturbed. During the whole procedure, the face of the corpse must be turned to the East. Gold should be put on the fingernails with the following words: "Oh, Osiris [and again the name of the dead person must be said], now you are receiving golden nails, your fingers are now of metal and your toenails of electrum. The Sun God Re's emanations come toward you, divine members of Osiris in truth. Now you walk on your feet to the House of Eternity and you lift your arms to the House of Infinity. By gold you are embellished and by electrum you are strengthened. Your fingers will become pliable in the House of Re and in the workshop of Horus." The text then continues without any further mention of the mummy. It uses the words "this God" when the corpse is meant. It says: "Now put [such and such an ointment] onto this God," etc.[18] The mummification is designed to give the deceased the quality of eternity and divinity; it is a divinification and immortalization of the personality, but every step is carried out absolutely concretely. It is an amazing concretization of phenomena which, in general, in other religions are rather looked upon as being invisible and belonging to an invisible realm.

There are steps toward such concretization in most primitive religions, magical concretization, but they are never carried through to such an extent. If you should ever go to the Valley of the Dead, opposite Luxor, where all the tombs of the Egyptian kings are located, and enter those chambers, you will see that all along the infinite number of chambers and passages are pictures of what the soul of the deceased undergoes before he becomes a Ba, an immortal star in the sky. There again every step is carried out completely and concretely on the ceiling of the funeral chamber. In those tombs you will see what we call the process of individuation represented on the ceiling of the funeral chambers. You can read every step of it, if you know enough comparative symbolism. I think that this concretization of those things which we would now rather call spiritual or religious ideas has to do with the fact that in Egypt the earth is masculine and the sky, which we regard as the spiritual realm, is more feminine.

What we look upon as material reality is, in a strange way, ignored or treated as being transient and insignificant by the Egyptians. For instance, in spite of all the money and labor they expended on building temples and tombs, they never, or hardly ever, built private houses of any durability; they simply lived in mud holes which went to pieces in twenty or fifty years. Earthly existence was treated as quite immaterial, something to be ignored almost completely. All the emphasis was put upon things which we would call spiritual reality, or things of the Beyond, or contents of the unconscious. There is therefore, in a way, a strange reversal of feeling toward life: for us this life, our physical temporal existence, is reality, and the other world is something relatively real to some people but completely unreal to many rationalists. When Jung traveled in Egypt, he was struck by this fact and commented to one of the guides who still led tourists into the tombs and who seemed to be quite a wise man, how strange it was that the Egyptians never took the trouble to build decent houses to last but took so much trouble to preserve the tombs for eternity. The guide, with typical Oriental wisdom and melancholy, smiled back and replied that in the one house you lived seventy years and in the other the whole of eternity, and was it not more worthwhile to build for eternity? He still had that same attitude to life. According to that attitude this life was just an unimportant episode; our present life and material existence was something impermanent and flimsy as compared with the archetypal representations and ideas, which to the Egyptians were completely and concretely real.

The North American Indians, particularly the Iroquois, seem to me to show a similar trend in their religious attitude, because—though it does not go so far as with the Egyptians—they have the same tendency to look upon temporal existence on this earth as something relatively unimportant and to stress the concrete reality of what we now would call spiritual contents. What I am endeavoring to emphasize, therefore, is that if a mythological concept is qualified as male or female, as being celestial or earthly, these are psychological qualifications without absolute reality or meaning in themselves; they too are simply symbolic qualifications. If something is said to be earthly, we should not understand that from the prejudice of what we call earthly, but have simply to understand what earthly means, namely: appearing in relatively concrete form.

Now, why should the Sky Goddess, Nut, be feminine in Egypt? What would that mean practically? I hope I have conveyed to you what it means if the spiritual God is the Earth God. I have interpreted what Geb is, but I have not yet interpreted what Nut is. In reading Egyptian religious texts you have probably been struck by their tremendous poetical and emotional expressiveness. The emotional quality is technically confirmed by the unusual amount of repetition. Now, the urge to repeat the same sentence twenty or thirty times simply expresses the intensity of emotion. People who are emotionally gripped by a story or an idea repeat it endlessly and cannot stop talking about it or telling and retelling it. Also, if people have had a shock—perhaps in a car accident—you just have to avoid them, otherwise you will hear the story of the accident twenty times over on the same day. It is a means of abreacting a strong emotional impact.

In North American Indian texts and in Egyptian texts there is an amazing similarity in this respect, for there is an unusual heaping up of beautifying adjectives and of emotional repetition. Those of you who have read Egyptian religious texts, or North American Indian texts, will know of this. It looks to me, therefore, as though what we would now call the celestial realm of Platonic ideas, the logos sphere, is to those people more an emotional feeling experience. That means it is more a question of establishing an emotional feeling, an atmosphere of relatedness toward those contents, something which is typically feminine and, in a man's psychology, belongs to the anima.

So where we have our spiritual heaven, the Egyptians have more an emotional atmosphere of religious experience, and where we have concrete reality, they have practiced concrete realization of what we now would describe as spiritual.

Standing above the heavenly Goddess Nut in the Egyptian cosmic structure, there is still the Sun God Re, who goes in his ship across her back. We should not forget that in our Iroquois myth, too, there are as many male Ongwe as female, and up there also is the Onodscha, the tree of light which gives light to the worlds above and below. So beyond the female again is a male principle. These structures should be looked at as qualitatively characteristic of what is close to consciousness and what is more removed from it, though not in an absolute sense.

Looking back to the Eskimo creation myth, you will remember that in heaven Father Raven was a human being, and that the only unusual feature he had was a little growth on his forehead which later became his raven's beak. It was only when he decided to descend into the abyss he had discovered—the abyss which corresponds to the hole in heaven in the Iroquoian myth—that he first made himself wings out of twigs from the trees and transformed himself into a raven. It is a very vague story because later, on earth, he is not a raven but a man with a raven mask: at a certain moment when he laughs, on discovering that a human being has come into reality, he pushes up his raven mask and shows his human face; then he puts his mask down again. This shows that even after having turned into a raven, secretly he is still a human being. So the raven is more like a mask, or a shell, covering him on the outside. Only the sparrow can go back and forth between the two worlds untransformed. In the Indian myth of Mennebosh, who wanted to convey certain wisdom of the medicine lodge to Algonquin tribes, he could not get through, so he had to teach the fish otter, and it was the otter which, coming up from the water, taught the human beings.

The common denominator of those stories shows that sometimes the contact between the Beyond and that sphere which we call reality is complicated, and it is not always possible for certain contents to go over the threshold unaltered; they cannot cross it without suffering certain changes. This sometimes corresponds to the fact that when you wake up in the

morning you may still remember that you had a
dream that was tremendously numinous and colorful
and full of emotion, and that it had many shades in
it, but what you actually get onto paper when you put
on the light and take your pencil is some miserable
fragment that seems no longer to convey the richness
of the unconscious dream experience, of which you
have still a kind of flavor in your mouth, but you cannot bring it out anymore. You do not bring it over;
there is a threshold difficulty which you cannot get
through. You may have had dreams which have given
tremendous enlightenment about a problem, where
you understood everything in a flash and knew how
it was all connected, and then in the morning you
could only remember that you had had the solution
in the night, but nothing was left!

When I was about sixteen or seventeen I got terribly worked up over a mathematical problem and in
the night dreamt that I saw the solution; I woke up
saying that I must write it down at once, for tomorrow I shall have forgotten. So, without even stopping
to put on the light in case I lost the impression, I got
out of bed and seized a pencil and wrote down what
I thought was the solution, making a terrific effort to
fight against the numbness of sleep, and dropped back
into bed, very relieved to think I had it down on
paper. In the morning I woke up feeling that I had it!
I got up and went happily to the table, and what had
I written? In trembling, almost illegible writing, I
read: two is three! That was one of the lousiest tricks
the dream spirit ever played on me! That is Mercurius
playing jokes on you in the night! We know that

mathematical discoveries have often been made through some such sudden insight. Henri Poincaré tells of several such experiences, and other mathematicians had them too, so it is quite possible that in my unconscious I had seen something real, but nothing at all came over the threshold.

This threshold difficulty has also to do with the fact that our consciousness is structured so as to represent things in a spatial and temporal order that does not exist for contents when they appear in the unconscious, where they seem to be present simultaneously. Adolf Guggenbühl-Craig made an interesting experiment. He put a recorder near his bed, and whenever he had a dream in the night, he would tell it to the recorder in his half sleep, and then in the morning, without listening to what was on the recorder, he would try to recall and write out the dream in the ordinary way. He wanted to find out whether we falsified our dreams. How much did we change them in writing them out? There was no striking falsification, though some details got lost or slightly changed, but the striking result was that on the recorder time was confused. For example, he would dream of being in a church and of doing this and that, and then of going into the church. But in the morning when writing out the dream, he would automatically rearrange it, writing that he went into the church where such and such a thing took place. So, in a conscious state he put a natural time order into the events which did not exist in the recorded report, where the time order was completely chaotic.

We might, therefore, work on the hypothesis that

in the unconscious there is what Jung calls a relativity of time and space and a certain spatial and temporal simultaneity of the whole content. This corresponds also to certain mystical experiences. For instance, Jakob Boehme, the great mystic, had a sudden enlightenment when looking at a tin plate in which a ray of sunlight was reflected. This threw him into an ecstasy, and he saw what he said was the whole mystery of the cosmos. All his chaotic stammering and bad style are really the effort to put into a spatial and logical time sequence this one experience which he grasped, and by which he had been overwhelmed in one second! Though he did not quite succeed in doing it, he spent the rest of his life trying to work it out, to put it into words and into a conscious system. This qualitative difference between things in the unconscious and the same things after they come over the threshold of consciousness probably creates the threshold difficulties. If the two psychic systems, the field of consciousness and what we call the unconscious, were qualitatively the same, there would be no difficulty for the content to come up from the unconscious. At the threshold, however, a certain difficulty is constellated, which you find also in creation myth motifs.

In the Raven example, getting over the threshold is an impoverishment: the Raven has his complete higher human form in the Beyond but can only appear on earth, at least outwardly, as a bird, though inwardly he retains his anthropos quality, the quality of a divine human being. A darkening, an impoverishment, takes place when he crosses the threshold. The

Iroquoian mother and girl again becoming one in crossing the threshold has to be seen in a similar light: there is a seeming regression or impoverishment—only one figure, whereas in the Beyond there had been a differentiation into two aspects. But it is simplified again when it comes over the threshold, so that some differentiation has to take place in the sphere of consciousness, that is, in the concrete earthly world.

This threshold phenomenon is not only found in creation myths; it is a general mythological motif which is found in other kinds of myths, fairy tales, and hero myths, where it is sometimes exceedingly difficult to get into the Beyond. Certain conditions have first to be fulfilled by the hero. In many myths and fairy tales there is not only a difficulty in getting into the Beyond but a terrific difficulty in getting back. Very often, for instance, a hero goes into the Beyond and finds the beautiful woman, but on his way back he falls asleep and an enemy steals the treasure again, or he loses it. A most famous example is Gilgamesh, who finds the herb of immortality and then, just in a moment of unawareness when he goes to bathe in a pool, he allows the snake to steal the herb back again. This is a threshold difficulty, this bringing back of something which has been found in the Beyond. So the threshold problem is not specific for creation myths. The general difficulty is between the realm of consciousness and the unconscious, in bringing over contents from one to the other.

From philosophical quarters, especially existentialist quarters, the objection is often raised that we talk of the unconscious as if it were something, though it is only a borderline or negative concept. In their opinion, we commit the same mistake as if we philosophically put up the concepts of being and nonbeing and then suddenly hypostatized the concept of nonbeing and talked about it as if it were something. Parmenides already got mad at this naiveté in thinking, where suddenly a concept was hypostatized when it really was only a borderline concept. Jung himself raised this question, and discussed it at length.

Can we say that the unconscious is a reality, since it only stands for that which is not conscious? We surely can say that a single content is either unconscious or conscious, but can we hypostatize this and talk about *the* unconscious, as if it were an *ens reale,* something which exists? But the very fact that a content which goes over the threshold and becomes unconscious *is altered in its quality,* and that when it comes up over the threshold and gets back into consciousness it is altered again, is one of the reasons why we are allowed to imagine the unconscious as a medium, or a *something.*

If I drop something here and it is wet when I pick it up, then I may safely assume that there is water down here, and the threshold is not only an imaginary line, but here is air and here is water. So it is with psychic contents. When they get forgotten, for instance, or repressed, they do not stay preserved in just the same form; they begin to alter in the unconscious, and vice versa: when you pull them up into consciousness, they again alter quantitatively. You see this illustrated in these myths. Thus we are allowed to talk about the unconscious as a real medium, as a psychic reality,

and to talk in this way is not just philosophical naiveté and it is not that we hypostatize an abstract
word. On the contrary, it is because of these threshold
phenomena that one is induced to think of the unconscious as something real in itself. When these impoverished contents come across the threshold of consciousness, we have to amplify (enrich!) them again in
order to understand them.

Associating around a motif means dipping it back
into the unconscious; you lie back and let any emotion, nuance, or memory come up which you may
have about this motif. The main thing is especially to
concentrate on the emotional and feeling qualities,
and not on definitions. You may make definitions if
you really must, but that is not the vital thing; you
have to try really to get back into the original richness
of what the picture conveys. That is why we amplify,
and that is the correct way to do it. Amplification
means getting back beyond the threshold as far as
possible and revivifying all those dim emotional ideas,
feelings, and reactions you have about something. For
instance, if you dream about such-and-such a street,
it is not enough to say that was the street in which
you lived as a child. That's all right, that has to do
with childhood memories, but then you must try to
get to the feeling you had when you came out of the
house. What was the street like and what did you
come across there? What did it smell like? Then only
you know what this picture means. Otherwise you
have not at all associated properly to your dream, for
you have to reconstruct exactly the richness which is
beyond and which got lost in crossing the threshold.

Then, according to our method, when we have done that, when we have enriched the dream and put it back into the emotional matrix from which it came, we have to formulate the interpretation, which means that we try, from the context, to reconstruct the central message of the dream, its meaning. Now we may use the other method—our Western abstraction—in trying to get the meaning of the dream into what you would call a sentence or a nutshell.

I always remember that when we did dream interpretation with Jung, he would let us interpret every bit of the dream, every scene, and then he would walk up and down and say, "And now, please, tell us, in one sentence, what the dream says! In one sentence!" It is the most difficult part of the interpretation, for theoretically it should be that the message is conveyed in such simple human language that it hits the nail on the head and conveys a striking message. If you fumble around and say it must have to do with this and that, and that it seems to mean this and that, you are on the right track, but you have not got the message yet. You have not arrived at the nucleus of the dream, which is like a letter or a telegram that has a definite message to convey and does not just throw a lot of pictures at you. By amplification you satisfy the emotional needs of the unconscious and the personality, but you have not satisfied the needs of the conscious personality and you have not strengthened the ego complex if you cannot do that second step, which is completely opposite from the first, namely to abstract it into a simple, understandable message. If we make these two steps of interpretation, then we deal properly with the incompatibility of the conscious and unconscious personality. That is making a synthesis through dream interpretation. We do justice to the unconscious phenomena and try also to do justice to the conscious part of the personality.

There is a threshold difficulty, a certain borderline, where it requires real effort to bring the two contents together. We know from physics that two particles of the same electric charge repel each other unless they are forced to approach each other beyond a certain spatial limit; then the opposite happens, and they fall into each other with a terrific power of adhesion. To use a simile: you have seen bubbles in your cup of coffee. There may be two which dance around each other and repel each other, and cannot combine; but then in a flash they rush and melt together and make one big bubble. To me this is an illustrative simile of what happens with unconscious and conscious contents. The ego complex has a certain tendency to repel the unconscious complex; you need a certain force to bring them together. Then suddenly you have the phenomenon of their coming together and of being enriched, of something having clicked. The right interpretation clicks and vivifies you. Every good interpretation should have a vivifying effect upon the conscious personality, a vitalizing effect. Suppose you have a dream where awful shadow figures appear, and you have awkwardly to realize that that is you too. Even that depressing dream, that sad message, has a vivifying effect, if you take it rightly, because now at least you know where the trouble lies and you know why you always stumble over certain difficulties in the outer world and in the inner world. So you have the reaction of not liking it, but still of knowing this is it! And that has a vivifying effect even if it is disagreeable. There is tension and sudden adhesion between conscious and unconscious contents. I think that the threshold phenomena in these creation myths and in other myths mirror this psychological fact.

4

The
Two
Creators

 We come closer to this problem of the threshold if we proceed to the motif of the twin creators, or rather of the two creators, for they are not always twins. In our Iroquois myth, when the woman arrived on earth she gave birth to a girl, and that girl later was impregnated by the spirit of the tortoise; during her labor pains she heard the twins talking in her womb. The one said to the other, "That is the place where we shall come out; it is the shorter way and the light is already shining through." But the other said, "Oh, no! We should kill our mother if we did that! We should go out by another way, the one which all human beings will take later. We will turn downward." The first speaker gave in, and the other said that was how it should be from now on. Thus the first quarrel arose. The second then said the other should go first, but the first one said his brother should go first, and so they fought with each other till the second gave in, turned over, and came out head first. The grandmother received him and then turned her attention to the woman for the second child, but the second twin did not come out the normal way but from under his mother's armpit. The apex of his head was

a firestone knife, and with that he pierced his mother and came out. This killed her. The grandmother was furious and said, "You have killed your mother!" But the firestone twin accused the other and persisted so vehemently in this that the grandmother finally took the innocent human-shaped twin and threw him away into the bushes; the one with the firestone body became her beloved son whom she nursed and cared for. The grandmother then took her dead daughter and out of her corpse formed the sun and the moon and all the other lights. The twin who had been thrown away into the bushes recovered and grew up and became the positive creator called Maple Sprout and was in constant battle and difficulties with Tawiskaron, the son with the firestone head.

There is a typical hero myth in which Maple Sprout creates the human beings, the maize, and all the good plants and teaches man all the cultural activities; Tawiskaron imitates him but only creates the crocodiles, mosquitoes, and other horrible animals. He also tries to create human beings, but they cannot walk and are demonic. So he becomes a real *simia dei* (ape of God) who undoes much of the creation of Maple Sprout. At the end of this great Iroquois myth there is a final battle between the two where they chase each other over the whole surface of the earth, and finally the good one overcomes the bad one, and the firestone demon retires from earth with his grandmother, the old earth mother, into the Eastern borders of the world, where he lives as a God of the dead. He becomes the God of the land of the dead and the Beyond and is there with his grandmother the earth, while

Yoskeha, the Maple Sprout, or Oterongtongia (according to other versions, but with the same meaning) is the real creator and savior God of this tribe.

Now this extreme polarization of opposites into good and evil, which one cannot help comparing with our myth of Christ and Antichrist because the opposition of good and evil is so strong, is not the usual type of a double creator motif. It is exceptional and unusual. The more usual type is that when there are two creator Gods the one is a bit more light and the other a bit more dark, one is a little more male and the other a little more female, the one is rather more dexterous and the other clumsier, or sleepy, or animal-like. But the opposites are not pulled apart into such a strong ethical opposition. Sometimes the opposition is very small. I want to give as an example a myth which comes from the North-Central Californian tribe of Achomavi.

> In the beginning there was water everywhere and the sky was clear and cloudless, but suddenly a cloud formed in the sky, condensed and changed into Coyote. Mist welled up and condensed, and out of this came the Silver Fox. They began to think, and by thinking they created a boat. They said, "Let us now settle here, and let us live in this boat as if it were a house." So they drifted about on the water for many, many years, and the boat became old and covered with weeds, and they got a bit bored with being in it all the time. "Lie down," said Silver Fox to Coyote, and the latter obeyed. While he was asleep Silver Fox combed his own hair and put the combings aside, and when he had a large heap of hair, he rolled it in his hands and stretched and flattened it out. He then put

it on the water, and it spread at once and covered the whole surface. Then Silver Fox thought that here there should be a tree, and at once there was one. He did the same with the bushes and the rocks, and then he weighed down the thin crust of the earth with stones so that it should neither rock nor curl if the wind pulled it around on the surface of the water. And he made everything right.

The boat landed gently on the edge of this new world, and Silver Fox called to Coyote: "Wake up! We are sinking! We are going down!" Coyote woke up and opened his eyes; he saw above his head cherries and plums and he heard the crickets chirping on the surface of the earth. Immediately he began to devour the cherries and the plums and the crickets. [Coyote is the trickster God in these tribes, very greedy and obscene.] After a while he asked, "Where are we? What is this place?" Silver Fox answered, "I don't know, we are now here! We landed on this shore!" Naturally, he knew, but he denied having created the world, because he did not want Coyote to know that it was his creation. So he said, "What shall we do now? This is solid ground. Let us go onto this earth and dwell here." So that was what they did. Silver Fox built a sweat lodge and lived in it.[19]

Here we have another type of the two-creator motif, where the one only contributes by sleeping and afterward by trying to eat up what has been created, while the other performs all the creative activities. This is reminiscent of our first myth, with the little sparrow and the raven; the raven did all the creative work, but the sparrow was there first. The sparrow is rather more active than Coyote because at least he goes down on Father Raven's orders and explores the earth below and helps in this way; but otherwise he does not contribute to the creation either. Yet in spite of this, at the end of the story, it is said: "Thus Father Raven created the earth, but the little sparrow was there first." And this sentence suddenly at the end of the story places an emphasis, as though the little sparrow was still the more ancient and the more important figure, in spite of his ineffectiveness in the creation. Here we have Coyote, a strange brother of the creator-fox, who only contributes his share by sleeping.

Coyote in the mythology of many tribes is the trickster god *par excellence*. Whole cycles are told of his deeds. You can find this material in the book Paul Radin, Karl Kerényi, and C. G. Jung published together on the divine trickster.[20] You will see from Jung's comments that he interprets Coyote as a shadow figure whose function it is to undo the consolidation of consciousness. Consciousness has the unfortunate tendency, inherent in its functioning, of solidifying, and affirming itself and maintaining continuity—its very essence must be like that if it is to function; but it has the disadvantage of constantly excluding the irrational, the primitive, the unwanted. So it needs a counterfunction in the unconscious, something which constantly breaks the consolidation of collective consciousness and thus keeps the door open for the influx of new creative contents.

Creative people often have a solid, strong ego consciousness and usually need some upheaval from outside—a depression, or an emotional upheaval from within, or even an illness—to get into a state where they can create. I have observed two types: one type is rather bohemian and is found mainly among creative artists, who practically live in a constant *abaissement du niveau mental.* They live in bohemian surroundings and do not conform to many of the social rules of collectivity and constantly live in the world of Coyote, the Trickster, so to speak, and are continuously open to new inspirations. But there is the other type of creative personality who has, in spite of his or her creative gifts, succeeded in adapting and conforming to collectivity and has built up a strong ego consciousness. Such people generally need a smashing-up experience before they can create again. It is inevitable, but if they know about it, then naturally as soon as they get the first symptoms of such a creative illness, they move toward it, they realize that something is coming up again, and thus they can defend themselves against the approaching onslaught of the shadow and the unconscious and can go to meet it. It was not by chance that Jung, for instance, wrote *Answer to Job,* the book which he thought of as his best, when in bed with quite a high temperature; when he had finished the manuscript he got up and was all right again. But it needed this kind of *abaissement du niveau mental* to bring out this creative work. It is highly emotional and needed such an illness to undo his normally strongly functioning consciousness. There are many other examples of this kind. Beethoven and Goethe would be typical representatives of the two types of creative people: Beethoven, who lived constantly close to the unconscious in a disorderly bohemian life, and Goethe, who, on the contrary, always needed to fall in love, with the accompanying crisis, before he could bring out another work. Goethe always tended to consolidate into the Herr Geheimrat, but his constant love experiences undid his consciousness sufficiently for him to become creative again. That is one of the main tricks of the unconscious, to undo a man's oversolidified consciousness, the anima making a hole in it!

Jung's comment about the figure of Coyote does not refer only to creation myths. It is striking that in this Achomavi cosmogony the Trickster God is there from the very beginning. We might make the assumption that at first there was not such a figure, just a creator, and that only after some time, when consciousness was well established and consolidated, did there come up from the unconscious a compensatory trickster figure to undo the hardening of consciousness. But apparently, as seen from this and some other myths which I shall tell you later, this is not true. The duality, namely a tendency toward ordered consciousness and a basic tendency toward a counterposition, something that acts according to emotion, moods, and momentary disturbances, a semi-animal figure, is there from the very beginning. It comes up at the same moment as a double movement of the birth of consciousness, just as when you stretch out your arm you move two muscles, one which contracts and one which does the opposite. So you can say that from the very beginning of consciousness, if there is that *yes* toward consciousness, there is also the *no,* the tendency toward undoing and creating a counterposition.

Before we proceed any further with this problem of

the dual creator, I want to relate some other myths where there are two creators. A tribe akin to the Achomavi, the Maidu tribe, also a North-Central Californian tribe (the two tribes have probably influenced each other to a certain extent), has the following creation myth: Earth Maker was swimming on the water. He was preoccupied and thought, "I wonder how, I wonder where, and I wonder in which country I shall find a world." "You are very strong because you think this world," said Coyote. And then the publisher adds: "Where Coyote suddenly comes from, the myth does not tell." Obviously Coyote, like Earth Maker, is eternal. Then Earth Maker and Coyote plan how they can create the world together, and so on. I am not going into the details of this creation.

In the creation myth of the Pima Indians there are also two creators. The one creator comes from a cloud, like Silver Fox, and he creates the world out of parts of his body. He is called Earth Doctor or Earth Magician, and from the very beginning has a rival called Elder Brother.[21] These two creators are again more hostile, as in the Iroquois myth of Maple Sprout and the firestone demon, for Elder Brother always tries to undo and destroy what Earth Doctor has created.

Among the Odjibwai, who belong to the Algonquin tribes, is a high God, Kitchi Manitu, and on earth are the two creators, Mennebosh and the Otter. So there are also two creator Gods, but with another one behind them, so to speak, who remains in the sky and does not take part in the creation.

Another Californian tribe has the following creation myth: In the beginning there was no sun and no moon and there were no stars. Everywhere there was darkness and water. A raft drifted on the water; it came from the north and two persons sat on it, Osma, the tortoise, and Pepeipe, the father of the secret lodge. Then a cord came down from heaven and along it came Earth Initiate. His face was covered so that one could not see it, and his body shone like the sun. He came down and did not speak for a long time. Finally, the tortoise said, "Where did you come from?" and Earth Initiate answered, "I come from above." Then those three create the world together. Here there are really three, but in the beginning before Earth Initiate comes down to start the creative process, two Gods drift on a raft over the water.

One finds the same constellation sometimes in creation myths from South American Indians. For instance, the myth of the Munduruku tribe from Central Brazil goes as follows: In the beginning of the world there was darkness, and out of the darkness came two people. One was called Karu and the other was his son Rairu. They are coeval, for one does not create the other, but they are coexistent. Rairu stumbled over a stone which was hollow like a cup, and he shouted at the stone. Karu, his father, told him to pick up the stone with which he had quarreled. Rairu did so and took the stone and put it on his head. It began to grow in all directions and to be very heavy, and Rairu said to his father, "This stone is already very heavy." The stone grew more and more, and Rairu could not walk any longer, but the stone still went on growing. It then took the shape of a cup which forms the sky, and on it appeared the sun. Karu hated his son Rairu for knowing more than he did—the son was wiser than his father. One day Karu shot an arrow into a tree and asked his son to go up the tree, for he wanted to kill him, and then it becomes a long story of a fight, but Karu does not succeed in killing his own son.[22]

This motif of the enmity between the two creators also appears in many African parallels.[23] The following African creation myth is told among the Basonge tribe in Africa: Nkolle and Fidi Mkullu quarreled (the latter is a divinity who appears in many African stories, a kind of high God of those tribes; Nkolle, as this story tells us later, is the eldest son of Fidi Mkullu). Nkolle said, "I have created everything!" Fidi Mkullu said, "No, I have created everything!" Nkolle said, "I can make everything!" Fidi Mkullu said, "All right, then go down and rule over the human beings."

Nkolle went down and became a great chief among human beings. He guided them, but mankind fell ill. He could not help. They suffered, but he could not help. The human beings said, "Take our pain away." Nkolle could not help. The human beings died and while dying they said, "Take our pains away." Nkolle could not help. He returned to heaven. The human beings went to Fidi Mkullu and said, "You must again be our chief." Fidi Mkullu then cured some, and others he helped to die quickly. The human beings said, "You are our true chief and remain our leader." Nkolle was the eldest son of Fidi Mkullu. As long as he was good, he had the name of Mwile, but when he became bad, he got the name of Nkolle

Nfule. Because Nkolle had become bad, Fifi Mkullu had sent all those illnesses.

The following is another creation myth of the Basonge tribe: Kolombo mui fangi, or Kolombo, was the one who made himself. Mwile, the highest God of this tribe, said to his people, "The people always talk about Kolombo mui fangi. I would like to see Kolombo mui fangi." The people went to Kolombo mui fangi and said, "Mwile wants to see you." Kolombo said, "I will come." And then he called all the animals and on a long, long journey went to the highest God, Mwile. When he arrived, Mwile asked, "Who are you?" And Kolombo said, "I am Kolombo mui fangi, the one who has made himself."

Mwile said, "That's not true; I have made everything. Do this." Mwile took some earth and spat on it till it was moist and turned it as you do to make a pot, and he formed a human being and put it on the earth, and it was a living human being. Kolombo also took earth. He spat on it till it was moist. He turned it and he formed it into a human being and also put it on the earth. It was a living human being. Mwile said, "Make your human being speak!" Kolombo said, "First make yours speak," and that continued three times. They quarreled as to who should make his human being speak. Mwile finally said to his human being, "Speak!" And the man spoke. Kolombo said to his man, "Speak!" But the man only moved his lips; he did not speak. Mwile said, "I am going to destroy my man." He put his hand over him, and the man of Mwile was dead. Mwile said, "Now you destroy your man." And Kolombo mui fangi put his hand over his man, and the man of Kolombo was dead too.

Mwile said, "I see that you can do this, but now go into this house and shut the door, and I'll burn down the house and then we shall see who you are. Because I have created everything, I can destroy everything." Kolombo went with his people into the house and said to two animals, "Make a hole through the earth back to my village," and to a bird which he had taken with him he said, "Lay your eggs on the floor before we leave by this subterranean escape." So he secretly left the burning house through the earth, and the eggs when they burnt exploded so that Mwile, who was listening outside, said, "Well that is good, now Kolombo is burnt down." The house was burnt down completely. Mwile went to the ashes and looked for the bones of Kolombo but saw only eggshells. A man came and said, "Kolombo mui fangi has escaped with all his people into the village."

Another creation myth, this one of the Baluba tribe, runs as follows: Kadifukke said to Fidi Mkullu: "You have not created me." Fidi Mkullu said, "I have created everything, I have created the earth. Why should I not have created you?" Kadifukke said, "You have not created me. I came of myself out of the earth." Fidi Mkullu said, "My son, go with Kadifukke to a tree." Kadifukke and the son of Fidi Mkullu went to a palm tree, and then they fought for power. (I am skipping this part because it does not really belong to the creation myth.) Kadifukke nearly killed the son of Fidi Mkullu but not quite. Then again Fidi Mkullu got furious with Kadifukke and imprisoned him in a house and tried to burn it down. Again Kadifukke escaped, as in the other story, through a subterranean passage. When Fidi Mkullu investigated the ashes, a man came and said that Kadifukke was not burnt, and Fidi Mkullu went and saw him still alive. Then Fidi Mkullu said to Kadifukke, "I am white, you are black." Frobenius, who took down this story, says that people do not understand this last sentence. If you ask them why the one says, "I am white, you are black," they do not know what that means. They shrug their shoulders and can give no explanation.[24]

The Masai tribe in Africa also has a dual creator myth. There a Black and a Red God quarrel about power. The Red God is called Naiterukop, the beginner of the earth, but he is not, the tribe says, as great as the Black God. So you see the creator is sometimes a bit less than the other, but he is still the creator. In Unyoro you also find a dual creator God; the second one is the Brother of God and First Man. There is a Great God and coexistent with him is God's brother, who is called Nkya, and who asks God to create the world. God would not have done it of himself, but Nkya, his brother, asks him to proceed toward the creation, which he then does. This myth is also found among the Masai, according to Hermann Baumann.

The motif of the hidden creator has given rise to a theory put out by Max Schmidt, the great ethnologist, which, to my mind, is deplorably distorting. In missionary and ethnological reports on primitive tribes it is asserted that a High God existed once but was later superseded by polytheistic deities.[25] As you have seen from the few examples I have given you, there is in some of these dual creator myths a tendency for one figure to be older and greater and more passive—the God who does not proceed toward creation but who stays in the background—while in other myths, creation is effected by a figure who then retires into the sky. The striking frequency of this motif has induced Father Schmidt to assume that at some time there was an original monotheism, that a monotheistic religion once existed even among the poor pagans, but that then, slowly, by a development of religious degeneration, monotheism was superseded by more polytheistic systems. For us, who look at these myths from a psychological standpoint, it is quite clear that we are not confronted here with the remnants of a historical development, nor is there reason to assume one in order to explain this phenomenon, but rather this motif of the dual creators is an archetypal one, to be found all over the world.

I could present some Indian and Gnostic parallels but have concentrated on Native American and African myths in this case because these stories are more vivid and colorful. But you could find them all over the world. Even in China there is the motif of the dual creator. All over the world there is the tendency to ascribe the act of creation to one figure who then retires and stays outside, while another figure steps into the act of creation. It seems to me quite obvious that this is an archetypal motif which describes the separation of individual consciousness from its unconscious background, the two together representing the preconscious totality. We have no reason, therefore, when we find such myths, to assume that there was

an earlier historical time when this "High God," as
Father Schmidt describes him, was formerly worshiped but is not any longer. That is a projection into
history of a psychological factor.

In the examples I have cited are two motifs which I
would like to illustrate by a drawing, because it is difficult to explain what is happening in those myths. It
would be easier to explain if we were to pin onto
them the labels of ego consciousness and shadow,
which is allowable because certainly in each individual those two figures would partly correspond to such
a classification, but I would rather call the one figure
the preconscious totality (C)—the whole thing in
one—that is, what Schmidt would call the High God.
On this figure the luminous spot, A, represents con-

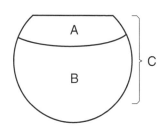

sciousness, or I would
rather call it the archetypal
tendency toward con-
sciousness. The tendency
toward consciousness
would be the son of the
preconscious totality, C,
but at the same time the

two exist in a natural union, because this tendency
toward consciousness stems from the whole totality.
You see, the drawing itself is already misleading because it illustrates a duality, but naturally this tendency toward consciousness is inherent in the whole
thing. Only when it becomes manifest is there a certain amount of contrast between A and B. This contrast is formulated in different ways. At first you have
two identical figures. Then, as in such African tales as

that of Kadifukke and Mkullu, where both contend that they have made themselves, when they try out their power one against the other, it is proved that both are equally powerful, and neither can destroy the other—Mkullu tries to destroy Kadifukke but cannot. They are relatively identical creators, but:

1. One is more active.	One is more passive.
2. One knows more.	One knows less.
3. One is more human.	One is less human.
4. One is a son type.	One is a father type.
5. One is male.	One is female.
6. One is good.	One is evil.
7. One is bent more toward life.	One is bent more toward death.

1. This is only a relative difference; *vide* Silver Fox and Coyote—the one sleeps and the other acts.

2. In the South American myth, for instance, it is said that Rairu, the son, knew more than his father, Karu, which is why the father tried to destroy the son.

3. The one is more human and the other less. We see this in the Eskimo myth, where the sparrow has no human characteristics throughout the story, while the Raven is really a human being who only temporarily turns into a raven figure.

4. The active one is more a son type and the other rather a father type—another differentiation which is to be found in some of the African and some of the South American myths.

5. The male-female contrast will be one of the final differentiations, but I want to give it a special chapter.

6. The contrast of good and evil comes in many degrees. For instance, in the Iroquois myth and also in

Nkolle and Fidi Mkullu, and in some other tales, the one really becomes destructive. It is interesting that in one of the African myths, where the one who is the son later in the tale becomes evil, they are both good at first, and it is only after some development that one becomes evil.

7. The one is more a God of the living, the other is more a God of the dead.

One would belong to the relatively more human aspect of the Godhead, the other to the less human aspect. When I speak of the son type and the father type, you should not think of the son as later than the father, for father and son are, as some of the myths definitely show, coexistent; so father and son are not meant to represent a time sequence, the father being first and the son later. The difference intended is shown by the fact that if you take the series to which the son type, or the human, belongs, those characteristics all show a tendency toward the creation of human consciousness—activity, increase of knowledge, stress on the good against evil, being more human and more creative. So that if we go back to our drawing, one part would characterize the tendency toward consciousness and the other, the passive, the one who knows less, the evil, the father type, the less human part, would be the preconscious totality taken as a whole. Father and son are only in relationship in the characteristic that somehow one has come out of the other, but actually, according to certain myths, they are self-created and are all simultaneously in existence from the beginning.

Here we get into difficulties, but people who have

some theological training will at once see that the same kind of archetypal constellation is to be found in the Christian teaching of Christ as the Word, being from the beginning identified with God and serving him, so to speak, as an instrument of creation. Christ as the eternal Logos—long before he appeared as Son on earth—was already in the creation and was even the creative activity of the Father. Therefore in the Christian mythology of the Logos we can recognize the structure of this same archetypal constellation which one finds in those primitive myths. To me they seem all to circle around, or to describe in a symbolic way, the mystery—which we shall never be able to solve—as to why there is consciousness and why consciousness has come from the unconscious, or always has been with what we now call the unconscious, and always existed in it. We only can say that in every human being we meet with the same fact, namely, a preconscious totality in which everything is already contained, including consciousness, and at the same time something like an active tendency toward building up a separate consciousness, which then, sometimes, in a Luciferian gesture, turns back to the preconscious totality and says: "I was not created by you; I made myself." This is shown especially in the African myth where Fidi Mkullu and Kadifukke or Nkolle quarrel about who made himself, and the quarrel ends without any decision.

To try to discuss, therefore, which was the first, consciousness or the unconscious, is the same as to quarrel about which came first, the chicken or the egg. Actually, if we make a synopsis of different myths, the two figures seem to make a relatively simultaneous appearance.

It is quite clear that *the unconscious* only makes sense if we presuppose consciousness. As long as there is no consciousness, there is no meaning in the word *unconscious*, there is no such thing! So as soon as we begin to speak about the phenomenon of consciousness, we set forth, logically, the counteraspect, the unconscious. Also, if we remember that the unconscious is full of luminosity, we can really say that, basically, they arc coeval phenomena which have not evolved out of each other in a time sequence, but existed from the very beginning as two coequal tendencies in the psyche. Yet the myths where the two creators are relatively equal and only quarrel about who was first, with no ethical shading in their quarrel, seem to stem, as far as I can see, from especially primitive tribes. Also, such stories have a vague, dreamlike quality, as, for instance, when Silver Fox goes on a dream boat over the ocean and then creates the world from the hair he has plucked from his body. The tribes with a greater cultural development seem to show a tendency toward creating a myth where the figure of consciousness carries the accent of being positive and good and the other figure of being negative and destructive. This ethical element, which does not enter into every tale but only comes in at a certain stage of cultural development, seems to me to mirror a *higher* stage of consciousness, in the sense that there is a certain differentiation of ethical awareness in it, and therefore a certain progress of consciousness is mirrored in it.

It seems to me tremendously important to look back especially to those natural primitive myths, where the two creators are not put into an ethical counterposition, because we tend nowadays to over-estimate consciousness. We have really reached a stage where in a one-sided way we think of the one as being the purely positive factor and the other the purely negative. But in looking back at those primitive myths we see that the problem of good and evil, the relationship of consciousness and the unconscious, the relationship between the activation of concentrated consciousness and the remaining in a dreamy, passive way close to the instinctual preconscious totality, is a much more complicated problem, one which we cannot cut apart with a sword, judging them as good and evil. Both sides really have a positive and negative aspect. What we find in the dream life of a modern analysand very often corresponds to this motif more than, for instance, to our counterposition of Christ and Antichrist, the good son of God and the evil, which is a specific and extreme position, and amounts to an overevaluation of consciousness. We even see that in some of these primitive myths there is a tendency to make the part which is usually evil the better of the two: the passive, the dreamy one, the one who does not enter into creation, is, so to speak, the High God who retires into heaven, and the active one is sometimes the more destructive, Luciferian tendency who breaks away from a harmonious preconscious totality.

The accents therefore are put in a very different form from that in the development of our civilization, and I think we have to learn about this relativity of the two in order to understand the human being in a more total way. Chinese Taoism, and also the Chinese movement of Zen Buddhism, for instance, place the accent completely on preconscious unconsciousness with its vague insights or cloudlike total awareness of things, which is evaluated above any cultural consciousness with its ethical and cultural activities. The great conflict in China between Confucianism and Taoism is also based on this duality, Confucianism stressing the importance of social and ethical order and behavior, and Taoism always stressing preconscious self-awareness of totality as the important thing.

In Taoism, man tries to become as unconscious as possible and to escape from creation as far as it is possible. A Confucianist, on the other hand, says yes to life and tries to fashion it according to some political or other standpoint. From a Jungian standpoint, one could say that this is, to a certain extent, the conflict which we see as being the difference between extraversion and introversion. An extremely introverted type of person tends to deny reality and to place a lot of importance upon a relationship to the unconscious. On the other hand, an extraverted person places emphasis upon the outer world and consciousness. Probably it is advantageous to take a not too extreme position, for we always have both sides within us. Thus we have both these Gods of creation in our own soul, and we must realize that both Gods have both for and against within themselves and that this is simply an insoluble paradox of our human existence. I am only touching upon these opposites to illustrate that this motif of the two creators includes one of the deepest problems of humanity, that is, the questionability of the development of a cultural consciousness in man.

The duality of the creator God crept in, even into our tradition, via the fact that the creation myth in the Bible has been amalgamated into one version from two versions: the text in which Yahweh is the sole creator, and the second version in which the creator is called Elohim. The verb accompanying Elohim's deeds is used in the singular, though the ending on *Elohim* is plural. If we take the Elohim as representing in our drawing the preconscious totality, it becomes clear, because this preconscious totality represents a multiplicity in the sense that it represents the totality of conscious and unconscious and therefore contains all the archetypes; it is multiple, containing all the Gods—Elohim—and it is one thing, because it is the preconscious totality. So this contradiction of the verb in the singular and the noun in the plural is really a wonderful way of expressing what this preconscious totality is, namely a unit-multiplicity which is, so to speak, not identical, and yet identical, with Yahweh, the active creator. As I tried to point out, our two columns are also identical; you cannot separate them, they are two that are still one, two aspects of one and the same thing.

In Gnosticism, there were several sects which believed that first there was Elohim, a high God who was good and completely spiritual and who was not involved in creation, which was brought about by the evil Yahweh, whom they interpreted as being a Luciferian, devilish figure.[26] This explained why creation is evil, so that, according to Gnostic teaching, Christ had to come down to redeem the people and lead their souls back to Elohim, to the highest and good God, who had never been involved in creation. This heretical teaching hooks into that one sentence in Genesis. There we can see that, in contrast to our enormously positive evaluation of creation (i.e., consciousness), even in those times there was this other evaluation that the passive one, the one who retired, the one who stayed out, is the positive figure, and the active one, the one who carried out creation, is a devilish, destructive agency.

This Gnostic idea is based on a feeling experience of reality as being evil. Those who feel that creation and human life are a complete failure and should not have happened, that it is deplorable that there is such a thing as the reality in which we live, will attribute the predicate of evil to the creator of our world. Probably in this Gnostic myth there is a certain amount of Far Eastern influence; in Buddhistic teaching reality is looked on as being evil, and ego consciousness is evil. The aim of life is to escape from it. In other civilizations also, there are similar tendencies to evaluate *creation* as a bad mistake, which should not have happened, that it was God's shadow which, as it were, got him into creation and that if he had been conscious of what he was doing, he would not have created this miserable reality. When it comes to a feeling, or an ethical, evaluation of creation, then it depends really on the human reaction.

In a Taoistic-Chinese myth which I will discuss

later, the Gods which represent consciousness are de-
cidedly evil, and those which represent the unconscious are good. The undertone, then, of this creation
myth tells us that creation is a catastrophe. It should
not have happened. To us Westerners, this would
seem to be a very strange idea. But if, for a moment,
we try to see it from the point of view of the animal
world at a time when man had not yet separated himself off from animals, in Neolithic times, for example,
when small herds of men shambled along among
other herds of animals and were not to any significant
degree different from any other herds, then one can
easily imagine that creation was less destroyed at that
time than it is today. This is especially relevant when
one acknowledges the fact that through the development of human consciousness, we are capable of destroying all forms of life on this planet, plant and animal life included, by means of radioactivity or the
explosion of an atomic bomb. If the world were to
end in this manner, which is absolutely within the
realm of possibility, then we would have to say that
nature's discovery of human consciousness (for
human consciousness is not of our own doing, rather
nature and the history of our own evolution have
driven us to attain this consciousness) was indeed a
catastrophe. Then it would have been proved that the
creation of man, mainly of conscious man, was a catastrophe, a disastrous, dire creation which, from the
point of view of life itself, would have been better if it
had not happened at all.

This is, of course, an extreme way of putting it, the
point of which is to make us shudder and to awaken

the doubt within ourselves that perhaps consciousness is not the last cry or simply good. Rather, that it is also something dangerous. Some races have experienced this more intensely. We will be returning to this theme of demonic consciousness and the demonic aspect of creation later.

In my drawing of the circle, the father type characterizes psychologically the totality of the preconscious psyche, in which the conscious and unconscious are one and where the active, more creative type would correspond to the tendency to form a more lighted field of consciousness, evolving slowly from the preconscious totality. The preconscious totality, the representative of the large circle, very often in myths later becomes the God of the dead, as, for instance, in the Iroquois myth of Maple Sprout and the firestone devil, Tawiskaron. The Firestone Creator, the evil one, is chased away from this earth and retires to the East, and there he lives with the Earth Mother in the Beyond, surrounded by ice. He is the great God to whom the dead go. So one can say that they return to this preconscious totality, to the father, the older thing, when leaving reality and the field of consciousness. This pattern is also to be found in certain African creation myths, for instance in the one where the two creators are the Red One and the Black One: the Black One is the God of the dead who stays outside creation and the Red One is the Creator God. The dead return to the Black One. Black is not evil here but, like Osiris in Egypt, simply the God of the dead, of the night, of the Beyond, death not being simply an end of life, but another form of existence in the Beyond. There the dead continue to live with the Black God, or in the preconscious totality.

The twin motif is naturally not restricted to creation myths. There are innumerable hero myths where there is a pair like Gilgamesh and Enkidu. In these two-hero myths there is a certain similarity to our two creators, for the one is generally more a shadowy type, like Enkidu. In Gilgamesh and Enkidu one finds that Gilgamesh is connected with the Sun God and Enkidu goes first into the underworld. Enkidu is connected more with death and is the more mortal of the two; he precedes Gilgamesh to the land of death, and he is an older type of man in his archaic, animal-like behavior. We must assume that this duality is a basic law of all psychological manifestations and does not appear only in the origin of consciousness, that is, in creation myths, but everywhere else also. There is, for example, in the teaching of the Gnostic Ophites the idea of two saviors; they say that there were two Adams, the original man who was created before time (i.e., the unconscious man), and human being who, through acquiring gnosis (consciousness), is reborn the pneumatic spiritual man and becomes identical with the first man. One text of the Ophites says that they have in front of their temples the statues of two identical men, representing the first Adam, who was there before any development took place, and the spiritual man—*anthropos pneumatikos*—who looks just like the first Adam. Here there is again the motif of the two: the one is the unconscious man in his preconscious totality and the second the spiritually reborn man who again reaches this totality, but in a conscious form.[27]

Jung defines the psyche as a conscious-unconscious totality. For him the word *psyche* means the totality of conscious and unconscious processes. Duality also refers to the problem of the psyche and matter. Matter and psyche appear in the psychological sphere as characterizations of conscious contents. That is, if we say that something represents spiritual contents of the psyche, including psychological contents, which have no material reality, or if we say of something that it has material reality, both things can only be perceived through the psyche; some we characterize as materially real and others as spiritually, or inwardly or psychologically, real.

If we try to go to the bottom of the problem, the only immediate reality we can perceive is the psychological reality; we cannot go beyond our contents of consciousness, but we tend to characterize certain contents in our consciousness as being materially real and others as being psychically or spiritually real. Both the material reality and the spiritual reality are ultimately transcendental, but not transcendental in some philosophical or theological sense; in Jungian terminology, transcendental simply means transcending consciousness, transcending the possibility of conscious awareness: they are *unanschaulich* (unobservable), which is a term from physics. The fourth dimension, for instance, would be *unanschaulich,* that is, we cannot form an inner image, an imaginative representation, of it. Its reality can be mathematically concluded; that is, we arrive at its reality by a process of logical conclusions, but we cannot represent it, for we have no immediate inner image of it. This is true also for the archetypes, which in themselves are also *unanschaulich*. We have no idea what they are; what we can observe are archetypal *images*, from which we conclude that there must be such a thing as archetypes which we cannot imagine in themselves. Therefore, Jung says that in their ultimate nature archetypes are *unanschaulich*, just as matter is because it reaches into the fourth dimension. The unconscious psyche is *unanschaulich* because the psyche and its images are the only reality immediately given to us, the only reality we can immediately observe.

The physicist Wolfgang Pauli has quoted this explanation of Jung's and has added a few clarifying points to it. I am taking this from a lecture given by Pauli on Jung's eightieth birthday.[28] There Pauli says that it is not the fact that one cannot imagine (meaning have a representation of) matter or spirit which creates logical difficulties, but what Jung says in the next sentence, namely that the psyche is "immediately given" (given *a priori*), because how could a conscious-unconscious totality be immediately given? The physicist, if he looks at it naively, would assume first that only the conscious contents are immediately given. What goes beyond seems to the physicist to be questionable, because he asks himself whether what goes beyond could not also include the material aspect. I have abbreviated Pauli's argument and have just given the gist of his statement. It is not really a criticism but only an additional proposition, namely that this conscious-unconscious totality also includes the physical world, that is, the world which can be observed by the physicist in certain microphysical processes. He says then that if one imagined the unconscious in opposition to matter, one would indirectly isolate the unconscious too much from the material aspect of reality. I think that Pauli does not contradict Jung here, because the latter says himself that material is only a characteristic of things on the subjective level; that is, we characterize certain things as material but cannot prove their existence immediately.

I am going into this because the problem of the pre conscious conscious-unconscious totality, which in our drawing would be the circle without the light field in it, would, in this view, include all reality in itself, not only the psychic but the physical also. This question is still an open one, and this is only a hypothesis which helps us to think about these factors. That we cannot get away from the basic structures of this pre-conscious-conscious totality is illustrated by one of the theories of the origin of the cosmos in which we again find the twin motif. There is a cosmogony in physics which has been worked out by Jordan and Dirac (Dirac deviates a bit from Jordan, so that in working it out more in detail there are certain differences) in which they start with the idea that the whole cosmos originated from twin particles—from two electrons which were twin particles. There was neither time nor space; the time-space continuum only comes into existence with some content. In microphysics one finds also that there is not a single type of particle which does not have its antiparticle.

You see in this cosmogony—projected onto matter—the same idea of the twin creators. Although this time it comes as a natural scientific idea and in this new form, one still can clearly recognize the same archetypal structure behind the idea, for this duality of all conscious-unconscious contents, as well as particles and antiparticles, shows a striking parallelism. It is therefore not really surprising that one finds this duality motif in all man's attempts to describe the basic processes through which our awareness of reality came into existence.

I should, however, say that the scheme we have made is somewhat suspect, for as soon as one delineates something and cuts out certain aspects in order to clarify others, something gets an overemphasis, so that every kind of delineation is a little wrong. I want you, therefore, to take what I have given as a relative illustration only; I will return to this point later.

I should like now to tell an individual dream about a creative problem, to illustrate or to bring us back to the more practical realm of the problem and also to show how these things work in reality. It should also serve to illustrate the extent to which the shadow is often involved in the initial steps of a creative process. With Silver Fox and Coyote, Kadifukke and Mkullu, and so on, in mind, you can appreciate the fun of the following dream.

There is a further point which the dream should serve to illustrate. In the Iroquois myth it was a woman who was the main agent of creation. She represents the female principle, both in women and in men. As is well known, Jung calls the female aspect of man the anima. As we will see, the anima plays an important role in a man's creative life. (The animus, on the other hand, is important for the creativity of a woman.)

It is the dream of a medical doctor, a general practitioner, who had a Jungian analysis, but then left for another country and proceeded quite well with his own dreams without more analysis. He is an introverted feeling-intuition type and therefore quite capable of fishing into his own unconscious; he got along all right, understanding, as he told me, about sixty percent of his dreams. He felt all right and had no apparent problems; his marriage and career were going well. But when he came to me he said he had been bored for some time and vaguely disquieted by the suspicion that he was beginning to be a successful *stuffed shirt;* everything went easily and was all right and he had nothing to complain of, but just that was, in a way, unsatisfactory. Then suddenly he got a terrific depression, which started on the morning after he had the following dream, which he could not understand. This was why he wanted an interview with me, to have it explained.

He dreamt that a colleague turned up in his consulting room (which is in the flat below the one in which he lives) and disappeared again. This colleague is a very extraverted American, interested in genetics and working on related problems. Then the dreamer is in his flat and feels very ill. His wife says that they must ask a gynecologist, and she rings up a gynecologist colleague, who comes at once. He is a rather tough, extraverted type, and begins at once to complain about the problem of giving certificates of or legal abortions to women. He says, "Is it not your experience also that women, when they come wanting to have a child removed, are so impossible, so difficult to talk to—they want the child and they do not want it? They do not want to look at the problem, they just want quickly to pay for a certificate. They are so obstinate and one has the greatest difficulty in getting them to talk and really to take the problem seriously; they just want a superficial solution, and one knows they will have the trouble again." And then the gynecologist goes on to say that for such a pregnant woman they had, with a razor, cut off inside her the head of the embryo (that's naturally *dream surgery*), but that the embryo continued to live; the pregnancy went on and the child was still there and continued to grow.

The dreamer joins in and says, "Yes, it's awful, I really would like to give up giving certificates for abortions, I know it is such a horror. The only thing you can do is take the time and make a terrific effort and talk to the woman and get right to the bottom of the problem; and then, generally, you find that she wants to keep the child. But it is such an effort that it practically cannot be done." With this the gynecologist left again. Patients are waiting in the waiting room, and the dreamer thinks he cannot work, he feels too ill. So he calls his wife and asks her if she could not help him. His wife laughs and shakes her head and says, "No, I have to clean my own silver, thank you!" So he turns away, disappointed, and wakes up in a deep depression, which continued from then on.

Obviously, if a woman calls a gynecologist for her husband it is because he is pregnant, so in spite of the fact that the dream does not say so, if he needs a gynecologist, it is quite clear that somehow the pregnant anima with whom he is, according to the dream, secretly identical, is the real problem. He would not need a gynecologist otherwise. In the dream, therefore, the whole discussion circles around the problem of pregnant women who want and do not want an abortion, which naturally refers to his anima and indirectly to him. But the interesting thing is that it does not begin with the anima—we know from the myth of the woman falling from heaven that the anima figure is the mediator for creative processes; here we see, in the short appearance of the American who studies genetics, first the appearance of a shadow figure. The dreamer had had from the government a chance to investigate a certain psychosomatic medical problem. When he started to work on it, a flood of interesting thoughts came to mind, and he quickly saw that through this work he could find out many very interesting new things. But for the dreamer the work has nothing to do with genetics; this must therefore be taken symbolically. He had studied the microphysical processes and mutations which lead to the origin of a human being and had made a special study of the problem—now so widespread—of bringing forth mutations by X-raying germ cells.

The problem is an extraverted one and concerned with the origin of life. That appears in the shadow figure of the extraverted American. Exactly as with Silver Fox and Coyote, you have the moment where the shadow turns up but does nothing; he is just there for a minute, but then, suddenly, the whole creative problem is started. I have often seen that in introverts the first impulse toward a creative idea or a creative activity is aroused by something which comes from outside; it comes from the shadow half of the personality. That is the first inspiration, so to speak. In this case it was quite clear: the government order to work out a certain problem came purely from outside, through his ambitious, extraverted shadow side, but it set the whole creative process in motion. When he started on the work, he suddenly felt pregnant with a lot of ideas of what could be done. He felt one should investigate this and that, and he got quite excited, but, being lazy, he quickly repressed the germination of these possibilities and tried to live on at the normal pace of his life.

We can see how the duality turns up first in the American and then in the gynecologist. The association to the latter was that he was a medical colleague, a rather tough, extraverted person, the tough surgeon type with not much feeling but great efficiency; so there again the shadow is involved. The shadow complains about the problem of legal abortions. This corresponds now to the negative aspect of this man's extraversion, the negative aspect of his shadow, which wants a short, clear-cut solution; the gynecologist says that in one case of a pregnant woman they had cut off the head of the embryo with a razor, but the child had continued to grow all the same. We found out what this meant: he had in a moment of impatience thought that he would just do what the government asked—in about ten pages—and send that off; then he would no longer be tempted to have creative ideas about this theme any longer. That would be cutting off the essence of the embryo, cutting off its head and all those creative ideas; just doing what he could grasp at once, what the government had ordered, and sacrificing the rest.

But the dream says that did not help, or the embryo continued to grow; this quick, rational abortion, finishing the task and then not having any more creative thoughts about it, would not work. Though this extraverted surgeon gynecologist is a shadow figure and close to destructive, because he is also close to suggesting the quick, radical suppression of a creative impulse, it is seen that he is absolutely necessary because, in a Luciferian way, he speeds up the inner problem! Our dreamer would have dallied with the idea whether he should or should not write down his ideas, or he would have gone about dreaming of his creative ideas forever, but for this brutal, primitive, extraverted shadow who from time to time would say that they should remove it or not remove it.

So we see how the shadow, or the dual creator, is necessary to produce the work. The whole conversation, instead of circling around the man's illness, circles about the obstinacy of pregnant women: how they really do not know what they want and are full, we would say, of animus opinions. Our dreamer just said they were obstinate and full of stupid ideas. This refers to the fact that the unconscious, and the anima as the carrier or the temporary personification of the unconscious impulses, has always this dual tendency

which wants, and does not want, to produce. It wants
to produce a creative idea; it offers it with the right
hand but takes it away with the left. That is where
consciousness has to interfere and either pull the fish
ashore or throw it back into the water.

This strange dual tendency of the unconscious to
bring something up and then not want to hand it to
consciousness has also to do with the problem that
every creative impulse is double. There is always a yes
and a no, an active and a passive aspect. Here the
active and passive aspects are mirrored in the dual attitude of those pregnant women who want and do not
want a child. Since the gynecologist and the man discuss the psychological problem of pregnant women
instead of looking at the man's illness, we can conclude that the problem of the pregnant women *is* the
man's illness; his anima is pregnant. His anima, his
feminine feeling side, is not able to make up her mind
if she will give birth to the conceived child within
him—that is, to his creative ideas—or whether she
will pitch them into the wastepaper basket, thereby
aborting them. This is his situation as the dreamer.
And it is expressed through a woman and exemplified
by a woman because, in the final analysis, it is not an
intellectual decision, but rather one which belongs to
the realm of feeling. With his feelings, he will have to
decide whether he cherishes these creative ideas and
will bring them lovingly into life, or whether he does
not care a bit about them and, because they are of
no importance to him, will discard them. Clearly, his
ambition alone does not provide enough drive in itself. Where creative ideas are concerned, this is al-

ways so. Wherever attempts are made to realize creativity through ambition alone, not much is achieved. Ambition has a sterilizing effect on creativity. So to be creative for reasons of ambition will not work. It requires love, a contribution from one's feeling side. And it would seem that he, much less his anima, is not able to reach the point of making this feeling contribution. But, apparently, "it" within him wants to keep this child.

That his general practice is pressing on him, I took objectively, for it is very difficult for a general practitioner to be creative when the telephone and the doorbell are constantly ringing and the waiting room is full of people. So there is a concrete problem, the temptation to escape into everyday work. Then comes another temptation, to escape by asking his wife if she could do it for him. Actually, he *had* asked her if she could write on the problem, but she was not at all inclined to do so. In the dream she says that she has to clean her own silver. This also in this case was to be taken on the objective level, for she had a special problem of her own and was working on that and so was not inclined to listen to his suggestion. The dream ends without any decision, so from then on he felt absolutely under the weather, in a very bad depression, just dragging himself along through life and calling himself a silly, meaningless stuffed shirt and not knowing what was the matter.

I was impressed because the dream shows in a nutshell, on a personal level, all the agencies we were talking about, and on a more archetypal level it illustrates the double tendency of the unconscious to create. In the dream the pregnant woman is the first step toward a creation, and then comes the illness of the dreamer. If you remember, our Iroquois chief felt so bad and so horrible when the woman got pregnant and so much better when he pushed her aside. Our dreamer tries the same thing; he tries to push the thing aside and say that now he feels better again and that now he has made up his mind. But with him it did not work in this way, because this embryo is in his anima—that means, in his own inside—and in spite of being beheaded, it is just happily growing on and on.

If a man's anima is pregnant, he can push her aside in one of two ways. Our dreamer pushed her aside in the wrong way by trying to look away and to do nothing about his problem and pretending that these ideas did not exist. The Iroquois Ongwe chief also pushed the pregnant woman aside, but in another way, for he pushed her onto the earth, where creation begins. Whenever there is a creative constellation in the unconscious, that is, when the unconscious has conceived a child, if we do not put it out in the form of a creative work, *we get possessed by it instead.* You see it in the case of our dreamer, who, because he did not proceed to write down his ideas or do creative work, became ill himself, like a pregnant woman. He got possessed by a pregnant woman and felt like a woman in the last months of pregnancy. So one can say that if the man's anima has become creative, then he has to disentangle himself from his pregnant anima in the right way and proceed toward creation; that is, write down, for instance, the ideas he has. If, instead of feeling sick and hanging about like a sick woman, he had asked what was happening to him and why he had those ideas and what he could do about them, then he might have looked up further material or literature on the subject, etc. In that way he would, in a manner, have disentangled himself from the pregnant state, and that would have been the right way of pushing the anima out into creation. The other way would be to repress the problem and do nothing, but then one becomes identical with the state the unconscious is in. One gets identical with the pregnant anima in a disagreeable form, and I would therefore say that he felt as the chief did before he had pushed out the woman, absolutely miserable and getting worse and worse.

There are, therefore, two ways: either to repress or to disentangle by expression. There is another point. If one is still entangled with a preconscious creative process, one is secretly inflated. Men then have a belly like a pregnant woman, but psychically, which is an inflation. A pregnancy is, so to speak, an inflation. People sometimes resist becoming creative because one's *would-be* creativity is always so much more impressive and important than the little egg one lays in the end when birth takes place. When you are full of would-be ideas, then you feel you will go far beyond whatever Jung said; you will bring out an idea that will revolutionize our whole age, and so on. That is what one feels—quite legitimately, by the way—when one is pregnant, because the whole unconscious is contaminated with this preconscious creative idea. You carry the whole Godhead in your womb, so to speak. But then when you sit down and do the hard work of setting forth your idea, there is a terrific disillusionment, and what you finally produce is generally a sad remnant of what you felt it to be when it was still inside your own psychological womb. Inside it feels tremendous, but when you bring it out there is always a relative reduction. *Parturiunt montes nascetur ridiculus mus,* as the Latin proverb says: The mountains have labor pains and a ridiculous little mouse is brought forth. This is a typical state, but the only thing to do is under all circumstances to bring the mouse out, for sometimes it is more than a mouse. Sometimes it is only a mouse, to be sure. But you can never decide ahead what it will be, and the only way to check whether it is a living child or a rather miserable, crippled abortion is to bring it out. In our human society we may not do away with crippled children, but we may do away with crippled ideas and throw them in our wastepaper baskets if they do not amount to anything. Or, if one has reached this stage, one has to give birth and then deal with what comes out. But the birth is a deflation, because while you are carrying the new creative idea, it is still connected with the wholeness of the unconscious, and therefore you feel so full of ideas.

Probably, this high that one feels has its positive side. But of course, this is not always the case; the opposite state of being can also occur. In many instances, one's condition fluctuates between a jubilant high and a morbid depression; that is, at one point one feels one has really achieved something great, and at another time one feels very depressed. Every creative person has to go through this process to some degree. A further characteristic is that at the moment of creation, one is not able to assess what one has done. One just does not know its worth. Only after a period of about five or six years has one enough distance so that one can look at it as though another person had done it. At the time of creation, one is either too close to, or too far away from, one's work. It is too new and fresh. This is how such enormous tension of the opposites originates, and these are also projected into the creation myths.

Sometimes the problem is also how much you can bring out, and how much you will have to leave behind. Every question you touch leads from hundreds into thousands of problems; you go deeper and deeper, and then have to make up your mind how much you will set out and how much you will omit, and how far you will make your investigations. And that is all cutting, deflation; it is a painful decision to make, and people very often prefer to walk about for years in the state of a would-be creative person, with an enormous belly but with all the disagreeable symptoms of constant irritation, wanting to vomit, bad moods, and restlessness.

Deus Faber

 One very prominent pair of opposites with the motif of the double creator is that of active and passive, and the tendency toward becoming conscious is to be understood as the active part. This active part is given shape especially in the *Deus faber* motif. *Deus faber* is a technical term which characterizes God as the craftsman or artisan, who as an architect, carpenter, or smith creates the world on the analogy of some skill or craft.

I will begin with a Chinese creator who is a master in all crafts. There is one creative power in this more recent Chinese myth, and the creator is called P'an Ku. It was thought that before the world existed only P'an Ku was there, in the form of a man. In pictures he is represented as having pointed ears and being covered with green leaves. He is a kind of cosmic Adam figure. P'an Ku was thought of as the creator of the world who at the same time became the world; when he died his body decayed and became the different parts of the world. I will go into that idea later, but I wish now only to comment on his active aspect, where he is represented as having a chisel with which he chisels and cuts out the whole world. This is a paradox since he makes and becomes the world at the same time, so that, actually, he in a way forms himself. He is a kind of divine artisan who shaped the mountain and chiseled out the sky. He is generally represented as being accompanied by a primeval tortoise and a phoenixlike being; these represent the basic elements of the world. He was also, as the creator God, sometimes represented with an adze, or with a hammer or chisel.

One *Deus faber* of Egyptian cosmogony is the God Ptah of Memphis.[29] He was supposed to have created the whole world, and even the other Gods, on his potter's wheel. Later he was thought of as dwelling in the heart and especially in the tongue of all beings. The Egyptians thought of the heart as being the seat of one's soul and one's consciousness. For this reason, language and consciousness and what we today would call our soul was thought of as having its origins within the heart. As God of the civilized world, Ptah is seated within the heart and tongue of all beings. One text praised Ptah in the following way: he became the tongue and became the heart of the God Atum—the original God—the great and powerful Ptah, who created even the Gods and their Ka. Thoth issued from him, Horus issued from him. He is the God whose heart and tongue are powerful. He is the best in everybody, the best in every mouth of all Gods and human beings, animals and snakes. He is that through which the heart lives and thinks; all he desires comes about.

The whole company of the Gods of Atum came out of his pots and from his fingers. On a potter's wheel he made pots out of which came the Gods. The Gods are also the teeth and lips of his mouth, for he announces everything. The eyes see, the ears hear, the nose breathes the air, and through them all it comes to the heart, but it is the heart which makes every decision, and it is the tongue which repeats the thought of the heart. That is how Ptah created all the Gods. Every divine word is the thought of his heart and came from an order given by his tongue. He created the spirits of life and nourishment and food everywhere. He created what one likes and also what one hates. He gives life to those he likes and death to those who are condemned. Every work of art made by human hands made by him. Legs and limbs move at his command.[30]

In another part of the same text, where it is said that Atum is the father of all the Gods, Atum himself admits that it is not he, but Ptah of Memphis, who created everything.

We can remember from the previous chapter the African tale in which the Gods created things by shaping them in clay. That is not quite the same as on the potter's wheel, but it refers also to things being shaped in clay; these tribes had no potter's wheel; they made their pots with their hands. Mwile and Kolombo mui fangi quarrel as to who made himself first. In this myth, Mwile takes some earth and forms a human being and then Kolombo does the same thing, and they compare them to see which is the best and then destroy the human beings again. So also in African myths, the God creates things from clay, like a potter.

Another craft sometimes mentioned in connection with cosmogonic myths is weaving, where the God weaves the whole world on a loom. This is mentioned in a comment by Sayana, a medieval Hindu commentator on the *Rigveda*. In verse 10.82 of the *Rigveda* the question is put as to the substance from which God created the world, and Sayana in his comment says that from the primeval matter God wove the earth. Weaving is not so often used as an image because it is naturally attributed more to a Goddess, weaving having always been a more feminine activity.[31] The image of weaving is therefore more to be found where a Goddess of nature is involved in the creation myth. For instance, you may recall the Goddess Nemesis in Plato's *Timaeus*. She is the Goddess of natural law. She sits in the center of the cosmos, and the axis of the cosmos spins around in her womb like a spindle.

Spinning and weaving activities are connected with the idea of nature. The Goddess of nature is the loom into which God throws the shuttle so as to weave the world. One of the pre-Socratic Greek philosophers, Pherekydes, has the same image: in the beginning there were Zeus and Chthonia, the Earth Goddess; the Sky God married the Earth Goddess, and he wove the whole world as a big mantle and spread it over an oak. The world is actually a huge coat, in Greek a *pharos*, which is spread over an enormous world tree, the oak; in it are the ocean and the earth and everything else—the sum of it is reality. The whole world has, so to speak, been woven by the Godhead.

We find this idea of the world as a huge colorful woven cloth again in the Indian concept of the veil of Maya. In Indian philosophy, Maya is, in fact, the Goddess of the world of appearances who, to some extent, conjures up the dramas of the world of appearances. In later, more pessimistic philosophical systems, she is interpreted as being illusion, to some degree a fantastical being which, with the help of meditation, one can make dissolve. Or one must turn away from her as one would turn one's back upon some deceptive stage-play. In her original form, Maya was simply the flaming world stage-play which, as a Goddess, she performed as a dance for God. The masculine God is pure light and knowledge, and his Goddess, Maya, spread the veil of the world of appearances out before him.

The carpet weavers of the Orient also had the idea of weaving the world carpet. Carpet weaving has a deeply religious background. Vonessen writes, "It has been claimed that there is no Persian carpet in which there is not a mistake; indeed, the weavers deliberately make a mistake in their knotting to show that it is not their intention to compete with the weaving skills of the creators of the world, even within the context of a small doormat." We find the same thing among the Chinese. It was also their opinion that nothing on earth should be perfect, that in each entity there must be one small mistake, and this is why there is always some flaw to be found in the manufacturing of their artistic ancient vases. Perfection is only for the Divine, and therefore it is inappropriate when something is perfect.

Weaving and spinning are most often expressions for unconscious fantasy activity. Also in the negative sense, when one says about someone in German, "er spinnt" (he spins), one finds the root of this word for fantasizing behind it. Creativity always involves some form of fantasy activity which produces a web of associations. It unfolds like a path to which one suddenly sees connections, and one notices that this idea belongs here, and that explains this, and so, quite suddenly, one is confronted with a web of thoughts. This is also true of sculptors and painters, who see an image becoming increasingly enriched with additional ideas. This is why such people at certain points of their work have no idea how they shall continue. It shows that fantasy obeys its own laws, sets up its own connections, and then suddenly produces some fully completed object which, in hindsight, is experienced as incorporating a comprehensive wholeness.

Rather late in history there appeared the idea that God greated the world as a sort of machine. In the religion of Manichaeism (first and second centuries AD), for example, it was thought that God had created the world as one enormous bucket wheel, so that all the souls lost in darkness might be scooped up and carried back up to heaven. The thought behind this was that while creation had already taken place, it was a sinister chaos. Therefore, in order to redeem the world and to save the light, he built the world in the form of an enormous bucket wheel, literally a kind of machine by means of which those parts of the Godhead which had fallen into darkness could be carried back up to the light.[32] This theme quite often appears in dreams or fantasies of modern people who are familiar with machines. Sometimes it has a negative undertone, in which case the world would appear to be a meaningless mechanism which runs on pointlessly. But very often, if one looks closely at the context, there can be a positive ring to it. Then one sees the underlying idea that creation has come about for a purpose, for some specific goal to be achieved, just as man has invented machines to achieve some specific goal. This is perhaps a more seldom motif, but it nevertheless does occur.

Very frequent also is the image of a smith, the earth having been created as a smith forges reality. So P'an Ku, in certain Chinese representations, carries a hammer; he forged or hammered together the earth. In some commentaries of the *Rigveda,* God is characterized as a smith who forges the world into shape. The image of the smith is also alluded to in the *Enuma Elish,* where there is an interesting connection. The God Marduk fashions the world from the dead body of Tiamat. He first slays her, and then from her corpse creates the world. Now, this dead body of the slain Mother Goddess Tiamat is also called Ku-bu, which is a technical term meaning embryo or ore; so in the art of metallurgy one finds Ku-bu; it was like working the corpse of Tiamat. You will find this with all the references and comments in Mircea Eliade's book *The Forge and the Crucible.*[33]

A verse in the *Rigveda* also gives praise to the creator of the world as a smith, as follows:

> Even as a smith the Lord of Prayer
> Together forged this universe:
> In the earliest ages of the gods
> From what was not arose what is.

In another verse in the same poem the creator is called the carpenter. One of the most familiar forms for us, because in our medieval art he is generally represented in this way, is the idea of the Godhead constructing or fashioning the world as a carpenter builds a house. Also in the *Rigveda,* in 10.81, is the verse: "Tell us from what matter, from which tree, it was that the God fashioned heaven and earth so that they remained firm and young forever and did not fall apart." The Sanskrit word for wood is the same as the Greek word *hyle,* which means both wood and matter, including the wood used for building. The Latin word for matter is also the same, namely *materia,* which also means the building material, wood as building material, the wood which is already cut and prepared for use in building. So in our languages the first matter, the material from which the world was fashioned from Indo-Germanic time onward, has been the carpenter's material, wood. Very often, therefore, in medieval art God is represented as a geometer with a circle in his hand. He sits on his throne above the world, making a plan like an architect for building a house, and in that way he fashions, or creates, the world.

The God who fashions the world as a dead object is mostly found in civilizations which have a rather developed technical aspect. Also there is a tendency in these pictures of the *Deus faber* to use the idea of creating the world like a carpenter or smith as a simile only, and not to take it as concretely as other creation myths do. I think we can conclude from that that creation myths where the God appears as a craftsman mirror a stage in which consciousness has already to a certain extent developed as an independent power apart from the unconscious. Thus in such pictures the Godhead is no longer immanent in the material world, but exists outside it and treats the world as his object, as a craftsman uses his material. To us this seems so self-evident because our whole tradition has trained us to think always of God as being outside the world and shaping its dead material in some form. But upon making a general survey of creation myths, we see that this type of God mirrors a rare and specific situation; it mirrors a state where consciousness has already markedly withdrawn, as an independent entity, out of the unconscious and therefore can turn toward the rest of the material as if it were its dead object. It also already shows a definite separation between subject and object; God is the subject of the creation and the world, and its material is the dead objects with which he deals. Naturally we must correct this viewpoint by putting it into its right context, namely, that the craftsman in primitive societies never imagined himself to be doing the work himself. Nowadays if you watch a carpenter or a smith, he is in a position to feel himself as a human being with independent consciousness, who has acquired from his teacher a traditional skill with which he handles dead material. He feels that his skill is a manmade possession, which he owns. If we look at the folklore and mythology of the different crafts in more primitive societies, we see that they have a much more adequate view of it. They all still have tales which show that man never invented any craft or skill, but that it was *revealed* to him, that it is the Gods who produced the knowledge which man now uses if he does anything practical.

There is a beautiful tale among the Australian aborigines which says that the bow and arrow were not man's invention, but an ancestor God turned himself into a bow and his wife became the bowstring, for she constantly has her hands around his neck, as the bowstring embraces the bow. So the couple came down to earth and appeared to a man, revealing themselves as bow and bowstring, and from that the man understood how to construct a bow. The bow ancestor and his wife then disappeared again into a hole in the earth. So man, like an ape, only copied, but did not invent, the bow and arrow. And so the smiths originally, or so it seems from Eliade's rather plausible argument, did not feel that they had invented metallurgy; rather, they learned how to transform metals on the basis of understanding how God made the world.

Always at bottom there is a divine revelation, a divine act, and man has only had the bright idea of copying it. That is how the crafts all came into existence and is why they all have a mystical background. In primitive civilizations one is still aware of it, and this accounts for the fact that generally they are better craftsmen than we who have lost this awareness. If we think that every craft, whether carpenter's or smith's or weaver's, was a divine revelation, then we understand better the mystical process which certain creation myths characterize as God creating the world like a craftsman. By creating the world through such a craft, he manifests a secret of his own mysterious skill.

In one African myth the word for God is even identical with skill and capacity. The Godhead is defined as that thing which appears in man as the mystery of an unusual skill or capacity. It is something divine, a spark of the divinity in him, not his own possession or achievement, but a miracle.

Because of the relative separation of subject and object in creation myths which characterize creation as fashioning through a craft, certain people have felt that this kills a part of the aspect of creation, because it turns one part of it into a dead object. When you handle material you treat it partly as inanimate material. This process has reached its highest form in our civilization, while in other civilizations there are still at least remnants of an idea that the objects have a life of their own. We have the illusion that it is a completely dead object, which we can handle according to our mood. To illustrate the questionableness of this attitude, I want to give you a simile of the Chinese philosopher, Chuang-tzu, who created an opposite creation myth. It is a relatively late text and is a kind of protest against an overevaluation of the idea of the craftsman creating the world. Unfortunately, the English translation which I have deviates very much from the German translation.[34] Explanations which are added I owe to the Sinologist Dr. Ariane Rump.

It is called "The Death of —" and then comes a word which in English translation is given as "Chaos" and which Richard Wilhelm translates as "the Unconscious": "The Death of the Chaos-

Unconscious." The Master of the Southern Sea was the one with many facets. In the English translation he is called Brief. In German it is the *Schillernde* (iridescent). If someone is *schillernd*, it means that he has many moods, many facets to his personality; he has not only one idea and one purpose in mind. It seems as though someone had not a reflective consciousness with one definite purpose in mind, but rather a vague personality with changeable moods—now this and now that—which is why the English translation is Brief. The Master of the Northern Sea was in the English translation Sudden, while the German is *der Zufahrende*, the one who seizes quickly. If I *zufahre* without thinking of what I am doing, then I just seize something, so you see what it characterizes. The one is the thing which has no definite purpose in mind, but flickers around in different moods; the other is the one who seizes something too quickly, who interferes too soon. In the middle was Hwun-tun, which is translated as Chaos, or the Unconscious; it is the preconscious totality, that vague thing which you could as well call conscious or unconscious or chaos, or preconscious order; it is the unknown thing in the middle.

Brief and Sudden often met in the middle space of Chaos-Unconscious. Chaos-Unconscious was always very friendly toward them. Brief and Sudden now wondered how they could reward the kindness of Chaos-Unconscious. They said that all human beings had seven orifices, so that they could see and hear and eat and breathe, but he had nothing of the kind, so they would try to make them for him. Every day they drilled a hole into Chaos-Unconscious, and on the seventh day he was dead. That is the end of the story.

So you see, they wanted to be very kind and shape Chaos into a beautiful being who could hear and see, which means make him conscious. By trying to make him conscious, they nicely killed him! This is an exceedingly meaningful creation myth of Chuang-tzu, which strongly compensates our viewpoint of the God shaping matter into form and beauty out of chaos. It means killing something, killing the specific life of that world material, destroying it in some ways. It does make it into something shaped and conscious, but destroys it at the same time. This is naturally a typically Taoist text; Taoist tradition has a general tendency rather to emphasize the value of the unconscious in opposition to consciousness. I think that puts the right counteraccent against our myths of the God who fashions the world out of dead material, and it naturally mirrors the questionable aspects of our civilization with its overevaluation of craft, technology, and consciousness.

I now want to insert some short definitions of certain key words in the text.

Shu: Here there are two explanations, either (1) heedless, hasty, sudden, brief, or (2) mottled: iridescent, with the colors of green, blue, and black.

Hu: Suddenly, unexpectedly, carelessly, hastily.

Hun: Turbid, or torrent, or the whole of, complete.

Tun: Confused. Therefore, *hwun tun* means approximately: confused, unintelligible, unclear, and muddy—not yet separated, but in a harmonious union. Also explained as being without cause or reason, bottomless, the root cannot be seen. Both parts of the name carry an illuminating implication, namely that of water.

An interesting parallel to the motif of haste is found in an Islamic text which comments on the creation of Adam. The text is handed down by Masudi, who says that when Adam was created, he lay around as a lump of clay for 80 years. Then Allah gave him human shape, but his soul was still lacking. He then lay around for another 120 years, after which Allah breathed the breath of life into him. But the breath had not yet completely filled Adam's body. He wanted to get up, but was not quite able to do so and therefore fell back; thus it is said in Surahs 17 and 21 of the Koran: "Man was created in a hasty manner," and only when Allah's breath had completely penetrated Adam's body could he get up and praise him. There you see the idea that there is a strange kind of imperfection in the act of creation, which in China is attributed to the hasty impulse and which comes again here in this Islamic motif of the creation of Adam.[35]

These two heedless and hasty creators, who, in fact, are to become the murderers of Hwun-tun, readily bring to mind a scene from our first Eskimo myth: the moment when Father Raven wakes up as a human being in the darkness and feels around and becomes conscious of himself. Then, still in heaven, he first makes a figure out of clay, but this figure immediately begins to dig around in the earth: or, as it is said in the tale, "it had a hot-headed and violent temperament, not like Father Raven." The latter then makes a hole in the heavens and lets it fall through, and it becomes the evil spirit. This part of the text shows that the evil spirit is Father Raven-God's first creation and that it is indeed a being with a violent and impatient temperament. This would be a parallel to the Sudden we spoke of above, to a reckless being who simultaneously wants to bungle things. This clearly points to a shadow aspect of creativity.

To come to a more practical aspect; I have seen personally that one of the greatest problems in any kind of creation is to be able to time the creative urge properly. When you are caught in something creative, you generally tend to be so overwhelmed by it that you become hasty and want to put it out all at once. There is an inpouring of ideas, and you fear that when you begin to write you will not get them down quickly enough and will so lose half of them again. If you are the more intuitive type of creative person, it is particularly difficult, because the writing or painting hand cannot follow the flow of ideas quickly enough. This is not only the case in verbal creation; the same thing happens in plastic arts also. One sees a picture or something in stone and what it should look like, and one wants to get it quickly out of the stone, or down on the paper or canvas, fearing to lose the inner sight of the thing, for if it cools down and loses its freshness, you are lost! You cannot call it back into your mind again. So you must forge it, or create it, in the moment when it is red-hot, just when it is there and offers itself. At the same time, just that feeling that it must be done now when it is pressing seduces one very easily into a hasty way of creating, either a sloppy way of writing or a hasty way of giving any kind of artistic expression, and by that, naturally, one ruins it completely. One has to redo it two or three times, trimming it and cleaning it up, but sometimes one ruins it so that one cannot bring it out at all. So this feeling of hasty explosion is one of the dangers and difficulties of most creative impulses.

In the scientific field there is the same danger, in the form of jumping to conclusions and generalizing. One aspect seems to fit things very well, and then you generalize; everything is the same idea. This gives rise to those theories which are so monomaniacal, where one idea is hammered into every object, and if the object does not comply, you even cheat, because it must fit. That is hasty creativeness. In the history of science, for instance, most misguided ideas in which humanity has been caught sometimes for many hundreds of years were caused by an (in itself right) idea which was so hastily generalized that it thereby blocked further investigation. One is so emotionally filled with a new discovery that this danger of killing everything by applying it in a too heedless and hasty way is one of the greatest dangers in creative activity. And it is very difficult to discipline. Jung, for instance, wrote his books very slowly, in handwriting. If you look at his manuscripts there is very little correction. He did not write more than a page or two an hour, very carefully, pausing after every sentence. I watched that for many years and swore I would do the same, for I think it is the only right way, but I haven't succeeded, and even now I cannot do it. It is a battle of life and death to hold back this Mr. Hasty. You can laugh at

me, I don't mind, but try it yourself before you laugh
too much! A creative impulse is so powerful and grips
one emotionally so strongly that one has at the same
time to withhold emotion, whereby you can naturally
overdo it and go too slowly. And if you hold back
your horses too much, it happens that the idea disappears, or it loses the freshness of the first insight and
goes dead.

Thus to time the creative process properly, so as to
be accurate, reflectively conscious, and aware of every
detail, but at the same time not killing it by holding
back too much, is one of the greatest arts. On it depends, to a large extent, how far one can develop
one's creativity in the right way without killing the
object (the material) or the original revelation.

Now, this Hasty with his violent temperament has
a further very important meaning. Creativity is, in a
certain sense, always very close to something devilish.
We can see this today most readily, perhaps, with our
technological discoveries, which illustrate how man
always tends to exaggerate. We need only consider
the extent of the destruction and pollution we have
caused to the environment as a result of this hasty
exaggeration of our technological discoveries. We can
say that our progress in human consciousness has re-
peatedly been characterized by such catastrophic
hasty exaggeration. In this connection, one might also
consider what has taken place in the field of psychia-
try and all the sins that have been committed in this
field over the last fifty years. It is impossible to describe the numerous things which were tried and
highly praised until, two or three years later, when it

was shown that the latest innovation did more harm than good, it was then dropped, and always it was simply a matter of trying something new again.

This characteristic of being hasty has a direct connection to creativity: one cannot be creative without a certain creative fever taking hold of one, without feeling excited and full of enthusiasm. Indeed, on the one hand, this is essential. On the other hand, if I do not develop a large moral sense of responsibility, then all will turn out negatively because of this hasty and heedless manner of being. And this is why in our creation myths we so often have this double meaning, even right from the outset. As in the myth of the Firestone, for example, who is also so hasty and impatient, as the story shows, when both brothers argue while still in the womb about being born. Firestone says, "I see light, let us now go that way." But Maple Sprout God says thoughtfully, "No, we do not want to do that, for we do not want to kill our mother," and then gets himself into the normal position an embryo must have in order to be born naturally. But Firestone cannot wait and tears his mother apart, and she dies. He is the hasty one, the one without patience who chooses to take the shortcut and thereby represents the destructive. That is the shadow aspect of creativity.

There is concrete evidence of this in the fact that many creative people have something demoniacal about them. Their partners would have a lot to say about this, for a creative person can be ruthless, and to some extent he must be so, for he needs all his energy for the object of his creativity and has not enough vitality to cover all of life's other demands. For example, if we think about an explorer or an inventor who focuses all his concentration upon that one thing which he is after, we cannot blame him even; but on the other hand, it is clear that there may be a demoniacal aspect present when one is creative.

There is a further point which needs to be looked at. When a content from the unconscious surfaces, there is a tendency for it to try to break through not on a symbolic inner level, but rather on the level of concrete reality. To illustrate my point, a terrible example which actually happened comes to mind. In a psychiatric hospital, a schizophrenic patient behaved in such a peaceful and friendly manner that he was given permission to work in the garden of the director of the hospital. In the process, he made friends with the director's little daughter. They used to talk together and became good friends. But one day, the man fell into a state of great excitement and took a knife and cut off the little girl's head. There was no court case, for it was known that he was insane. But he was asked why he had done such a thing, and he said he had heard a voice, the voice of the Holy Ghost, and it had told him to do it, and so, of course, he had done it. And he showed no sign of remorse.

If we psychologically analyze it, this voice was, in itself, something absolutely positive and constructive, and one could say it was indeed the voice of the Holy Ghost. But then the question is raised, what, in fact, was really meant? If, for example, he had been my patient and he had come to me with a dream content which told him to do such a thing, I would have said,

"Yes. That is right. You are still behaving like a little child, and now this childish side of you has to be killed." This would mean that such a voice is to be understood as a challenge on an inner spiritual level. Instead of doing what he did, this man should have sacrificed his own childish, naive attitude toward life, not the real child.

When an impulse from the unconscious comes up, it is always accompanied by a drive to realize it in a concrete manner. This is a general truth. We see this most often, for example, when transference phenomena occur during psychological treatment. When one is a patient and falls in love with one's doctor and dreams of making love, it is a sign that one needs to experience greater human closeness, a better human contact. But most often a patient gives it a more concrete interpretation and would like to realize it immediately. This is not because of stupidity, but rather we know that "it" within us is driving us. It is a certain demoniacal force, but if it were to be realized in such a concrete manner, the patient would be the first to be disappointed. But one is unable to restrain oneself and does not notice that it is meant to be understood symbolically. This is how it is with most contents from the unconscious. They are always accompanied by this hasty drive to carry the thing out immediately. This is the demon. This means that one must always first of all think about it and say, "Just a moment. Let's wait and see what wants to be realized."

In a letter, Jung even went so far as to say, "Demonic powers are archetypes in an initial stage of moving toward consciousness." This means that all archetypes, as they begin to move toward consciousness, have demoniacal aspects. It is only after the threshold into consciousness has been broken through and the content has been integrated that its positive meaning becomes apparent. This also means that that which is demoniacal is not something absolute. Rather, it is a stage to be passed through for those unconscious contents which are moving up toward consciousness. And this explains why it is that creative people are very closely exposed to demonic, devilish forces, for in them, archetypal contents are breaking through the threshold into consciousness. This is also why one very often sees that before there is a creative concretization, there is a creative disturbance and certain demoniacal impulses appear. I once knew a creative man who, before he could proceed with his creative work, suffered from attacks of malice—one cannot put it any other way—which meant that he verbally attacked each and every friend that he had. As he was a very intelligent person who could speak in a very pointed manner, he was able to maliciously wound each one of his friends when he met with them, the result of which, of course, was that they all walked out on him. Only then, when he was completely alone again and nobody would have a bar of him did he try to establish contact with them. But naturally, nobody had any time for him. Then he would return to his room, and this was the point at which he was able to do something worthwhile, but only then. Out of sheer loneliness, with no one wanting anything of him, he was able to give birth. Other people do the same thing, but to themselves, alone within their own four walls. They have depressions and feel deeply discouraged. They feel worthless and nothing has any meaning. And only then, when they are completely floored, can they begin to work.

I once knew an artist, an extravert, who worked as a graphic designer. In his precreative phase, he was overrun by a mad sexual possession. He used to run out of the house and sometimes rode around the entire day in a tram staring at all the women. He was able to laugh at himself about it and say, "Now it's got me in its grip again." And when this state had passed, he was then able to produce really beautiful things. An explanation of this behavior is that there is a certain energetic charge which cannot yet come out in the right place and therefore gets diverted into by-paths. Then one has to know that there is a charge inside oneself, but one should not let it take a wrong path, but must contain it until it comes out in the right way. But, of course, this requires strong self-discipline.

The First Victim

 This last creation myth of Chuang-tzu leads us to another motif which I want to take up here, namely the motif of *the first victim*. As we have seen, poor Hwun-tun, Chaos and Unconsciousness, was the first victim. It is not possible to create something without destroying something else at the same time, and the Chinese, especially the Taoist philosophers, who are so fully aware of the questionableness of human consciousness, have therefore quite rightly stressed creation as a sort of murder, the murder of a kind and innocent being, because Hwun-tun is characterized as especially kind, friendly, and innocent.

The motif of the first victim is also found in the *Enuma Elish,* where chaos, the monster Mother Goddess Tiamat, is slain by Marduk; out of her corpse the world is created. She is a first victim. Here the victim is not the God but the Goddess. The same idea, but in a different aspect, is contained in the oldest Hindu cosmogony, where the world is created as a sacrificial act. According to certain Hindu cosmogonies, the first being was a primeval giant called Purusha (the word simply means person or man).[36] In certain other texts, according to some commentators, he is identified with

Vishnu, but in the main text he is generally just called Purusha—man. The whole cosmos has the shape of Purusha, of a man. He has a thousand heads and a thousand feet and extends even beyond the earth and covers the whole world. Out of his body the whole world was created. But the act of creation is treated as a sacrificial rite, in which the first man, or Purusha, was the victim. He is cut up, and each part of him becomes a part of the universe: his head becomes the sky, his navel the air, his feet the earth, from his mind springs the moon, from his eye the sun, and from his breath the wind. Thus *they*—suddenly there are many creators, "they" meaning the Gods—fashioned the world. One text says Purusha is the whole world: what is, what has been, and what shall be. One-fourth of him is all creatures, and three-fourths are the world of the immortals in heaven. Sometimes in later Sankhya philosophy, Purusha is the soul in matter, as opposed to matter. I do not want to go into the subtleties now; I want rather just to point out the idea that the material from which the world is created is a divine victim.

Our Chinese God, P'an Ku, is also not only the artisan who created the world, but the first victim as well, and from his corpse the world is created. When P'an Ku wept, one text says, his streaming tears made the yellow Yangtse River; he breathed and the wind blew; he spoke and thunder roared; he looked around and lightning glanced from his eyes. The weather would be fine when P'an Ku was in a good temper, dull and cloudy when he was cross. When he died, his remains fell apart and formed the five sacred mountains of

China. His head became the Ti Mountain in the east, his body the Sung Mountain in the center, his right arm the Heng Mountain in the north, and his left the Heng Mountain in the south. His two feet became the Hua Mountain in the west. His two eyes were transformed into the Sun and Moon, his fat melted into streams and seas, and his hair, taking root, covered the earth with plants. So although P'an Ku is in some myths and mythological representations the artisan, he is here the victim and the material of which the world is made.

The same motif is found in old Germanic mythology where Ymir is the primeval giant. The name Ymir means the up-rushing noise of boiling water in a cauldron, the gurgling sound of something boiling over. In German it is generally translated as *Urgebraus,* the noise of a storm at sea when the waves roar and make such a boiling noise. One translation says:

> Out of Ymir's flesh was the earth fashioned,
> from his gushing gore the seas,
> hilltops from his bones, trees from his hair,
> heav'nly sky from his skull.[37]

Thus the world was shaped from the parts of Ymir.

We know that Wotan and two of his brothers, Vili and Veli, slew Ymir, or Odin did it (Odin is the Nordic name; in German it is Wotan). These three brothers were the sons of Borr. Ymir is a sort of giant. Those three are the first who are not giants but Gods. How the children of a giant suddenly become Gods is not explained, but it is clear that they are more potent powers in the world than giants. According to Saxo-

Grammaticus they slew Ymir, and in his blood all the other frost giants were drowned. Then the three brothers dragged Ymir into the original chaos—*Ginnunga-gap*—and formed the earth from him. They took the skull and made it the sky, held up by four dwarfs. Sometimes, therefore, in later kennings (riddles in verses) the sky is called the skull upheld by four dwarfs. Nordic poetry is full of such indirect allusions.

In the *Voluspa* a variation of this myth says:

> In time's morning lived Ymir,
> Then was no sand, sea, nor cool waves;
> No earth was there, nor heaven above,
> Only a yawning chasm [*Ginnunga-gap*],
> nor grass anywhere.

Ginnunga is akin to the German word *gähnen* and the English word *yawn*. It is a kind of vast, open gap, an open mouth, just as the word *chaos* comes from a root which means to yawn—the yawning abyss.

> Then Borr's sons [the three mentioned] upheaved
> the disks
> And shaped the beautiful Midgard [the earth];
> From the south the sun shone on earth's stones,
> And from the ground sprang green leeks.

Another text says:

> Out of Ymir's flesh was shaped the earth,
> The mountains out of his bones,
> The Heaven from the ice-cold giant's skull,
> Out of his blood the boisterous sea.

More details were added later, but in such later sources we are not quite sure how much the medieval

Adam legends may have influenced Germanic traditions. Very early, with Christianization, a lot of legendary material spread concerning the biblical figure
of the first man, Adam, who in the Midrash (Jewish
legends) and in Islamic lore and traditions is described
as a kind of world-giant. In certain versions his body
goes from one end of the world to the other.[38] We find
the beginning of this cosmic aspect of Adam in legends which say that God took the clay, or the dust, to
shape the body of Adam from the four corners of the
world. Not only did he take the dust from the four
corners of the world, but it was in four colors: red,
black, white, and yellow. (Notice that they are the
same as the main colors in alchemy.) From the red he
made blood, from the black bowels, from the white
bones and blood vessels, and from the yellow he
formed the body. God brought all this dust together
so that whether man wandered from east to west or
from west to east, or if he found some other place
where he wished to stay, the Earth could not say,
"Here you cannot dwell because you have not my
substance." So the Earth cannot chase him away from
any place.

In certain early Jewish traditions it is said that the
first man reached from one end of the world to the
other. There you see an opposite motif: it is not only
that the material comes from the different corners of
the world, but that man was really spread over the
whole world, and only after the Fall, after he had
sinned, did God make him small, when he was reduced to his present size. In the Talmudic and Mid-
rashic traditions, however, Adam remains as tall after

the Fall as before. You can find this idea in the Kabbalah as well. It is said in the *Sefer Gigulim,* a Kabbalistic text, that the head of Adam and his throat were, at the time of creation, in the middle of the Garden of Eden, but his body was spread over all parts of the world. He is also generally regarded as having been androgynous, like the first man who is described in Aristophanes' speech in Plato's *Symposium.* According to others, he was not androgynous but had two faces and God cut him in two, an idea that reflects the influence of the Platonic tradition. In the Kabbalistic conception, Adam was not only as big as the world, but contained in him all the souls of all human beings which ever existed—namely, 600,000. Slowly they emanated from him, but originally every human being was contained in the first Adam. There are even amusing details. In rabbinic literature the souls hung all around his body, some in his hair and others from his nose, and all over him; from there they were born into the world. Here the first gigantic human being is not slain, but after the Fall he is reduced and made small, which is a certain variation on the theme of the slaying of the first monster.

If we make a survey of these first victims, we see that they belong mostly to the second of the two creator columns, the passive side. The idea is already contained in the word *victim:* he who is pushed out of reality, the one who does not continue to exist, but who retires, or is reduced or cut up. He belongs to a former appearance which has now disappeared. We must now ask ourselves what this motif of the destruction of a gigantic human form or humanlike being means psychologically. I think the meaning is relatively transparent: this primeval being represents an aspect of a preconscious totality, sometimes whole and sometimes, as in the motif of Tiamat, more the passive aspect, which is destroyed for the sake of the further development of consciousness. Every step forward toward building up more consciousness destroys a previous living balance. This is true even in the case of a neurosis and is one of the reasons why one is very attached and loyal to his neurosis and has generally great feeling trouble in separating from his former neurotic situation. One of the great therapeutic difficulties is that there is a certain instinctive resistance to being cured, because in this disturbed state of relative unconsciousness or unadaptedness the human psyche tends to establish a certain balance, a certain harmony. The neurotic system is a compensation. Maladjustment, for instance, is compensated by megalomanic fantasies. But there is always a certain amount of balance, and whenever progress, or a widening of consciousness, is intended, the former balance must be destroyed. That is why we speak in therapy of the healing crisis, and why people often complain when they are analyzed that they get worse and worse, that before they went into analysis things were relatively tolerable, but got so much worse that they feel they should never have touched psychology. Also, at the beginning of an analysis the parents sometimes come and say that previously their son or daughter was at least tolerable, but now it is absolutely impossible to have him or her at home anymore. The neurotic balance has been disturbed by the process of bringing up a new form of consciousness, and it is only when this new widened form of consciousness has become dominant that the conflict subsides.

Every bit of progress in consciousness, every creative process, every widening and changing of the conscious attitude, first destroys a primitive original totality and a certain balance within the whole system. Because we look at the conscious-unconscious psyche as being a relatively closed, self-regulating system, it is understandable that such processes always split it up. You find this motif in a different form again in the myth of the noble savage—the balanced, harmonious human being from whom we have deviated through our development toward higher consciousness (Rousseau). To a great extent this is probably a pure projection.

Whenever this primeval giant who represents the totality is destroyed, there are, with one exception, also figures of destroyers who are Gods. Only in the myth of P'an Ku the text runs: When P'an Ku died, his head became the Ti Mountains, etc. He died himself, so to speak, without any outer cause. But in the case of Hwun-tun it is Brief and Sudden who destroy him, in the case of Ymir it is the three Gods who slay him, and in the case of Tiamat it is Marduk who, with the help of the wind, tears her to pieces. In the case of the Purusha it is sometimes Vishnu and sometimes, in other variations, simply "the Gods" in general, who destroy the primeval giant.

This probably gives us a hint as to why the preconscious totality, an early form of the Self, is destroyed, and perhaps can also hint where we should look for the origin of consciousness. If you look at it from the point of view of man's evolution, it is naturally a question why man is the only one of the higher mammals to have this strange quality of consciousness to so much greater an extent than any other being we know on this planet. If the Gods slay this primeval being (we could say that the Gods represent archetypal contents) it would mean that a single archetypal content, or group, destroys the original total balance. Looking at it as a diagram, we would have to think of the preconscious totality as a continuum.

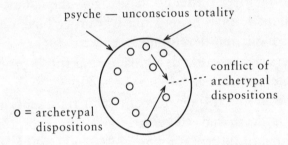

When we use the word *psyche,* we think of it as something like a continuum, while at the same time, naturally, it contains all the different archetypes or archetypal dispositions which correspond to what in animals the zoologist calls the patterns of behavior. Now, the totality of the patterns of behavior in animals and in man are not harmonious. Already on the animal level you see that different patterns and different dispositions can conflict and collide. In other words, even an animal suffers constantly from conflicts, let us call them unconscious conflicts. You can see that easily enough. For example, if you watch a broody hen and approach her when she is sitting on her eggs, you will notice at once that she gets into a dual attitude: the normal instinct of flight and self-preservation, and the maternal, brooding instinct, which tells her to stay on her eggs. She gets into a tension and stares at you and then suddenly flies away screeching: the instinct to escape has overcome the brooding instinct. Or it may be the other way around, and she may stay quiet and not show fear anymore; you can stroke her and see that the brooding instinct has won out. Sometimes the conflict goes on for some time, and if you know the expressions of such a bird, you can see how she is torn between the two instincts, one of which after a time turns out to be the stronger; then there is an either/or reaction. Here comes the phenomenon, the problem of the displaced reaction, about which I spoke before when I told of the two birds which wanted to fight but, since fear and aggression were in complete balance and neither could overcome the other, a third reaction appeared and both birds went to sleep. Here the two conflicting instinctual patterns were absolutely balanced. Generally that is not the case, for usually, after a while, one or the other wins out and there is a reaction. Another well-known conflicting pattern is that of a sexually excited male deer or stag, who will run straight into a hunter. It is well known that a man with his gun must keep out of the way; it has even happened that a huntsman has been knocked down by such an animal. In such cases the animal loses its natural instinct of self-preservation, for the one instinct, sex, sweeps away all the others. Naturally, all the other instinctual patterns—

self-preservation, hunger, and so on—are only repressed for a time and come up again, but at the moment the one is so prevalent that all the others subside.

We must not, therefore, think of the higher mammals as in any way harmonious beings with a harmonious set of instinctual patterns; the harmony of instinctual patterns in higher animals is only very relative and on occasion can fall into conflict. Probably we are no exception in this respect, and in us as well the different instinctual dispositions can collide and disturb the total balance of the system. Now, what we call in zoology patterns of behavior are what we can watch from the outside, namely the actual behavior: flight, mating, feeding, nesting, and so on. The archetype, according to Jung's definition, is the accompanying inward aspect of the pattern of behavior, namely emotions, feelings, and inner representations, including even abstract concepts; that would be the archetypal disposition, and those archetypal dispositions collide and fight exactly as instincts or patterns of behavior do. That is why in so many mythologies one finds a war of the Gods, or a war of the Titans. It is not at all that the heavenly world, or ghost world, is free from wars; on the contrary, innumerable myths all over the world show the Gods warring with each other. Sometimes there are two types of Gods: Gods fight with Titans, or Gods of the light fight against Gods of the darkness, ghosts of springtime fight ghosts of winter, and so on, mirroring the basic disharmony of even the archetypal unconscious patterns in man. When Heraclitus therefore says that the origin of existence and the father of all things is war, he is in this sense right.

In this connection I want to cite a text which in its higher philosophical evolution is a bit different from the primitive texts but is still very illuminating on this problem of the warring patterns. It is the creation myth of a Gnostic sect which called themselves the Sethians. This sect existed at about the time of Christ. They had sacred scriptures of their own, called the "Holy Book," or the "Paraphrasis of Seth."[39] This book states that originally there was the cosmos shaped from three interwoven principles, which again contained a tremendous number of other principles. One principle was the light above, another the darkness below, and in between was pure pneuma, a purely spiritual force which spread a balsamic, wonderful odor into the darkness. The darkness itself was similar to a frightful mass of water, but not deprived of intelligence; darkness knew quite well that if one separated her from the light she would be empty, without power and weak, so she always tried to reach the light and to contain some sparks of it. (I am skipping parts which do not bear directly on our theme.) All three principles contained an infinite number of other powers which were reasonable and capable of thought. They all remained quiet, as if resting in themselves, but as soon as one of the principles came near them, then the unevenness of their order produced a certain movement and energy; this movement resulted in a collision of powers. When they collided, they made the impression of a seal upon each other. Through these collisions of powers, images were formed. Through the infinite number of powers and the infinite number of collisions there were produced an infinite number of images. Those images are the ideas of different living beings. Ideas are here not meant in the philosophical modern sense of the word, but in the Platonic sense, the *eidola,* the archetypal images of all beings which would exist later. In the Iroquois language the Ongwe, whom I mentioned before, are also the prototypes of everything which will exist later.

So you see, in this cosmogony of the Sethians it is clearly stated that the archetypal patterns in the human psyche result from the collision of instinctual, or energetic, impulses, and that already in the original totality there is a mass of collisions which slowly form certain patterns. This seems to me to mirror what we know from the psychological viewpoint, namely that the collision of different archetypal patterns probably stands at the original of consciousness. If we speak in an anthropomorphic way, we could say that the higher mammals with their colliding instinctual patterns are only relatively well adapted beings, because there are departures from perfect adaptation as a result of the collision of patterns. Thus it is obvious that the invention of a "central office," which would regulate colliding patterns, would be of the greatest value.

Actually, we could say that is what has happened in man: he has the beginnings of a conscious ego with which he can regulate such collisions. That is what we call subjectively the free will of the conscious personality. Jung defines free will as a certain amount of energy which is at the disposal of the ego. If the ego has a certain amount of energy at its disposal, then it is in a situation where it feels it has subjectively what we call a free will. Philosophically, the existence of a free will cannot be proved, because whatever you do, subjectively feeling that it is a free decision, your detractor can always say that it was an unconscious pattern which made you feel like that. So we cannot argue from a philosophical point of view about the problem of free will; there are just as many pros as cons; it is a question which from an intellectual standpoint can neither be proved or disproved. But as a psychological phenomenon we can speak of the subjective experience of feeling free and of having made a free decision.

Take the case of a mother whose house is on fire. The situation is the same as that of the hen on her eggs—her first movement is to run downstairs and save her own life, but then she remembers the sleeping child upstairs. Subjectively she will feel that she decides to go back and save the child. The man who does not believe in free will can say that it is just her mother instinct overpowering the self-preservation instinct—she had no decision in that, she only felt as though she decided. One cannot prove it, but as a subjective experience we are capable of having an instinctual conflict between running away and saving the child. We often feel afterward as if something had decided at the last moment, "No, that's what I am going to do, not the other."

If you ask people who have been in such critical situations, they will sometimes quite honestly admit that they did not themselves decide, but that something impelled them to run back and save the child. They say they cannot take credit, something which was stronger made them save the child from the burning house. But another person will equally honestly say that at a certain moment she realized the situation and decided to do it. So there we have to believe in the person's honesty, and in a certain case it will be that the maternal instinct impels the mother to save the child, and in another sense she had enough freedom and could have let the child be burnt but consciously made up her mind to save it. Sometimes we act in a completely driven way; instinct makes us act and we feel it subjectively. We know quite well we haven't any merit in what we did, for a stronger power carried us away, while at other times one remembers having made up one's mind at a certain crucial moment. So free will is in that way a subjective experience of having energy at our disposal.

We define the ego simply as one complex among others, the ego having a certain amount of energy at its disposal which goes to support one or another instinctual impulse. At a certain moment we decide to support this or that impulse. The minimum of energy at the disposal of the ego decides, so that in this way the ego becomes the central bureau which interferes when the instinctual patterns collide and can sometimes save the situation. Naturally, the ego sometimes misuses its power and, like all people who sit in offices, represses things which it has no right to repress. The real function should be only to be the central bureau of decision in case of collision, but it naturally oversteps its powers and does all sorts of mischief and interferes in things or processes which are none of its business, like all officials who poke their noses into things which are not their business. Here the ego is a mirror of the disease of our conscious civilization. But one sees why nature invested in human consciousness, speaking in anthropomorphic language, and one sees its tremendous value because in certain moments of disharmony and colliding instincts it can bring about a reasonable solution by reflection. The colliding instinctual pattern and the war of the Gods is a mythological motif to which I will come back later in another connection. For the moment I want to use this motif only to produce possible evidence as to why this original totality had to fall apart, why there is such a thing as a first victim. Certain instinctual patterns became stronger than others and disturbed the harmony, and therefore the original balance had to fall apart in order to build up a higher form of consciousness.

The origin of the ego complex is a very mysterious thing about which we know very little. Jung, in the introduction to his book *Aion,* gives a basic description of the ego, beginning by saying that it is a mysterious factor in the human being and that we do not know what it is. We can only define it as the center of the field of consciousness, in the sense that all the contents which are associated with the ego are conscious; those which are not associated with the ego are not conscious. Jung then says that the origin of the ego is unknown, that it probably originates from collisions of the body with the outer world.[40]

For instance, a child cannot judge distance: it sees

something it wants and stretches out its hand, but the thing does not come to it, so it howls at the top of its voice. It has a conflict! It has a deep pain because it cannot get the toy which is beyond its reach. And so, slowly, it learns how far its body goes. It bites itself and then realizes that it has bitten itself. There are all those collisions, which first are based on bodily collisions. By this means there is built up what the Freudians call the body ego, that is, awareness of the body, of oneself. Even adult people, if the question is put, "Who are you?" will touch their bodies. It is a genuine gesture to demonstrate the ego: this is me, and this is not me. Afterward the same collision occurs with the inner world, but that is a process which comes a bit later, namely that this which has already been built up from the physical collisions then begins to collide with inner factors, and that is where one comes to the problem of education.

I would like to illustrate this point with an example. Let's imagine that a child desperately wants to steal a piece of chocolate, for his greed is driving him to do it. However, the child knows that he may not do such a thing, or does not even want to do it. He is then on a collision course with his own desire. Many modern psychological theories maintain the view that at this point one's superego plays a role. This would be the case if the child's parents had strictly forbidden him to steal the desired piece of chocolate. But let's imagine that the child wants to steal the chocolate from his own little sister, in which case the boy is not so certain that his parents have forbidden him to steal it. Then it is possible that the child's own genuine af-

fection for his sister, together with a genuine feeling
of not wanting to take the chocolate away from her,
collides with his own wish to eat that piece of chocolate. This represents a genuine collision between the
ego and its inner world.

I remember an unforgettable experience from my
own childhood in which I collided with my own inner
world. I had a violent temper and was exceptionally
impatient. Once, when I was about six and a half
years old, I wanted to draw our dog. The dog was
lying on an easy chair, fast asleep. I got myself into a
good position and began to draw when all of a sudden the "stupid" dog moved. The drawing I had already begun, was, of course, no longer correct, and
so I had to start all over again, which I did, and the
dog slept on. I was at peace and happy to draw him
in this different position, when suddenly he moved
again. This process repeated itself about four times.
Then I stood up and gave the dog a hard slap. Now,
our dogs at home were always treated in a most fair
and decent manner so, as a result, the dog was deeply
wounded and indignant. He had done absolutely
nothing wrong. His conscience was clear. Consequently, he sat up and stared at me long and hard
with a look of indignation and reproach. He could
not fathom what had happened and quite obviously
thought, "She's mad." This reproachful look of the
dog went straight to my heart, and I felt miserably
ashamed of myself. It was quite clear to me that I had
had no right to hit him, for he had only moved and
shifted his head a little bit. This was such a collision
with my own impatience and my own violent temper-

ament, as I described above, and I have never forgotten it. I promised myself that I would never do such a thing again, and I never have. Everybody has certainly had this experience as a child of how one collides and falls into a conflict with not only the outer world and the conventions of society, but also, through certain impulses, in a very real way with oneself and one's own morality.

So the child knows he should not take or touch something; he has a tremendous desire to do so, but education has trained him not to, and then it collides with his desire; he has an inner conflict. He wants the chocolate and is forbidden to take it, so the desire to take it collides with the inhibiting force of consciousness. There is a whole chain of further collisions with the inner world, with desires, with impulses, with affects, etc., which beat like waves against the mainland of the ego and are always pushed back. That is all we can say with a certain plausibility about the formation of the ego. Through these collisions, slowly one complex which is stronger than another builds up and forms what we call the ego. There is the famous illustration that a child first speaks of himself in the third person, calling himself John, or Jack, or Billy, and suddenly, but only after some time, begins to say "I." He first sees himself only as mirrored in what others say about him, and then this feeling of "me," "I," "It's me," slowly build up.

It seems that the power which builds up the ego is one special complex, namely the Self, and not the other archetypes. If you watch childhood dreams, let us say of children from their fourth to their twelfth

year, you see that their future conscious attitude,
what you could call their future ego form, appears as
an image which is projected outside, generally in the
form of an older brother, or the gang leader—all of
those figures about whom the child would say that
that was what he wanted to be. He wants to be a tram
conductor, or a stationmaster and wear a red cap and
wave the trains on and off, etc. All those figures could
be called model egos or, more accurately, models of
what the next step of ego development will be. For
instance, if the boy wants to wave the trains on, that
is the next form; that is, he is capable of ruling the
hitherto mechanical processes of his psyche. It is a
typical ego idea—now *he* is the one who says what
will happen and no longer Father or others in authority. If you look at this model ego from its more general archetypal amplifications, it is the same thing as
the Self. The symbols of the model ego and the symbols of the Self are in early childhood—and in the
general phase of youth development—the same thing.
For instance, children dream about a gang leader
whom they admire, but in the dream the gang leader
has magical powers, or is radiant like a sun hero, or
something like that, which shows that this figure is
not only the gang leader whom the boy knows from
school, but also the Self. For him, that figure means
at the same time the Self, because it has supernatural
or even divine qualities in addition to ego qualities.
So the identity of the model ego figures in youth and
of what we normally call figures of the Self in mythology indicate that the impulse which mainly builds up
the ego is that center which in later life we call the

Self. In the first half of life it acts as a force which builds up the ego.

That process of ego building can be disturbed. In schizophrenia, as is well known, the ego complex cannot any longer maintain its head office position, so to speak, and it gets drowned among the other colliding archetypes. The ego gets drowned in the collective unconscious, it gets overrun by archetypal patterns. Then, also, there is a falling apart of the personality, and that is the moment where the war of the Gods, the war of the Titans, starts up again. I have often noticed that when I refer to creation myths and motifs, the people who have no psychiatric experience think these motifs in creation myths seem very weird and far away from reality, whereas to people with psychiatric experience they sound very familiar. That is understandable, because if there is a chance of somebody getting out of a schizophrenic episode, you meet in him all the processes of creation myths. If a patient comes out of his episode, his consciousness rebuilds itself, and then he has creation myth dreams, or at least dreams with motifs from creations myths, which indicate that consciousness is building up again and with it the awareness of outer reality. Naturally it is important to understand those processes, because then you can support his ego consciousness as it comes up again and re-creates the reality function.

The ego complex, if it gets drowned in the war of the Gods, is, so to speak, lying helplessly among the corpses of the battlefield; the Titans and the Gods step over it and kick one another over its head. Very often when people come out of the episode, they say that they were always present but could not manifest themselves. I know, for instance, of schizophrenic people who have been in a padded cell and who when visited by their families showed no signs of recognizing them, so the visits were given up because apparently the person did not notice that Father and Mother were there, or anything else. But many years later, when they had worked themselves out of it, they could say, "Yes, Mother came then, she wore a white dress and this collar, and she said this and that." I know of one person who, when asked why for God's sake she had not shown any sign of recognition, said, "I couldn't," and used a very good simile: "It was as if I were under the sea and noticing everything, but I could not wave to you. I could not make myself heard or noticed and I could not give a sign that I understood and was seeing my family and heard every word that was said, and I knew that outwardly I looked completely dumb." That was the drowned ego! It was still there but only as a potentiality; it had a certain awareness of what was going on but was incapable of taking its position of dominating the chaos and the different Gods. This explains why there are also those terrific changes of mood. At one moment there is a positive God on top, a Euphoria, and the next moment a devilish Titan rules; then they attempt murder, and the regulating ego is a weak, helpless thing which can no longer manifest within the chaos. It is overrun by the archetypal powers.

This possibility of conflict, the possibility that the primordial totality can fall apart, is probably *one* reason for the building up of the ego as a controlling power. The ego has here the original function of counteracting the chaos and the falling apart into meaningless conflicting patterns. That is its positive function, and that's why a conscious human being is better adapted. For instance, a person who does not dissociate in a moment of conflict and does not fall into an affect is a higher personality and always wins out in the end. We call him the one who can keep his head. When a ship goes down, he is the person who can keep his head and whose ego does not at once fight to save his own life while everybody else drowns, but who sometimes can save the whole boat, while people with a weak ego go off into one of the patterns of behavior. One sits in a corner and cries and prays, and the other shoves everybody aside and gets into the lifeboat himself, and so on.

As we know, Jung applied a final viewpoint in looking at psychological factors; he looked at the psychological fact from the causal standpoint *and* from the final standpoint. For instance, we look at a neurosis as being caused by certain parental and childhood experiences, in the Freudian sense, and then look at it additionally from the final standpoint and ask, "With what purpose?" We look at a neurosis as having a purpose as well as a cause, and its purposiveness is very often to produce a state of higher consciousness. A conflict causes higher consciousness. You see that every time you treat somebody. There comes Mr. X who has a conflict, but if he gets out of his conflict properly, he will afterward be more conscious. He will have a higher standpoint of consciousness, and suffering the conflict will have brought that about. Or you can look at it from the final standpoint and say the conflict was arranged in order to make him reach higher consciousness.

There is a certain plausibility in both standpoints. The first, the causal, is clear. Naturally, every conflict forces one into a higher form of consciousness. But the final objective is not so clear unless you know dream interpretation very well. For instance, it can happen that someone is in a peaceful, well-adapted state in which everything is O.K., but he gets dreams of an oncoming conflict. You wonder why. Why, when everything is all right, does the devil arrange a conflict? Because he is bored, or what? The person has a dream showing you a conflict, you interpret it, and the analysand says, "But I have no conflict! I am all right!" I say, "Wait." Two days later the conflict comes to the bursting point. He has a conflict then, and the dream announced it beforehand. There you have a certain justification for looking at the conflict from a final standpoint, as if it were an arrangement with a certain final purpose in mind. But naturally this is only a category of looking at it. Neither causality nor finality can be proved to exist objectively. They are only heuristically useful ways of looking at psychic processes. In biology, too, you can ask why people have stomachs and can get a long explanation, but if you ask for what purpose do people have stomachs, it makes even more sense. In explaining the function of organs, the final standpoint is useful in elucidating and establishing connections.

The problem of conflict has also to do with learning and the capacity for learning. It has been said by be-

haviorists who studied the learning capacity of higher
animals that this capacity increases when the patterns
of behavior become less mechanical, when they have
a certain plasticity. When a pattern of behavior is very
mechanical, the animal cannot learn. A very good example of the stupidity of a mechanical pattern of behavior is the wandering of lemmings. Lemmings, like
many other rodents, have an impulse from time to
time to gather together and wander in a procession
and change their territory. When they get into this
wandering mood, they get completely possessed, and
if by bad luck they come to a precipice, or to the sea,
they just wander down the precipice or into the sea,
there is a mass suicide, and not one lemming is capable of asking itself what it is doing and of turning
around. They just go into the sea and drown; there is
no learning capacity—they are like a wound-up
watch, and zoom—off they go! Now, there is the
other fact that among certain animals there is a certain plasticity in the pattern of behavior, within a certain range, and a learning capacity exists.[41]

The great entomologist Henri Fabre had the idea
that the pattern of behavior was completely mechanical. He watched a certain type of wasp which built its
nest in the sand, the sand wasp. This wasp makes a
series of holes in the sand; then by a certain poisonous
injection, inserted at a specific point, it paralyzes but
does not kill a caterpillar. The sand wasp lays a para-
lyzed caterpillar in each hole and then lays the eggs
on it. When the larvae come out, they first feed on the
caterpillar, which is slowly eaten up alive—it is a most
sadistic business—and afterward the mother wasp

feeds the young. Sometimes the caterpillar has received a bit too strong an injection and dies, and then there is a big stink, everybody dies in that hole, and one of the nests is ruined, but the mother wasp is apparently such an idiot that she mechanically continues to carry food into every hole. Fabre, who watched this process, often said, "There you can see the mechanized pattern of behavior, like a wound-up watch, and she does not know what she is doing at all, no plasticity, complete mechanical behavior!" This observation has been rechecked, and one sees what a part prejudice plays in the observation of nature, for Fabre's theory was believed, and copied, and recopied, because it suited the mechanical image of that time. It has now been observed that the sand wasp feeds along mechanically about four or five times and then goes along, once, on what is called an inspection tour. Without taking any food with her, she goes along observing every hole and after that feeds only the live larvae. So the only thing she cannot do is notice and feed at the same time. Now, that *we* also cannot do, to a great extent, I think!

Thus, already on the very low level of the sand wasp there is a certain capacity for learning, for getting information and adapting the pattern of behavior to it. So very low down in the animal range there exists a certain amount of plasticity in the pattern of behavior. The behaviorists say that, in general, the more the patterns are loosened up, the less mechanized, the less they are tightly organized, the greater the learning capacity. When the mechanical patterns are blurred and indistinct and not working very strongly, there is plasticity and the learning capacity comes in. Anthropoid apes have a very blurred pattern of behavior and accordingly a very high capacity for acquiring individual experience. We human beings have also paid for our learning capacity and higher consciousness by having relatively indistinct and weakened instinctual patterns. One cannot have the penny and the cake!

Arthur Koestler's *The Sleep Walkers* is a history of the prejudices which have sometimes reigned in science. It gives a lot of evidence to show how a relatively emotionally convincing prejudice has just been copied for a thousand years. In the 1960s a congress of medical doctors of the materialistic trend decided *ex cathedra* that asthma has no psychological cause or implication whatsoever, but that it is a purely physical fact and you should go on injecting dust specimens, and so on. The fact that there exist purely psychotherapeutic cures for asthma is absolutely ignored. I can, for instance, bear witness to one which I treated myself, where by not touching the physical setup and only analyzing the dreams, the asthma completely and definitely disappeared. But such cases are not taken into account. The analysand has not changed his way of life or anything, he has only gone into psychotherapy, and his asthma has disappeared, definitely and completely. But such a fact is simply ignored because it does not fit the *Weltanschauung* of those men. So our learning capacity is very, very small, which is why Jung always quotes the saying, "Les savants ne sont pas curieux" (Scientists are not curious).

Subjective Moods of the Creator

 This chapter has to do with the reactions, moods, and thoughts which lead to creation. As you remember, it is sometimes said that the creators awaken to consciousness, other times that they seem to be bored and therefore create. For instance, Silver Fox and Coyote created a boat by thinking; out of boredom they think that now something must happen, so Silver Fox created the world. We will collect, then, the different reactions and moods or thought impulses which have, according to the myths, led to the creation of the world. Strangely enough, the one pattern which one would think would perhaps be the most simple is not the most frequent one, that is sexuality, though the analogy of the man and woman who together create a child is naturally to be found in creation myths. For instance, Father Sky and Mother Earth, or Father Sun and Mother Moon, beget the whole world. Or there is the Great Spirit and his woman. A North American creation myth says that they had four children, and the four children also created, and so on, and in this way the world was created.

Naturally, we find, especially in many primitive societies, the myth of world creation through the sexual act. It is a beautiful analogy of how out of nothing, so to speak, something is created in a completely natural way. But it is, in a way, unsatisfactory, because to explain the origin of a human being by saying, "Oh well, that's through the sexual union of man and woman," does not explain what is really going on. It is a verbal explanation which covers up a complete mystery, namely the actual origin of the human being. Thus all the creation myths which attribute the origin of the world to the sexual union of father and mother very quickly skip over the beginning and go on to the next step. It is therefore a way of explaining creation when, for one reason or another, one does not want to go deeper into the question. It is just an easy way of explaining one miracle by another, "Oh well, that was just a father and a mother, and just as the child comes from the father and mother, the world comes from a father and a mother, isn't that obvious?" Such myths generally put an enormous emphasis on the further steps of the creation, and the beginning is glibly or quickly put aside with the image of sexual union.

I will cite a few examples. The South American myth of the world creation in the Quiché: their famous mythological sacred book the *Popol Vuh* says that in the beginning there were no human beings, no animals, birds, fish, no trees, no stones, no plants and no wood, only the sky was there. The face of the earth was not visible, only the sea was silently there under the sky. Only Tepeu Kukumatz was there, the builder of the cosmos, father and mother, surrounded by green and blue feathers. Her name was Kukumatz because she was a great wise being and with her was the heart of the sky. In darkness and night Tepeu and Kukumatz came together and spoke to each other. Thus they pondered upon it and agreed that, together with light, man should also come into being. In this way, they decided upon creation, upon the growth of the trees and creepers, upon the beginning of life and the creation of man. They created animals which could not speak, but they wanted to create man so that the Gods would be praised. Thus they decided to consult the oracle of two magical Gods to find out how and where they could try to create human beings again. At the beginning of the prophecy, the old God and Goddess said, "Lie down together, speak so that we hear, decide if wood should be gathered so that the creator and the one who molds may work with it, and see if what comes out of it shall sustain and nourish us." The oracle then spoke and made known, "Your creations out of wood will succeed, they will speak and be understood on the face of the earth." "So be it," was the answer given to this speech. And immediately the wooden beings were created. Then she and the heart of the sky together created everything. This creative couple is identical at the same time with the sky and the water surface. Then, also, the Maya of Yucatán say: In the year and the day of darkness, when there were no days and no years, when the world was still sunk in darkness and chaos and the earth was covered with water, and on the surface was only clay and foam, one day appeared the Stag God, who had the name of Puma Snake, and the beautiful Stag Goddess who was called Jaguar Snake.

They had human shape and great magical power; they united sexually, and from that the world originated. There are Jaguar Snake and Puma Snake, but they are really two human beings who are Gods.[42]

In such cases, the two beings, the father and the mother of the world, are always "just there"; it is not explained where they come from—they are given *ex nihilo*. Then it is simply said that they generated everything, but the "how" is not described, and if creation was begotten through the woman who then gave birth—that is entirely skipped. That is why I say it is so unsatisfactory. In these man-woman myths, they do not go into the details of what really happens. They think that by saying that it is a man and a woman, that's enough. What is lost is the wonderment! This is a terrifically shortened version where all the wonderment, the amazement, over the numinosity of creation is not expressed; perhaps it is felt, but it is not expressed in the myth. But these myths which begin in a sexual way generally lay enormous stress on later events. For instance, that the wrong kind of mankind is created, then destroyed, then another is created, then there are big fights, and so on. That is told at great length and with great emotion, but the beginning is disposed of in two sentences. To me this is unsatisfactory. I like to wonder, and to express my wonderment, so I prefer those myths which do not dispose of the mystery of the beginning in such a brief way.

The next step, and it is unique so far as I know, is given in the Egyptian myth where the original God created the following quaternio of Gods through masturbation. This is at least logical, for he is alone and has no wife. There is one God and not a duality at the beginning, and therefore, having no wife, the only way he could create the world was by masturbation. Out of the original water, Nun, came the Sun God. He masturbated and spat out two Gods—Shu and Tefnut—and they created Geb and Nut.[43] In one version he spits and forms the quaternio of Gods with his spittle, and in another he masturbates and collects his semen in his hands and thus creates the quaternio of Gods: Heaven and Earth, Shu and Tefnut. The original God is called Atum in this version. On one side there is the need to have one being at the beginning and not a couple, but there is also the inclination to explain the origin of the world by the sexual act. For the Egyptians masturbation was an obvious and fitting image and provided a solution by which they could keep to monotheism: through masturbation one God creates everything.

I now would like to turn to the different types of emotion which lead to creation. One possibility is that the God feels uncomfortable, or has a feeling of uneasiness, as for instance in some North American Indian myths. There is also the Maidu, where it is said that the Earth Maker swam on the water and was anxious, "I wonder how, and I wonder where, and I wonder in which place we could find land in this world?" Here the first reaction of the creator is a kind of anxious restlessness, "I wonder, I wonder how we could, and where we could" do something. This is a rather unusual reaction and not often found.[44]

A more frequent feeling which initiates the creation

is loneliness. For instance, the Winnebago, a subdivision of the Sioux Indians, tell the creation myth as follows: The Great Spirit felt lonely. So he took a part from his body, from the region of the heart, and also a little bit of earth, and from that made the first man. Afterward he created three more men and then a woman, who is this earth, the mother of all Indians. The four men are the four winds. At first they are very irregular and wild, but later they become more controlled. Then the Great Spirit populated the earth with animals and after that created man and woman. The man received tobacco, the woman corn, and so on. There is a long process showing how the Great Spirit is also the instructor of mankind in all the problems of civilization. But the primary motivation is that the God felt lonely and for that reason created the world.[45]

This theme occurs in many variations. The Klamath Indians, for instance, say the same thing. They say that there was first one God, the only being who had intelligence and thought, and he created everything through his thought and through wishing, by wishing for things *because he was lonely*. A certain Inca tribe says that the creator lives in heaven, which he never leaves because he has to order everything. He created heaven and earth because he felt lonely, and then created helpers who had the same attitude as he had, and they created the rest of the world. Here again we find the same motivation: The God felt lonely.

This idea also occurs in India. In the *Brihadaran-yaka Upanishad* it is said that the world is created through the sacrifice of the horse—I mentioned this when I spoke of the motif of the first victim. In the fourth part we find the following creation myth:

> In the beginning was Self (Atman) alone, in the shape of a person. [The word for person is *purusha,* meaning a human being in the shape of man, or person. Müller translates *Atman* as "the Self," so you could also say that in the beginning Atman was alone in the shape of a person, or in the shape of *purusha.*] He, looking around, saw nothing but his Self. He first said, "This is I"; therefore he became "I" by name. Therefore even now, if a man is asked, he first says, "This is I," and then pronounces the other name which he may have. And because before all this he (the Self) burnt down all evils, therefore he was a person (*purusha*). [That is a play on words, because *ush* means to burn down, and *purusha* is interpreted as that which burns all evil.] Verily he who knows this burns down everyone who tries to be before him. He feared, and therefore anyone who is lonely fears. He thought, "As there is nothing but myself, why should I fear?" Then his fear passed away. For what should he have feared? Verily fear arises from a second only. But he felt no delight. Therefore a man who is lonely feels no delight. He wished for a second. He was as large as man and wife together. He then made this, his Self, to fall in two (*pat*) and thence arose husband (*pat*) and wife (*patni*) [again a play on the word]. Therefore Yagnavalkya [the wise man whom he is instructing] said, "We two are thus (each of us) like half a shell." Therefore the void which was there is filled by the wife. He embraced her and men were born. She thought, "How can he embrace me after having produced me from himself? I shall hide myself." She then became a cow, and the other became a bull and

embraced her, and hence cows were born. The one became a mare, and the other a stallion, the one a male ass, and the other a female ass. He embraced her, and hence hoofed animals were born. The one became a she-goat, the other a he-goat; the one became a ewe, the other a ram. He embraced her and embracing each other through the whole of creation they produced all kinds of animals and beings.[46]

Here we are concentrating on the beginning of the story: the Purusha, the primeval being, is lonely and afraid and feels no delight. Again the motif of fear comes up, but it is very well characterized. It is not fear of something, fear of an object; he even argues about it and says that as there is no second person, why should he fear? He tries to rationalize his fear away, as we do when we are afraid. It is that deep, irrational fear which comes up when one is alone and which we all experience if suddenly left in complete stillness and loneliness, when most people get terrified without knowing why. One begins to fantasize that one is being watched, and one looks around. This is irrational fear, for one knows quite well that it is non-sense, that one does not fear anything, and yet, all the same, one is afraid. Actually, in us, the reason for this fear is the coming up of the unconscious.

If you are alone, a lot of your life energy, normally used up in relating to outer things, one could say the whole "social energy," is suddenly dammed up and has no outlet and therefore flows back into and constellates the unconscious. That is why in all religions isolation is one of the means by which to meet the Gods, or the ghosts, or the spirits, or by which we become initiated into inner experience. The first step in most religions, whether shamanistic experience, or the sweat lodge experience of Native Americans, or the search for revelation of the North American Indian on the top of a mountain, or monastic life in the Far East and in Europe, or the first monks in Egypt, was always the impulse to isolate oneself, because then the inner experience wells up.

The fear of loneliness is at the bottom of prison phobia. Being imprisoned alone for a long time is something a lot of people cannot stand because it threatens to cause them to go off their heads. Those are the people who are not capable of letting the unconscious come up as "a something" to which they can relate. The only way to overcome such an irrational fear is to try to visualize the unconscious, or to let it speak as a voice and listen and let it tell you things; then you can overcome the first irrational fear of feeling that if you hear voices and so on, you are going crazy. If you can stand this first impact, which seems intolerable for the rational mind, then the prison phobia, or whatever it is, is easily overcome. It is a question of standing the first impact. But before the unconscious reaches that amount of load, so that it breaks through in a hallucination or a voice, or any of these manifestations, there is generally first of all a state of terrific tension where such an irrational fear gets one.

I myself many years ago could not do active imagination and, having read about the monks in the Egyptian desert, thought that the only thing to do was to imprison myself completely and try to dam up the unconscious as they did. I confined myself in a hut in the mountains in the snow in winter, but I was so introverted that going once a day to the village and buying bread was quite enough extraversion to make me feel wonderful, and the unconscious didn't dam up enough. To have a few words with the woman at the baker's shop and say, "Yes, it's a nice day today, there's a little *Föhn* [a warm wind], the snow is melting," was quite enough, so no monk's experience wanted to come up. So then I had to get canned food and dried bread and not go out at all, not even to the baker's shop, and then it did dam up. I got a terrific phobia of a burglar! This fantasy got worse and worse, especially at night when I always had the idea that a burglar would come to the hut, which could not be properly locked up. On the third night, in terrible fear, I slept with an ax near my bed—I had nothing else, but I had that for chopping wood—and there I lay with the ax beside me, trying to imagine whether I would have the courage to hit the burglar over the head if he came! That became absolutely intolerable—I got so terrified that I couldn't sleep anymore—and then suddenly I thought, "But, my God, that was what I wanted!" And then I visualized the burglar and began to talk to him, and the whole feeling of fear collapsed.

I stayed a fortnight in that hut and didn't need to lock the door; I slept like a log. I realized that I had come up there to have such experiences, and when they came I was terrified, but then I learned to talk to this burglar. I saw him quite clearly with my inner eye. And that is how I think one could overcome this kind of panic. It is the trick of letting the thing in, in whatever form it comes up, to let it become objective. And then, moreover, one is not lonely anymore, one has an inner partner to talk to, and exciting talks the whole day. On the contrary, one is quite occupied by that.

This is the moment when the "one becomes two," (Nietzsche) which is described when the Atman-Purusha falls apart into husband and wife—into the two halves. It is the moment where one has to realize that this thing one fears is objective. It is so beautifully described here: The wife fills the void, and then embraces the Purusha. It is the void which one fears, but in the moment when one allows the unconscious to break into that void and fill it and become an objective partner, the loneliness, and with it the irrational fear of loneliness, is gone. Then it is just a matter of talking to the inner partner. That is also why Jung often quotes the famous saying of the alchemists that whoever is lonely and isolated from the crowd and cannot join other people will find an inner friend to join and guide him. For the alchemists it was Hermes Mercurius who helped them in their lonely enterprises of making the philosopher's stone. But there is the first prestage before the unconscious can take this shape of being a real object; this is a transitional stage where one has, or suffers from, the irrational fear which is actually the well-known fear of ghosts, and the fear which all primitives experience. It is also the fear of something new and of the unexpected.

Normally, the relationship of a living being, including higher animals, to the outer world and to social surroundings, that is, to other creatures of the same species, is conditioned by patterns of behavior. Animals, for instance, are conditioned by inborn patterns of behavior toward their fellow beings, including the prey which they have to kill. An animal has no problem of relationship, since everything is regulated by instinctive patterns of social behavior. We, being tribal animals so far as we now know (in the excavations of the earliest times of man one always finds tribes, tribal formations), are also conditioned to relate not only to other human beings but to objects, to everything, and fear befalls us when we have no pattern of behavior by which to relate. That explains the fear of the unknown, because the unknown we do not know how to meet. If it's a human being you know, you can react in this and that way. If it's a tree, or an animal, you can react, you are conditioned to all these things. But if it is the unknown, then you feel a void inside, you don't know what it is and therefore don't know how to react. That gives this strange, lost feeling; one is an empty space, so to speak.

The fantasy which crept up in my mind was very obvious and cheap—the burglar-animus—but it was a very fitting fantasy, because the German word for burglar is *Einbrecher,* one who breaks in, and the one who breaks in is the unconscious. So the burglar symbolizes the invading unconscious, that which invades the realm of consciousness. As soon as you can visualize it, or hear a voice or something, then the worst is overcome, because then you have your patterns of behavior and can relate. If, for instance, it is a burglar, then you have all the patterns of relation to a human being at your disposal. The unconscious has then already taken shape, has transformed itself into something to which you can relate. But before, while you still are in the state where there is just tension, a damming up of energy, there is terrific fear. Actually, many people, even those in analysis, never overcome this fear of the unconscious and rationalize it away. They never let the impact of the unknown come near them and even use psychological concepts, Jungian or Freudian, to block it off. They say, "Oh, this is my animus," or "This is my shadow." They use the mind as a defense mechanism, which is naturally very suspect.

Sometimes in analysis, when you try to convey something to an analysand of which he is afraid, then, instead of listening, he will pour out a whole sermon, and talk and talk and talk, so as to leave no hole in the conversation where you might place the terrible thing. He is terrified of something, so he tries to talk it away. That is even a neurotic symptom, for some people out of unconscious anxiety have a kind of constant word diarrhea. They are afraid of something and constantly have to fill the empty space around them with a lot of hot air—because silence would bring up the real thing, which is terrifying because unknown.

But fear, according to our Indian myth, is the basis of creativity. Anybody who cannot stand the impact of the unknown naturally is not capable of creating anything new, or of letting something new come up, something creative. If he cannot stand this preliminary stage of panic or fear, he will never become creative, and that is one of the blockages of creativeness. Some people can never face this terrible moment of being overcome by the unknown, and for that reason cannot get into active imagination, talking to the unconscious.

Now we come to a theme very closely related to this anxiety and feeling of loneliness, and which one finds very frequently in myths, namely the motif of crying. The creator cries; his first reaction before or while creating the world is to cry. An African myth, a creation myth of the Baluba, which in a way is a bit strange because all the beings are already there, also brings in this motif of weeping: In the beginning there was a big, empty plain; there was no bush, no grass, no tree. All the animals cried: the antelope cried, the birds cried, the leopards cried, all cried because there was nowhere they could hide. Now, there was an old woman who had running, evil-smelling eyes who said she would save them if they would all lick her eyes and heal them. The animals agreed to this, so the antelopes came and licked her eyes, the parrots, the leopards, all of them came, until she was healed. Then the old woman took a calabash with seeds and threw the seeds over the land. From these seeds came all the vegetation, and every animal now had its dwelling place, and so all animals were saved by the old woman.

This is not a creation myth in the proper sense, because earth and the animals already exist and there is only the creation of vegetation. I have included it because the motif of crying is essential. Through the crying of the animals the surface of the earth is changed from a desert into a dwelling place. Crying is also commonly found in North American Indian creation myths. One comes from a subdivision of the Algonquin tribe. It runs: In the beginning there was nothing but water; no land could be seen. On the water was a boat, and in the boat was a man who cried because he had no idea of what his fate would be. And the Moshus rat came from the water and said, "Grandfather, why are you crying?" And then she fished up the earth for him. That is the famous Indian way of bringing up the earth. There the first reaction of the creator God is to cry, out of anxiety before the unknown, because he does not know "what his fate will be."

Then there is the Winnebago creation myth where it is said that what our father sat on when he came to consciousness is uncertain, but his tears began to run; he began to cry, and he saw nothing. There was nothing, and then his tears formed the earth below. In other versions he takes up the earth and forms the surface of the earth. In another Winnebago myth, his tears fall down and form the lakes, and then he begins to wish. He wishes for light and there is light, he wishes for the earth and the earth becomes real, and so on. From then on he creates everything just by wishing.[47]

I have actually seen in analysis that sometimes people who are meant to do some creative work get into these crying fits. They don't know why they cry, or it is rationalized by some kind of self-pity, but they completely dissolve into tears and then suddenly pick up and begin to be creative. It is one of the ways of first dissolving consciousness and getting closer to the unconscious which plays a great role in alchemy as well. One of the beginning stages of the alchemical work is very often the *liquefactio,* the turning into liquid in order to undo the *prima materia,* which is often hardened or solidified in a wrong way and therefore cannot be used to make the philosopher's stone. The minerals must first be liquefied. Naturally, the underlying chemical image is the extraction of a metal from its ore through melting, but *liquefactio* often has the alchemical connotation of a dissolution of the personality in tears and despair. The *liquefactio* state is mentioned in the beginning of the work as a melting of the metals, and the alchemists say that during this part of the work the alchemist is sad; he sits in the nigredo and has melancholic thoughts; he is in the *afflictio animae,* in the sad and desperate subjective state which accompanies the melting of the metallic ore. This sheds light on what crying means, namely, that it effects an *abaissement du niveau mental* through which the creative content of the unconscious can break through. That is especially the case with people who tend to have a consolidated or rather rational conscious habitual attitude and therefore need a liquefying process in order to approach the layer where the unconscious can come up and speak to them.

One of the further reactions is *desire,* and together with that something which a Hindu text calls *hunger.* I think hunger is important because it has a wider connotation than desire and really expresses more accurately what, in my experience, the word *desire,* which is used in other texts, means. It is not desire for a definite object, like a man desiring a woman, or anybody desiring a particular thing; it is wanting something without really knowing what. It is like an open mouth wanting something without having a specific object in view, or a specific fantasy in mind yet. In the second section of the *Brihadaranyaka Upanishad* there is such a creation myth: "In the beginning there was nothing [the translator adds "to be perceived"] here whatsoever. By death indeed all this was concealed, by hunger, *for death is hunger*."[48]

This is naturally the specific Indian way of thinking, namely that through desire you, as an individual, create your karma, you come into existence. That is why Buddha later taught that by sacrificing every kind of desire you can leave the world and return to nirvana. Desire is, so to speak, the beginning, the root, of all evil, the root of all existence. And this existence down on earth and in reality, seen from the spiritual standpoint of the Hindu, is death. To get lost in reality, in life, and in this world through desire is, from the standpoint of the spiritual man who has retired out of it, a form of death. That is why hunger, desire, and death are identical in this old Hindu text. Death thought, "Let me have a body." You see, he wants something again! Then he moved about, worshiping. From him, thus worshiping, water was produced, and he says, "Verily there appears to me, while I worship, water." That is again a play on the word. Water is called *aka.* "Surely there is water, or pleasure, for him who thus knows the reason why water is called *aka,* verily water is *aka,*" and so on. In this way, then, the first being, Death or Hunger, divides himself into a threefold form and from there creates the whole world. This kind of *basic, existential hunger* one might call it, is here the root of the whole creation. I think before I interpret it we will go to a few somewhat more differentiated Gnostic texts where there is the same idea.

The great founder of a Gnostic sect was Simon Magus, who was one of the rivals of Saint Peter. They had a flying competition. In the cosmogony of Simon Magus—we have only fragments—is the idea that in the beginning there was an absolutely eternal and incorruptible power outside everything, not yet even formed into an image. This power Simon Magus called fire or desire. It is *the* basic cosmic principle which creates and pervades everything, and it is also the cosmic Self. Simon Magus says it subdivides itself into above and below, creates itself, increases itself, seeks itself, finds itself, is its own father and mother, its own brother, its own husband, its own daughter, its own son, father-mother, one, the root of all things.[49]

And then Simon Magus goes on: Fire is the origin of all creation because the origin of creation is the *desire* to create, which comes into everything which enters existence, and this desire to create comes from fire. So there is first this preconscious totality which contains the ego and the unconscious and everything in one, which is male-female, which is the one thing, which is before, and the thing which is afterward, all in one. And from there the movement is started by the fire, because fire is the desire to create. That is why the desire of even temporal earthly creation is called "burning in a flame." When you fall in love you begin to burn. He makes a play on that word and says that even in the most ordinary use of the word, when you fall in love and therefore want to create or generate, you burn. Thus fire or the desire-fire is the beginning of everything. Fire, Simon Magus continues, is in itself a oneness, but it appears in two forms. Here again is the subdivision into a duality, a discrimination. In the man it changes into blood which is warm and reddish, like the fire, and into the semen; in the woman into milk; in both it brings forth creation. Fire, according to Simon Magus, is also the origin of consciousness, of the Logos. It is, as he says in a later place, a little spark which goes on increasing to a tremendous power and then becomes a whole Aeon, a divine creative force. Elsewhere Simon Magus says there are two origins of the cosmos, namely the great power which is the all-ordering spirit and the great thought which is feminine and brings forth everything by birth. In between there is the pneuma.

If we sum up this complicated text, we see that the first movement out of this preconscious and harmonious totality which rests in itself comes from the fire of desire, or the desire which has a fiery form, which again has two aspects. One text of the school of Valentinus, another Gnostic author, runs as follows: In the beginning there was the *Autopater,* that is, the father of himself, the "self-father" in the sense of being the original being and the father of everything, having no father himself, being himself his own father. He contains the whole cosmos and rests without consciousness in himself. Here again is the unconscious

God symbolizing the preconscious totality. He, the never-aging, the always young, male-female, embracing the cosmos, but unembraced by it, lives with his Ennoia, a female power, within him. His Ennoia wanted to burst the fetters of eternity and therefore awoke in him, or became aroused in him; he felt the desire to embrace her. (The female power, which is within the Self-Father, tries to arouse in him the desire to unite with her.) Then he unites with his own greatness, which is the Ennoia, and out of him, the Father, came the Aletheia, the truth, and Anthropos, man.

Aletheia, the truth, which is a feminine being in Greek, and the Anthropos, man, are the first two children, and they create a whole series of further groups of male-female beings. I am skipping this part because I wish to concentrate on this first impulse. *Ennoia* in Greek means a thought which has not yet taken on the form of words, which has not been verbalized.

If you observe yourself thinking, you will notice that first you have a kind of insight, an awareness of a thought, which you then verbalize. For instance, if you are thinking alone in your room, you generally speak or write or say things; thus often your thoughts have already taken on the form of what the Greeks would call the Logos, the word. But before a thought is verbalized, there is already an inner awareness of it. For instance, I say *er-er-er,* which implies that I already have the thought in mind, and then have to make the transition of verbalizing it. Generally you first do this inside yourself. The Greeks studied this process of thought and watched their reflections, what happened when they thought, and they came to

the conclusion that there is a kind of antethought
which is the Ennoia. It is the first, silent awareness of
a thought. This awareness of a thought, or of a thought content, is a phenomenon of the threshold of consciousness; it is half conscious and half unconscious. It is
therefore fittingly personified by a feminine being, Ennoia, the anima, because that is what the anima does
in a man; the anima is that antethought being. That is
why Jung speaks so often of the anima as being *la
femme inspiratrice*, the inspiring woman, because she
is that inspiring factor within that brings up creative
thoughts in a man. If it is projected, then naturally
he feels that it is the woman, the outer woman, who
inspires him. But that is because he projects his anima
onto her; she then personifies this Ennoia, this antethought stage.

The Ennoia, according to Valentinus, is also called
Charis, which means grace, and Sige, which means
silence; these are two feminine words in Greek. So she
is Ennoia, this thought awareness, grace, and silence.
In this stage when Ennoia comes up, you do not talk,
either outwardly or inwardly; you are in a kind of
brooding meditative silence in which you become
aware of a creative thought.

The text goes on: This Ennoia awakens in the Autopater (in the unconscious father figure) a sexual desire
to embrace her, and from there they create Truth and
the first man. This is a complicated form of something
which has been defined in those primitive myths in a
simpler way, but which, in itself, is just as fascinating
and just as true and in a way much better defined,

because there we see the intermediary processes between the unconscious and conscious.

Another rendering of the same teaching of the Valentinians tells us that in the beginning there was the unfathomable Aeon who was there before everything, in the very beginning, the original father and Bythos, the abyss. He was invisible and nothing could embrace him or grasp or surround him; he was eternal, not generated; he rested for an immense time in deepest stillness. From the very beginning Ennoia was with him, whom they also called Charis and Sige—Grace and Silence. Suddenly Ennoia conceived the idea that one should produce from this Bythos a sprout, something new, a *sperma* which he should put into her womb. After she had received this seed and had become pregnant, she gave birth to the Nous. Here not the Aletheia, the truth, but the Nous, the cosmic mind, is created, but as a divine power. From then on he became the father of all things.

We have really already made a transition to a new motif, namely from desire to thought. We have seen that the Ennoia, the antethought, the thought which is still kept inside and borne inside, awakens in the father the desire to unite with her and create, so that there is a certain unity between the sexual desire and the creative thought in its very first existence or in its first coming up. We already studied a very primitive North American Indian myth where Coyote and Silver Fox created a boat by mere thought, and Silver Fox continued after that to create alone, but the first act of creation was done by thinking. Creation of things by thinking is to be found also in several other varieties of North American Indian myths. For instance, there is a Zuni creation myth where it is said:

> In the beginning of things Awonawilona was alone. [He was the very first high God of the Zuni Indians; he is a creator and the one who preserves everything.] There was nothing beside him in the whole space of time. Everywhere there was black darkness and void. Then Awonawilona conceived in himself the thought, and the thought took shape and got out into space and through this it stepped out into the void, into outer space, and from them came nebulae of growth and mist, full of power of growth. After the mist and nebulae came up, Awonawilona changed himself through his knowledge into another shape and became the sun, who is our father and who enlightens everything and fills everything with light, and the nebulae condensed and sank down and became water and thus the sea came into existence.[50]

Here one sees the idea that the creator first conceives a thought in himself, which is very similar to the Gnostic myth of Ennoia, and then the thought is exteriorized and comes out of him as a second being which fills the dark void that surrounds him. Then comes the opposition of the principles of consciousness and the unconscious, namely the sun and the sea, the sun being a symbol of the principle of consciousness, not of ego consciousness, but of consciousness as a whole, and the sea as its opposite. But before the sun of consciousness there is no sea of the unconscious. Again, the simultaneity, where really there is no unconscious before consciousness, and vice versa. The unconscious has its being only as the opposite of consciousness. Before, there is only this all-embracing totality which contains both, the totality in itself. It is similar to the Indian myth where Purusha, with his feminine partner, fills the void and then unites with her, though here it is not a sexual embrace which leads to creation but the existence of the sun in one form and the sea in another, which from then on create the rest of the world.

It is striking that creation by thought is found mostly in Gnostic creation myths, in North American Indian creation myths, and in some Asian Indian creation myths, which to me shows that it exists predominantly in the realm of introverted civilizations. The Gnostics are the introverted thinkers par excellence of the early Christian era. They are more of the thinking type than most of the other early Christian movements and, with few exceptions, definitely introverted. The North American Indians also constituted a relatively introverted civilization, where the emphasis lies on the inner potentialities of man. In Asia that is self-evident. In all these realms there is a tendency to describe the creation myth as an inner process, an inner thought process in the Godhead. They even try to search back into their own minds and come to insight and reflection, in the literal sense of the word, by bending their thoughts backward toward the inside and toward the subjective factor, to watch and describe the process which precedes a creative idea or thought.

This is mostly worked out in the East where there is the idea of creation through *tapas,* mentioned in the *Rigveda. Tapas,* which is used, for instance, in the different yoga schools, nowadays really means a specific form of meditation, but originally it meant to give warmth to the inner, to brood, so to speak, upon yourself; we would say to give libido to yourself. *Rigveda* 10.29 states that in the beginning there was only water, and in the water was a living germ. Out of this living germ everything was born through *tapas*. One had a loving desire, and from this first thought, or loving desire, came the first seed. Darkness at first was covered up by darkness, this universe was indistinct and fluid, the empty space that by the void was hidden, that One was by the force of heat engendered—*tapas*. Desire then at the first arose within it, desire which was the earliest seed of spirit. (What is here translated as "desire" is *tapas* in the text.) The bond of being and nonbeing, sages discovered searching in their hearts with wisdom. Who knows it truly, who can here declare it?[51]

This text is really not at all clear; it is a very vague formulation. There is the watery dark mass covered by darkness. *Tapas* is sometimes rendered by desire or by the force of heat; the one is engendered, and that one is a germ. Later, in certain commentaries, it is looked upon as being a seed and in others as being an egg. The Sanskrit word is *retas,* the seed, or the spirit—the spiritual seed from which all generation comes.

Tapas also means to sweat over something. In certain yoga exercises, the yogin can heighten the temperature of his body and voluntarily produce a feverish state. There are interesting reports about this feat by Alexandra David-Néel, who, in a Tibetan monastery, actually witnessed a competition in *tapas* by the pupils as to who could dry more wet blankets on his naked body. This degeneration into sport is only an outer aspect of something else, namely that in many of the yoga meditations *tapas* is used as a way of keeping back all the life energy, not only of physically heating up the body, but of getting into a mood of complete concentration of energy. One could therefore to a certain extent call *tapas* a concentration of all psychic energy onto one point, thereby creating psychological heat or accumulation, and by this means there is creation. This is an increase of what we have already had in those Gnostic texts in the idea of Ennoia, namely an introverted act of thinking which is a becoming aware of thought inside—not exteriorizing it through the word, but keeping it inside and meditating or brooding on it.

We have now run through most of the moods of creation, and to end up I would like to give a Maori sequence of creation, a Maori cosmology, where you will see a strange combination of all these factors. Some Maori myths simply have a list of the first beings, or the first things, which existed, in a kind of genealogy. There is a very long series of the powers which first existed and then only a report of the creation. To translate such vague Maori concepts is naturally very difficult, but there is a list which, summed up, runs in this way: The first being among them, after the separation of heaven and earth, mated with Ru (that is a power, but I have no translation for it), and they first gave birth to Kanapu (that is the light in lightning) and Whatitiri (which is the rolling of thunder, the noise of thunder), then Hinenui te po (the power of the earth) and then some other children

called Tawha-re-riku, Kukupara, Hawaiki (which is
the word from which *Hawaii* comes), Wawauatea,
and so on. All these powers are different animals of
the sea and at the same time partly also moods.[52]
We have a Hawaiian parallel which lifts all this
onto a subjective level. In Hawaii that same list runs
as follows:

> The first being is called Te Ahanga—the swelling of an
> embryo in the body; it is the growth of an embryo.
>
> The second being is Te Apongo—greed.
>
> The third: Te kune iti—inner conception, a conception
> which takes place inside;
>
> Te kune rahi—preparation;
>
> Te kine hanga—the impulse to search;
>
> Te Ranga hautanga—ordering, as for instance of the
> cells in a growing body;
>
> Te iti—the very, very small thing, the germ of an
> embryo;
>
> Te kore—not yet anything;
>
> Te kore te Whiwhia—not yet without any basis, but
> with a tendency toward existence;
>
> Te kore te Rawea—not yet without satisfaction; that
> means a not-yet in which there is a kind of feeling of
> frustration;
>
> Pupu—a welling up, as of boiling water;
>
> Ta ua—being depressed in sadness, or being imprisoned
> in a too-narrow uterus;
>
> Tama-a-take—making roots, to make roots;
>
> Te kanoiie o te uka—the vulva; and
>
> Te kawiti witi ⎤ Summed up by the translator as sex-
> Te katoa toa ⎬ ual organs. The last one he puts in
> Tira wai he kura ⎦ brackets—the penis of the red blood;
>
> Muri-ranga-whenua—married to Mahu-ika.

Those are the ancestors of the whole tribe, who carry, as if in an endless series of boxes, all the later generations inside them. Taranga then marries Ira-whaki, Maui potiki marries Hine rau mau kaku, and so on.

What follows now are the names of creative demiurgic Gods; I am not going to give you all those bewildering names, which are not important for us. What *is* infinitely important, to my mind, is the beginning, the swelling of the embryo, and then greed, which we had in so many other myths. Then "inner conception"—a conception which takes place completely within—that would be a little like Ennoia. Then preparation, something completely vague. Then the impulse to search; that is the anxiety which we had in the other myth: What, where, how . . . ? That kind of frustrated anxiety. Then something like order, but the order of cells, as for instance in a very primitive creature, a few cells order themselves in a circle, or in some form. The very, very small thing, the sperm of an embryo, the not-yet, but with a tendency toward being, the not-yet, with a feeling of frustration, and then all the others. Then depression also, as one of the essential aspects, the being narrowed in depression.

This Hawaiian list is so beautiful because it is a strange mixture: the origin of actual biological life, with the cells, for instance, the penis, and all the sexual aspects, the growth of the embryo, and mixed up with it the psychological aspect of the search, the desire, the germ of a thought, the not-yet but wanting to exist, and all these tendencies. It is a complete mixture of inner and outer factors, one more proof of how the birth of reality cannot be separated from the birth of our awareness of reality. Therefore it is described as a simultaneous process. The preforms of sexual union, as well as of creative thought, are described with great sensitivity and differentiation.

It is well known that sexuality and creativity are very closely linked in a human individual, and one very often sees that disturbance of one disturbs the other. Sex and creativity, especially in a man—though I would say also in a woman—are in a strange way linked; they are the two aspects of one and the same pattern. Sex would be on the spectrum the infrared end, and spiritual creativity on the ultraviolet end of the scale. You see sometimes, quite concretely, that a man who does not use his creativity properly can, for purely psychological reasons, become impotent, and his impotence can be cured if his creativity is released. If somebody tells me of a symptom, such as biting fingernails, or impotence, or scratching the forehead, or something, I just make a mental note, but I don't take it very seriously; it is not the thing upon which I concentrate because it is generally only a symptom of something which coincides with a deeper problem. In many cases where impotence was the apparent main problem for which people went into analysis, I have seen that the dreams ignored this aspect completely and instead nagged the poor analysand about not using his creativity, or for using it in a wrong way. If the dreams do not speak about the symptom, then I say to myself that that is not the main thing, that it is only an emanation of the problem, and we should concentrate on what the dreams speak about. In several cases there has been the gratifying experience that

after some time the analysand said, "By the way, my
impotence has disappeared as well!" One does not
concentrate on it, but it cures itself "by the way" too,
while the main work is to bring out the creativity or
to get it into its right shape. Then suddenly sexuality
functions normally again. It is quite understandable,
because if somebody has a creative gift and does not
bring it out properly, he might by that create a blockage of emotion which could also manifest in the physical realm, for without emotion the physical motivation falls away.

This is not a rule—do not think that *every* case of
impotence has such a cause; it is not always the reason, and there are a thousand others. But I have seen
many cases where this was connected and where one
sees what the Hawaiians seem to know very well,
how deeply the emotion of creativity and the emotion
of sex are intertwined and have a similar root. Another way in which the two are sometimes wrongly
intertwined is, as I have seen in different cases, where
a man overdid sex to escape creativity. That is another possibility. You could say that he had an accumulation of superfluous energy and so felt tense and
laden; then, if he was not capable of bringing it out
on a creative level, he instead overdid sex. He is not
happy in it and it is not gratifying, but mechanical,
and means getting rid of a state of tension and then
accumulating and getting rid of it again and again, in
a kind of vicious circle, a nervous-tension circle, because the other outlet, the mental or artistic, or whatever kind of creativity is meant, has not been opened.
As soon as this is opened, the other thing stops, or

becomes normal—it takes on normal measure—but these two patterns, the pattern of sexual behavior naturally understandably, and the pattern of creativity, are very closely intertwined.

To sum up, feelings of frustration, fear, loneliness, and boredom are some of the motifs which we find pretty often in creation myths. We can say that they all belong to what the alchemists call the *afflictio animae,* the depression and sadness which precede a creative act. In the individual case this is generally what we call an *abaissement du niveau mental,* which so often comes before an important content of the unconscious crosses the threshold of consciousness. This is partly an energetic phenomenon. Imagine that an important content, a big energetic load, is on its way up over the threshold of consciousness. When it approaches the ego complex, it attracts libido from it, because, like mass particles, it has an effect upon the other particles: that is, complexes. They affect each other like particles—and this content therefore attracts libido away from the ego, causing it to feel low, tired, restless, and depressed, until the content breaks through.

The opposite of crying—laughter—I have found in only one example, in a text from late antiquity, probably from Hellenized Egypt. We cannot date it and do not know its exact origin; it has been handed down to us in a papyrus now kept in Paris, containing magical recipes, invocations, and incantations. Mixed in with these are outstanding texts of Hermetic philosophy and late syncretistic religious documents.[53]

The text, which begins with a number of names of

angels and invocations to the Godhead, says: "The first angel praises you in the language of birds, ARAI, ARAI. The Sun praises you in the holy language LAILAM [Hebrew] with the same name: ANOK BIATHIARBARB-ERBIRSILATUBUPHRUMTROM." In 36 letters, it means: I go before you, I, the Sun, and it is through you that the sun boat comes up.

Out of the sun boat comes the baboon, which greets you in the language of the baboons, "Thou art the number of the year ABRAXAS," and so on. I give you this, not that it is important for us, but to show you the setting of the text, the atmosphere in which it comes up. But now comes what interests us. A paragraph says: And the God laughed seven times. The Greek word here means to laugh loudly; it is not merely a smile. The God laughed seven times: Ha-ha-ha-ha-ha-ha-ha. God laughed, and from these seven laughs seven Gods sprang up which embraced the whole universe; those were the first Gods.

When he first laughed, light appeared and its splendor shone through the whole universe. The God of the cosmos and of the fire. Then: BESSEN BERITHEN BERIO, which are magic words.

He laughed for the second time and everything was water; the earth heard the sound and saw the light and was astonished and moved, and so the moisture was divided into three and the God of the abyss appeared. The name is ESCHAKLEO: you are the OE, you are the eternal BETHELLE!

When the God wanted to laugh for the third time, bitterness came up in his mind and in his heart, and it was called Hermes, through whom the whole universe is made manifest. But the one, the other Hermes, through whom the universe is ordered, remains within. He was called SEMESILAMP. The first part of the name has to do with Shemesh, the sun, but the rest of the word is not explained.

Then the God laughed for the fifth time, and while he was laughing he became sad and Moira (fate) appeared, holding the scales in her hand, showing that in her was justice. So you see, justice comes from a state between laughing and sadness. But Hermes fought with Moira and said, "I am the just one!" While they were quarreling, God said to them, "Out of both of you justice will appear; everything should be submitted to you." Then Moira took the first command of the world with a long magic name which I cannot even read and which contains forty-nine letters.

When the God laughed for the sixth time, he was terribly pleased, and Chronos appeared with his scepter, the sign of power, and God said to him that he should have the glory and the light, the scepter of the ruler, and that everything, present and future, would be submitted to him.

Then he laughed for the seventh time, drawing breath, and *while he was laughing he cried, and thus the soul came into being.* And God said, "Thou shalt move everything, and everything will be made happier through you. Hermes will lead you." When God said this, everything was set in motion and filled with breath.

When he saw the soul (who "he" is, is not clear, but it was probably God), he bent down to the earth and whistled mightily, and hearing this, the earth opened and gave birth to a being of herself. (This is interesting. There are seven creations by the God, but the eighth creation comes from the earth.) She gave birth to a being of her own, the Pythic dragon (that is the dragon which is buried under the Delphic oracle), who knew everything ahead through the sound of the Godhead. And God called him ILLILU ILLILU ILLILU ITHOR, the shining one, PHOCHOPHOBOCH. When he appeared, the earth swelled up and the pole stood still and wished to explode. And God saw the dragon and was afraid, and through his fright there came out Phobos (terror), full of weapons, and so on.

This is the one and only creation myth where God laughs. But in the most important places, namely when Hermes, the guide of the psyche, and the soul, the psyche, are born, he not only laughs but also feels bitterness in his heart, or he cries. It is a double state in which the Godhead is between laughing and crying. Opposites always attract each other and tend to turn into each other through enantiodromia. We know also that laughing and crying in us are very similar states, and that one very often falls from one into the other or has both impulses at the same time. This union of opposites in the emotional state is the real origin of the psyche and of her guide, Hermes. We could interpret it as the first creative preform of conscious realization, because Hermes at this time was thought of as the inspirer, the one who gave and guided with the right ideas, gave the right word at the right moment, the creative inspiration. He is also the God of intelligence, in the widest sense of the word.

You could say, therefore, that the psyche and conscious intelligence came from these mixed states of the Godhead, when he laughs and cries at the same time. If we sum up all these different states, we see that practically all the important emotional states from which we suffer are collected in the different creation myths. Very closely connected with the emotions and moods are accompanying physical reactions such as spitting, vomiting, shedding tears, and ejaculation. Emanating something from our body, which is naturally the most primitive way of producing or creating something, has been used as a symbol or as an analogy for creation. In modern dreams and fantasies as well as in schizophrenic material, the act of defecation most frequently symbolizes creation. In *Symbols of Transformation* Jung describes the vision of the schizophrenic patient in which God is defecating the whole world.

The Kokowarra of Queensland tell the following creation myth: there was a black giant, Anjir, who had an enormous bottom, which was, however, without an opening. While Anjir slept and dreamed, a man came out of the wood called Jalpan (this is a divine primordial hunter and bush spirit), and he felt that Anjir was uncomfortable. With a piece of quartz he bored an opening into his bottom. Immediately a black mass came out. It was alive, and out of it came the black people, the Kokowarra. Anjir was very relieved and went south, where he disappeared and died.[54]

The bridge between the moods which I have described and the physical secretions and productions is what we call emotion. We should not forget the original meaning of the word *emotion*—Latin *emovere*—as that which moves one out of something, which makes one move. To sum up, emotion seems to be the absolutely essential basic factor in all creation myths, together with its concomitant psychological feelings and physical reactions. Emotion is generally symbolized by the element of fire, one of the most frequent symbols of libido or psychic energy. Here I can refer to *Symbols of Transformation,* where Jung amplifies endlessly the union of fire, word, libido, creativity, insight, and intelligence, an associated complex of contents which circle around the symbol of psychic and emotional energy.[55]

To be cut off from one's emotional basis always means complete sterilization. Whoever cannot connect with his emotions feels, and is, sterile. There is no creativity and no essential realization of anything psychologically without emotion. Thus, to indicate emotion the psyche uses the symbols of fire and light, for there is no enlightenment, no new realization, without an emotional prestage. It is therefore not surprising that in some more elaborate creation myths—we could rather call them theories—the element of fire has been regarded as the actual creative factor. I will mention only the most famous one, namely the cosmogony of the Greek philosopher, Heraclitus, for whom the whole world consisted of fire. Everything came from fire and will be transformed into fire at the end of the world, or rather there will be many worlds which in sequences, or rhythms, always arise out of fire and in the end will be burnt up in a big conflagration. One of the fragments handed down says literally that everything is an exchange for fire, and fire the exchange for everything, just as gold can purchase every kind of merchandise and for merchandise gold can always be obtained again. You see already in this association that gold, fire, and money all point to libido, the most exchangeable basic factor—psychic libido. As Heraclitus says, everything will be turned into fire. There are two opposite powers which lead to the origin of all things, war and battle. They lead to conflagration and then again to peace; the one is the way upward and the other the way downward. When fire condenses itself, it becomes moist, and if it condenses still more, it becomes water. When water condenses it becomes earth. That is the way downward. If the earth dissolves again, however, then it becomes water, and if water evaporates it becomes air, and that is the way upward.

Here we see fire's nonphysical and nonchemical aspect, namely as the intelligent substance of the world, that which contains and brings intelligent order into all things. Heraclitus identified it with his concept of the logos, and the logos in this way is ordering, conscious thought which can be expressed in words—*logos* really means "word." So from this accompanying association you see that for Heraclitus fire is also the world intelligence, the rational order in everything. That we can make rational connections is due to the logos quality of the basic substance of the world, the fire.

This idea directly influenced the Gnostic philosopher, Simon Magus, whose cosmogony runs as follows: In the beginning there was the Godhead; we could call it a preconscious totality, about which is said:

> I and Thou are one, Thou before me, I the One who comes after you. This power is one, it separates itself toward above and below, it generates itself, it increases itself, it seeks itself, it finds itself, it is its own Mother, it is its own Father, it is its own Brother, it is its own Husband, it is its own Daughter, it is its own Son, Father-Mother one, the root of the universe. From the fire the origin of the whole creation comes, the origin of everything is the desire for creation.[56]

Here is an element which we have already discussed in the Hindu texts I read: desire as one of the great motivations, one of the emotional states which motivate the Godhead, which induce the Godhead to create the world. There is the same thing in Simon Magus's writings. "Origin is the desire toward creation, to become something, and this desire springs from the fire." There you see the associative connection between fire and desire, which again is obviously a subjective psychological fact which we use in everyday language. Fire is an analogy for rage, for love, for excitement, and especially for desire in love. That is why the desire for generation is spoken of as being "set on fire." The fire is a oneness but appears in two ways, in man as blood, which is reddish like fire, and in the semen, or, in the woman, what becomes milk. Then he also explains that this fire at the same time contains a rational element, and it too, as with Heraclitus, contains a logos element in itself.

Here Simon Magus is directly influenced by Heraclitus. I might just remind you that one of the most widespread and recognized cosmogonic theories in physics was that of George Gamow; he did not explain the origin of the universe, because he was modest enough not to try to do something which he could not do, but he said that at the beginning of the whole universe there were fiery gas nebula from which everything arose. So you see, the same image is still basic in a hypothesis of one of the most widely recognized cosmogonic theories. It is not the only one. As I mentioned before, another theory has the primitive atom from which everything arose, a twin pair of neutrons. So the fiery gas nebula is not the only original matter modern physics thinks of, but one of them. So you see that we have not gone very much further. For the ultimate questions we still resort to archetypal images, though we shape them differently and connect them with facts differently.

Some other theories believe in a kind of constant coming into existence of more and more matter, that there is a creative process which still goes on, what the theologians, for instance, call the *creatio continua.* You find it in Chinese philosophy, in the idea of synchronistic events, in which the Chinese are interested, which are part of a *creatio continua,* and you also find it in Jung's idea on synchronicity, for synchronicity could in a way be brought into connection with the theological idea of the *creatio continua.* In primitive myths I do not see many analogies, except that in most primitive societies one is absolutely ready, and I would say accustomed, to believe in miracles and every miracle, in a way, is a *creatio*. I mean that the highest God, or even a minor God, interferes and produces something which has not existed before and which had no natural cause, did not come from this or that natural cause which already existed, but something new is put into the world.

I know of no primitive myth which conceives consciously of no beginning. One could say that if there is no beginning it is because the people have not thought about it. There are certain myths which say, for instance: One day the antelope cried, other creatures cried, and then the old earth mother came and she had blind eyes and the antelope and other animals licked her eyes and she created the earth. Here there is no beginning; the antelope and the earth and blind old woman are already there. There are many in which one can presume that some stuff is already there and that no special event is the beginning. But that, I would say, is an unreflective "no beginning," for there is no point of beginning accentuated, or no reflection about the beginning. Wherever there is conscious reflection there is also the formulation of the beginning. This agrees with obvious psychological facts, because the unconscious has no beginning and no end, save in consciousness. As soon as I ask when it began, there is an act of consciousness, and then I have to set it in some way, which makes a beginning. Or we can say now, looking backward, that there never was a beginning. We now, for instance, say that there is an unconscious, but no primitive man would say that! First you have to become conscious, and then question the existence of consciousness, before you can speak of an unconscious. Until you have made those three steps, there is no unconscious. Therefore, to say now that there was no beginning would be the third step: first one forgets to think about it, then one thinks about it and sets a beginning, and then one undoes one's own thinking again and says that there could not have been a beginning. That would be a differentiated thought form.

Very closely connected with the fire theory of Heraclitus and Simon Magus, which is still the archetypal image behind Gamow's hypothesis of the world origin, is also the theory of Anaxagoras, the Greek philosopher, according to whom the whole world existed as a complete mixture of matter in which all material elements were connected in one, with movement and order brought in by the spirit. The spirit is a kind of whirling movement, or it creates a whirling movement by which the original material particles order themselves into the different visible elements we see now, though in their original state they were what he called *homomoeriae*, little particles which all had the same character and only through the ordering will of the spirit did they become the different visible substances. This is a cosmogonic image which is in some ways akin—in its archetypal basis—to that of Heraclitus and Simon Magus.

This image of the fire, of the fiery world and of fire which at the same time has ordering and thought qualities, is also found in myths which have not directly to do with cosmogony, for instance, in the fact that Hephaistos, the God of artistic creation in Greece, is a smith and the master of the fire and that in many primitive societies it was originally the smiths, the men who handled iron and fire, who were the great medicine men. Mircea Eliade's book on shamanism contains all the documentation and literature on that. In many African and Siberian tribes there are traces of a tradition that originally the great magicians and medicine men and the spiritual rulers of those tribes were the smiths, who because they handled the fire had the title of Master of the Fire. You see, therefore, that it is fire, and not iron, which is the dominant thing; the title shows that fire is the fascinating element. There are still Bantu tribes where there is a constant power struggle between the smith of the village and the medicine man. Those two still fight each other for power, and it is still a problem whether somebody whose cow was stolen should go to the smith or to the medicine man. The smith still has the role of the older medicine man and therefore is still sought after and partly looked up to by people who want magical help. Some tribes subdivide tasks, and theft is handled by the smith and illnesses by the medicine man, etc., but among the Bantu tribes there is still an actual fight, for the transition has not been quite made from smith to medicine man. But it looks as though the smith, as master of the fire, had been the earlier spiritual leader of the tribe. Eliade gives a lot more documentation about the connection between the medicine man, shamanism, and the activities of the smith. This shows that the idea of creativity, of production and of fire, and the connection of fire and superior intelligence, also played an enormous role in these fields of human activity.

Akin to the idea of fire, which we naturally would interpret as libido, or as psychic energy, especially in its emotional manifestations, is the Hindu concept of *tapas,* which I mentioned before. *Tapas* is translated in different forms, but in English texts generally as brooding. Max Müller, in his translation of the *Upanishads,* says in a footnote: "I have translated *tapas* as "brooding" because it is the only word in English which combines the two meanings of warmth and thought. Native authorities actually admit two roots, one *tap,* to burn, the other *tap,* to meditate." Here he brings a number of examples to show the two roots, but to me it is conceivable that really there is only one word *tap,* which meant both from the very beginning and then got subdivided into the two aspects of the word. There are many places, for instance in the *Mundaka Upanishad,* where it is said, "The Brahman swells by means of brooding [by *tapas*—here again there is the motif of swelling which we had before in the Maori myth], hence is produced matter, from matter breath, mind, the true, the worlds, and from the works performed by men the immortal," and so on. Then in the *Aitareya-aranyaka Upanishad* it is said: God was there and he thought, "There are these worlds, shall I send forth guardians of the worlds?" He then formed the Purusha, taking him forth from the water. He brooded on him (that is, he exercised *tapas* on him), and when that person had thus been brooded on, a mouth burst forth like an egg. From the mouth proceeded speech, from speech *agni,* fire (4th adhyaya, 1st khanda).[57]

Germs
and
Eggs

 In connection with *tapas* we come to a new theme, the motif of the germ or the egg upon which the Godhead brooded and produced the world in its present form. On this subject there is a very good paper by Franz Lukas, "Das Ei als kosmogonische Vorstellung" (The Egg as a Cosmogonic Idea).[58] It is a bit old, but still useful.

In connection with brooding, *tapas,* which means to give warmth by a meditative concentration of thought, the picture of the egg or germ comes up as the object upon which one is brooding. This is found in the very oldest Indian texts. In the *Rigveda* (10.82), for instance, one of the verses says, "What germ primeval did the waters cherish, wherein the Gods all saw themselves together [you see, the germ contains all the Gods together; they are still united in a compact oneness], which is beyond the earth, beyond that heaven, beyond the mighty Gods' mysterious dwelling?"

This idea of a germ, which is then sometimes definitely called an egg, comes up in the cosmogonic poem of *Rigveda* 10.21, and there the germ upon which the Godhead broods is called the *hiranyagharba,* which is generally translated as a germ of gold, the golden germ. It is a notion which one finds many times in Jung's writings always mentioned as a symbol of the self. The egg is sometimes identified with the whole universe and sometimes more especially with the rising sun. For instance, in the *Chandogya Upanishad* 3.19 it is said:

> In the beginning this was nonexistent. It became existent, it grew. It turned into an egg. The egg lay for the time of a year. The egg broke open. The two halves were one of silver, the other of gold. The silver one became this earth, the golden one the sky, the thick membrane [of the white] the mountains, the thin membrane [of the yolk], the mist with the clouds, the small veins the rivers, the fluid the sea.

Thus the sun is born.

Also in the cosmogony of *Manu Samhita* 15 it is said:

> The primeval God transformed himself into a golden egg which was shining like the sun and in which he himself, Brahman, the father of all worlds, was born. He rested a whole year in this egg and then he parted it into two parts through a mere word. From the two shells he formed heaven and earth, in the middle he put the air, and the eight directions of the world, and the eternal dwelling of the water.

Thus sometimes the Godhead is more outside, brooding on the egg, and sometimes he himself enters the egg and is in it. Accompanying this image is always this idea of cutting it apart. This egg was then also identified with the golden germ in the *Rigveda*. The writings I have just cited are later, but they were recombined with the motif of the *hiranyagharba,* the golden germ, upon which the original Godhead brooded.

The old Phoenician cosmogony contained the same motif. The Phoenicians believed that the basic substance of the world was ether, which was thought to be the lighter and brighter sphere of air, the air above the dust and cloud. The higher air, so to speak, was the ether and the basic substance of the world, and in it was the wind as a moving principle, which was filled with the desire of creating—there too is the motif of desire. He produced two beings, Chusoros and the egg. *Chusoros* means the artifex, the opener. And he, this Chusoros, broke the egg apart and made from its two halves heaven and earth. Here the egg is not the very first origin but is again the basic substance from which a creative God forms the cosmos.

One notes that in passing from East to West this story at once becomes more active. Here a God breaks the egg; it is not a God who is in the egg. It is the more extraverted activity of the *Deus faber,* who breaks the egg and forms heaven and earth from it. In one Persian text, generally dated from the time of the Sassanid dynasties, which would be from AD 200 to 600, it is also said that heaven, earth, and water, and everything under the heavens, were formed as the bird's egg comes into being. The heavens are above the earth, and the earth which resembles the yolk of an egg has been formed by the creative act of Ahura Mazda and is inside the heavens. These Indian, Persian, and Phoenician traditions probably have some historical connection with each other.

In India the egg is connected with the sun, which in certain later texts is called the Son of the Egg. The motif of the egg is also found in some Egyptian cosmogonic systems. According to one Egyptian cosmogony the first primeval mass of water was called Nun, which contained all the male and female germs of all future worlds. In the beginning the original spirit dwelt in those waters and penetrated them at all times; it could not be separated from them, being identical with them. The water contains the creative world spirit.

In most Egyptian systems the creative world spirit is identified with Atum. This spirit felt the desire for creative activity and therefore personified himself in the figure of the God Thoth, the Egyptian Hermes, who began to order everything. Through his thought activity, four divine couples came into existence, which formed the first cosmogonic group of eight: Nun and Nunet, which are then seen after the event as the creative and birth-giving matter; He and Hehet, who are the creative eternity and eros principle of pneuma; Tek and Teket, who personify the darkness of space; and Nenu and Nenuet, who personify non-movement, stillness. They are the fathers and mothers of all things. The first act of creation then began by making an enormous egg which was held in the hands of He and Hehet, who represent the eternal and creative aspects of the time principle. To a certain extent they correspond to the Hellenistic God Aion, who also contains the creative aspect of the time principle. From this egg sprang the Sun God Ra, who then became the immediate cause of all life on earth. Here the egg is not the very first essence of the universe, but is an essential step in the act of creation: after the eight divine principles have sprung from the original spiritualized water principle, they create the egg and from the egg comes the sun. Here again there is the association of the egg with the sun.

The same motif is also found in some Orphic texts. The origin of the Orphic traditions and mysteries is not very clear to us historically. It precedes the birth of Greek philosophy, and we have to date it between the eighth and sixth century BC. Aristophanes' comedy *The Birds* makes fun of one of these Orphic cosmogonies, but from it we can learn something of this old theological tradition. First there was Chaos and night and the dark abyss and the second Tartarus, but earth and air and heaven did not yet exist. In the immense clefts of the Erebos—that is, the deeper abyss—night with her dark wings gave birth to a wind egg. From it sprang in the course of time the God Eros, the one who arouses desire and who has golden wings on his back. He was similar to a whirlwind.

This is a very complex picture, in which there are the motifs of desire and the whirlwind, of the wind moving in a circle. He united with large Tartarus and with nocturnal Chaos and produced first a generation of Gods. Before Eros united them, there were no Gods and no immortal beings existed, but once they had been united, the heaven and the ocean and the earth and the immortal generation of the blessed Gods came into existence. We also hear from a late report of a Church Father that, according to other Orphic

traditions, one of the first Gods was Chaos, who produced the original God, the never-aging Chronos (the
time principle). Chronos produced an egg from which
sprang a hermaphroditic God with golden wings who
had on his sides the head of a bull and above his head
an enormous snake which looked like the form of all
images. Theology praised this firstborn God and
called him Zeus and the orderer of all things. He was
also called Pan. Pan is here probably a misinterpretation or a late interpretation or identification. Actually
this monstrous hermaphroditic God which springs
from the egg in Orphic cosmogony is generally called
Phanes, the shining one. Again the connection with
the Sun. What comes from the egg is a shining being,
whether it is the Sun or the Orphic God Phanes. In
later editions he has been mixed up with Pan as the
God who means the whole universe, which is what he
stood for in late antiquity when he was no longer just
a goat-legged demon of the woods.

The image of the golden germ, or the egg, is perhaps not so difficult to understand psychologically as
some of the other images, because we can easily recognize in it the motif of the preconscious totality. It is
psychic wholeness conceived as the thing which came
before the rise of ego consciousness, or any kind of
dividing consciousness. It is an archetypal idea which
in philosophy lies behind the Aristotelian concept of
the entelechy, the germ which already contains the
whole thing. In Aristotle and his followers one finds
that they used as an illustration the acorn, which already contains the whole tree, or the seed, or, most
frequently, the egg which requires only the addition

of warmth, for it contains everything else in itself. The mystery of the seed of the tree, or the seed of the flower, or the egg which contains so much unexplained mystery, is naturally an appropriate archetypal image to express the preformed totality which contains everything, the details of which are not yet manifest. We find the egg also as an image of the self, but in its form of not yet being realized. It is, so to speak, only a germ, i.e., something potentially existing, a possibility of realization, but not the thing itself.

As soon as the image of the egg comes up, it is associated with the idea of concentration: *tapas,* brooding, and the birth of intelligence. We see, therefore, that when this motif appears, it does not mirror a very primitive psychological state, for it is already the result of a certain amount of concentration of attention. I have seen the same thing practically in analysis, where the motif of the egg very often appears in a state where one could say that the human being has, for the first time, a chance of reflecting upon himself. People are sometimes practically incapable of really basically reflecting about themselves. In the most literal sense of the word, *reflection* means to bend back, and this bending back upon oneself is not something one can decide to do; or, at least, many people decide to do it and nevertheless do not find themselves capable of it. In religious language one would say that it is an act of grace if somebody becomes capable of reflection. Sometimes you can observe somebody quarreling, or in despair about a financial or love situation, and the person talks and talks and talks about psychology, discussing dreams and so on, yet you always have the feeling that the "mad mind" is holding on to the problem and discussing it in this and that form and in between the person will say, "Oh yes, it must be a projection of mine, I am sure my shadow is making mischief in that!" But that is not reflection! When real reflection comes up, you can always see it the minute you look into that person's eyes, for he or she is quiet. Then people are suddenly quiet and objective about themselves and willing really to look at the thing. I would call that a numinous moment, which nobody can bring forth. It is a wonderful thing when it happens to someone, this suddenly becoming quiet and truthful and really "bent back reflectively" upon oneself, looking really for the bottom of the psychological truth, to find out the difficulties. The moment of reflection, of the possibility of becoming conscious—because only thereby is a progress in consciousness possible—this is the moment of the birth of the sun out of the egg. When the egg appears in a dream, then you know that this moment is approaching, that now the birth of consciousness, as an act of self-reflection, is at least possible, it is constellated. The libido is concentrating in one point and now it can come out.

It is not by chance that in the *I Ching* one of the hexagrams identifies the image of the egg with the sign for "Inner Truth." In Hexagram 61 it says that the image for inner truth is an egg with the foot of a bird on it, which means the bird sits on the egg to brood on it. That is the pictorial image to express what the Chinese call Inner Truth. By the realization of inner truth, it says, one can penetrate every difficult situation, one can even influence fish and pigs, which means that one can even master the uncontrolled animal and unconscious impulses if one finds one's way back to this basic germ of the personality, this germ of truth through bending back upon oneself.[59]

Hence the motif of the egg is often mythologically associated with the motifs of light and sunrise, or the appearance of Phanes, the shining God, because it is combined with the idea of sudden illumination. A progress in consciousness is possible, and through that the whole world is new. We know that every time a human being makes real progress in consciousness, makes this evolutionary jump toward a higher level of consciousness, the whole world for him has changed; relationships change and the outlook on the outer world and on his own situation changes. There is a complete rebirth of the world. The golden germ or egg motif shows the constellation of this possibility by an enormous concentration of energy in this one center.

The Twofold and Fourfold Division of the Universe

 One very often finds that after the egg has been created, it is divided, and generally into two parts. One becomes the heavens, the other becomes the earth. In India the earth is made of silver—silver is a feminine metal—and the heavens are gold.

In the Phoenician cosmogony, Chusoros divides the egg in two. The motif which is very close to this separation of the egg is that of the separation of the primordial parents. In many cosmogonic myths the first parents, Father Heaven and Mother Earth, for instance, first existed in a continuous embrace. They formed, as it were, a hermaphroditic being in constant cohabitation. In this state nothing could come into existence, because Father Heaven lies so closely on Mother Earth that there is no space for anything to grow between them. Mother Earth cannot give birth to anything because there is no space for it. The first act of creation is therefore the separation of this divine couple, pushing them sufficiently apart so that a space is created for the rest of creation.

In order to present an idea of this act of separation, I want to cite a creation myth which comes from an island of the New Hebrides. It is told by Sir Arthur

Grimble in a book entitled *A Pattern of Islands*. There are many versions of the myth, but this is an especially colorful one. The author reports how he heard an old man telling the ancient creation myth of this island:

> Dusk was falling as he told his story. All his audience save only myself has straggled away. . . . Taakeuta began, "Sir, I remember the voices of my fathers. Hearken to the words of Karongoa. . . .
>
> Naareau the Elder was the First of All. Not a man, not a beast, not a fish, not a thing was before him. He slept not, for there was no sleep; he ate not, for there was no hunger. He was in the void. There was only Naareau sitting in the Void. Long he sat, and there was only he.
>
> Then Naareau said in his heart, "I will make a woman." Behold! a woman grew out of the Void: Nei Teakea. He said again, "I will make a man." Behold! a man grew out of his thought: Na Atibu, the Rock. And Na Atibu lay with Nei Teakea. Behold! their child—even Naareau the Younger.
>
> And Naareau the Elder said to Naareau the Younger, "All knowledge is whole in thee. I will make a thing for thee to work upon." So he made that thing in the Void. It was called the Darkness and the Cleaving Together; the sky and the earth and the sea were within it; but the sky and the earth clove together, and darkness was between them, for as yet there was no separation.
>
> And when his work was done, Naareau the Elder said, "Enough! It is ready. I go, never to return." So he went, never to return, and no man knows where he abides now.
>
> But Naareau the Younger walked on the overside of the sky that lay on the land. The sky was rock, and

in some places it was rooted in the land, but in other places there were hollows between. A thought came into Naareau's heart; he said, "I will enter beneath it." He searched for a cleft wherein he might creep, but there was no cleft. He said again, "How, then, shall I enter? I will go with a spell." That was the First Spell. He knelt on the sky and began to tap it with his fingers, saying:

Tap . . . tap, on heaven and its dwelling places.
It is stone. What becomes of it? It echoes!
It is rock. What becomes of it? It echoes!
Open, Sir Stone! Open, Sir Rock!
It is open-o-o-o!

And at the third striking, the sky opened under his fingers. He said, "It is ready," and he looked down into the hollow place. It was black dark, and his ears heard the noise of breathing and snoring in the darkness. So he stood up and rubbed his fingertips together. Behold! the First Creature came out of them— even the Bat that he called Tiku-tiku-toumouma. And he said to the Bat, "Thou canst see in the darkness. Go before me and find what thou findest."

The Bat said, "I see people lying in this place." Naareau answered, "What are they like?" and the Bat said, "They move not; they say no word; they are all asleep." Naareau answered again, "It is the Company of Fools and Deaf Mutes. They are a Breed of Slaves. Tell me their names." Then the Bat settled on the forehead of each one as he lay in the darkness and called his name to Naareau: "This man is Uka the Blower. Here lies Naabawe the Sweeper. Behold! Karitoro the Roller-up. Now Kotekateka the Sitter. Kotei the Stander now—a great Multitude."

And when they were all named, Naareau said, "Enough. I will go in." So he crawled through the cleft and walked on the underside of the sky; and the

Bat was his guide in the darkness. He stood among the Fools and Deaf Mutes and shouted, "Sirs, what are you doing?" None answered; only his voice came back out of the hollowness, "Sirs, what are you doing?" He said in his heart, "They are not yet in their right minds, but wait."

He went to a place in their midst; he shouted to them: "Move!" and they moved. He said again, "Move!" They set their hands against the underside of the sky. He said again, "Move!" They sat up; the sky was lifted a little. He said again, "Move! Stand!" They stood. He said again, "Higher!" But they answered, "How shall we lift it higher?" He made a beam of wood, saying, "Lift it on this." They did so. He said again, "Higher! Higher!" But they answered, "We can no more, we can no more, for the sky has roots in the land." So Naareau lifted up his voice and shouted, "Where are the Eel and the Turtle, the Octopus and the Great Ray?" The Fools and Deaf Mutes answered, "Alas! they are hidden away from the work." [Even then there were such people!] So he said, "Rest," and they rested; and he said to that one among them named Naabawe, "Go, call Riiki, the conger eel."

When Naabawe came to Riiki, he was coiled asleep with his wife, the short-tailed eel. Naabawe called him: he answered not, but lifted his head and bit him. Naabawe went back to Naareau, crying, "Alas! the conger eel bit me." So Naareau made a stick, with a slip-noose, saying, "We shall take him with this, if there is a bait to lure him." Then he called the Octopus from his hiding place: and the Octopus had ten arms. He struck off two arms and hung them on the stick as bait; therefore the octopus has only eight arms to this day. They took the lure to Riiki, and as they offered it to him, Naareau sang:

Riikki of old, Riiki of old!
Come hither, Riiki, thou mighty one;
Leave thy wife, the short-tailed eel,
For thou shalt uproot the sky, thou shalt press
    down the depths.
Heave thyself up, Riiki, mighty and long,
Kingpost of the roof, prop up the sky and have
    done.
Have done, for the judgment is judged.

When Riiki heard the spell, he lifted up his head and the sleep went out of him. See him now! He puts forth his snout. He seizes the bait. Alas! they tighten the noose, he is fast caught. They haul him! he is dragged away from his wife the short-tailed eel, and Naareau is roaring and dancing. Yet pity him not, for the sky is ready to be lifted. The day of sundering has come.

Riiki said to Naareau, "What shall I do?" Naareau answered, "Lift up the sky on thy snout; press down the earth under thy tail." But when Riiki began to lift, the sky and the land groaned, and he said, "Perhaps they do not wish to be sundered." So Naareau lifted up his voice and sang:

Hark, hark how it groans, the Cleaving Together
    of old!
Speed between, Great Ray, slice it apart.
Hump thy back, Turtle, burst it apart.
Fling out thy arms, Octopus, tear it apart.
West, East, cut them away!
North, South, cut them away!
Lift, Riiki, lift, kingpost of the roof, prop of the
    sky.
It roars, it rumbles! Not yet, not yet is the Cleaving
    Together sundered.

When the Great Ray and the Turtle and the Octopus heard the words of Naareau, they began to tear

at the roots of the sky that clung to the land. The
Company of Fools and Deaf Mutes stood in the
midst. They laughed; they shouted, "It moves! See
how it moves!" And all that while Naareau was sing-
ing and Riiki pushing. He pushed up with his snout,
he pushed down with his tail; the roots of the sky
were torn from the earth; they snapped! The Cleaving
Together was split asunder. Enough! Riiki straight-
ened out his body; the sky stood high, the land sank,
the Company of Fools and Deaf Mutes was left swimming in the sea.

But Naareau looked up at the sky and saw that
there were no sides to it. He said, "Only I, Naareau,
can pull down the sides of the sky." And he sang:

> Behold I am seen in the West, it is West!
> There is never a ghost, nor a land, nor a man;
> There is only the Breed of the First Mother, and the
>   First Father and the First Begetting;
> There is only the First Naming of Names and the
>   First Lying Together in the Void;
> There is only the laying together of Na Atibu and
>   Nei Teakea,
> And we are flung down in the waters of the western
>   sea.
> It is West!

So also he sang in the east, and the north, and the
south. He ran, he leapt, he flew, he was seen and gone
again like the lightnings in the sides of heaven; and
where he stayed, there he pulled down the side of the
sky so that it was shaped like a bowl.

When that was done, he looked at the Company of
Fools and Deaf Mutes, and saw that they were swimming in the sea. He said in his heart, "There shall be
the First Land." He called to them, "Reach down,
reach down-o-o! Clutch with your hands. Haul up
the bedrock. Heave."[60]

And then comes the fishing up of the land which we have seen in the Iroquoian myth.

This gives a poetic impression of one of the many different myths of the separation of heaven and earth. The psychological implication is easy to understand if we take it cheaply or superficially because it is for us self-evident that every psychological process is based on a pair of polar opposites. This is really the basic idea of Jung, the new idea with which he outgrew the Freudian outlook. It contains his concept of psychic energy, which, like all energetic processes, is based on a polarity, or presupposes a polarity of two opposites. We are now so accustomed in Jungian thought to this idea that we tend to underestimate it and not think back on what it means, but if we read these creation myths with all their different pairs of dualities—the two creators, the two halves of the egg, the separation of the Father and Mother images—we see how widespread this idea is and that it is really one of the most basic archetypal images and underlies most conscious processes of discrimination: the discrimination of ego and the rest of the psyche, or of subject and object, outside and inside, and all other opposites.

In the myth of the separation of the parents, emphasis is laid on the fact that space is needed, so that the whole of creation can come into existence between heaven and earth. Heaven in general symbolizes more the spiritual aspect of the psyche and earth more the material aspect. In one of his late works on the structure and dynamics of the psyche, Jung defines the psychic realm of ego consciousness as lying between the material realm of the body and the archetypal realm of the spirit. This model of the psyche corresponds exactly with these creation myths. The psyche in this view is the *triton eidos* (Plato) between soma and spirit.

A splitting into two parts therefore precedes every conscious realization. Often also before an unconscious content becomes conscious, when it touches the threshold of consciousness, it tends to split into two parts: this is generally the step immediately before it wells up over the threshold of consciousness. This is connected with the fact that no psychological process is imaginable for us without an underlying duality or polarity. As long as the opposites are one and in union, no conscious process is possible.

This point links up with the viewpoint of the East, where the ultimate goal is to return to the condition which existed before this split into the opposites. For instance, the enlightenment called *bodhi* in Buddhist teaching and philosophy, or the enlightenment described as *satori* in Japanese Zen Buddhism, are attempts of consciousness to jump back in a kind of intuitive flash into the oneness which existed before the splitting into two. It is a state of *nirdvandva*, beyond the opposites, the return into the preconscious totality stage and getting away from the subject-object split which presupposes every process in ego consciousness. Most of the cosmogonies, however, describe the separation of the opposites as a positive, creative act.

The same motif of twofold division occurs in the Maori tradition, in a myth entitled "The Sons of the Heavens and Earth." It reads as follows:

The heavens which are above us and the earth which lies below us were the progenitors of men and the origin of all things, for formerly the heavens lay upon the earth and all was darkness. They had never been separated, and the children of heaven and earth sought to discover the difference between light and darkness [that is important—the children *sought* to discover the difference *between light and darkness, between day and night*], for men had become numerous but still the darkness continued. [Then there is a note by the recorder of the story with reference to the phrases "during the night," "the first night," "from the first to the tenth night," the meaning of which is that the darkness had been without limit and light had not yet existed.] So the sons of Rangi [the heavens] and of Papa [the earth] consulted together and said, "Let us seek means whereby to destroy heaven and earth, and to separate them from each other." Then said Tumatauenga [the God of war], "Let us destroy them both."

Then said Tane-Mahuta [the forest God], "Not so; let them be separated; let one go upward and become a stranger to us; let the other remain below and be a parent for us."

So the children of heaven and earth agreed to rend their parents asunder. Tewhiri-Matea [the wind] alone had pity on them. Five agreed to separate them; only one had pity.

Thus by the destruction of their parents they sought to make men increase and flourish, and in commemoration of these things are the sayings, "The night! the night! the day! the day! the searching, the struggling for the light! for the light!!"

So now Rongo-Matane [one of the sons—I am not including all the explanations] arose to separate heaven from earth, but failed.

Then Haumia-Tikitiki tried his strength, but failed also.

Then arose Tangaroa to rend his parents asunder, but was unable to do so.

Tumatauenga then tried, but was equally unsuccessful.

At last arose Tane-Mahuta, the Forest God, to battle against heaven and earth. His arms proved too weak, so bending down his head, and pushing upward with his feet, he tore them asunder. Then wailed the heavens and exclaimed the earth—"Wherefore this murder? Why this great sin? Why destroy us? Why separate us?" But what cared Tane? Upward he sent one and downward the other; and thence comes the saying, "Tane pushed, and Heaven and Earth were divided." He it is who separated night from day.

Immediately, on the separation of heaven and earth, the people became visible, who had hitherto been concealed between the hollow of their parents' breasts.

So now Tawhiri-Matea [the wind] thought he would make war against his brethren, because they had separated their parents, for he alone had not consented to divide the wife from the husband. [Here heaven and earth are suddenly called the wife and the husband.] It was his brothers who resolved to separate them, and to leave but one, the earth, as a parent. . . .[61]

The story which I have quoted reveals the reasons why the children of heaven and earth separated them: first, they had become too many and therefore the space between heaven and earth was too crowded; second, they were attempting to discover the difference between night and day, between darkness and light. This version portrays more clearly than any other the psychological aspects of the division of the universe, namely that the separation means an act of discrimination, an act absolutely necessary as a step toward greater consciousness, that is, for the differentiation of consciousness. Not only the first, but every succeeding step toward higher consciousness is preceded by a separation of the opposites. Words for this process of separation often begin with *dis-* (Latin for "apart")—*discrimination,* for example. This fact points to the principle that one cannot recognize or realize anything without separating and dividing. In myth this is connected with the need for wider breathing and living space: at first the closeness of heaven and earth was not negative, but it gradually became so because it was suffocating the increase of life.

We see again and again the need for a widening of consciousness. A wider and clearer viewpoint is experienced subjectively as doors suddenly opening and allowing breathing space again. It is the freeing of certain life processes. Unconsciousness, when outdated (for reasons which we cannot know), has a suffocating effect upon the individual. Young people, for instance, speak of being suffocated at home. The *participation mystique* with the family, the unconscious identity with it, is at first all right, and is a kind of amniotic fluid in which the embryo swims around, but later it becomes suffocating and one begins to feel one cannot breathe and needs a wider space. Sometimes people who live in small villages and little groups, or in tribes, experience the same thing: suddenly certain individuals feel suffocated. Psychogenetic asthma may even appear as a symptom in such a case, always an indication that a widening of consciousness is now necessary. In former times, this widening was generally effected outwardly, either by leaving the group or going to another group, but not as an inner act. Naturally, it can also be achieved, and even more efficiently, inwardly, by a widening of consciousness and by discrimination.

The same need exists whenever there is the necessity for outgrowing a projection. Jung says we may speak of projection whenever a disturbance of the archaic identity between subject and object appears. As long as I have opinions about anything, whether about the essence of matter or the character of my neighbor, or whatever it may be, and it seems to click with how this thing or object behaves, I will never be capable of really seeing the projection, because the behavior of the object seems to coincide with my views of it. It is only when I begin to have an inner uneasiness, a feeling that what I assert about this object is not quite right, when I have a kind of bad conscience about what I say, that I develop a state of mind in which I can ask myself, "Is this a projection? What would it be if the object were different?" One may therefore say that in the unconscious there already is present a new idea about the object, a new viewpoint which has grown and pushed the old one out. It is like plants which have a little seed cap on them when they come up out of the earth, and if you try to pull it off too soon you destroy them. But, after some time, they push it off themselves and the new shoot appears. So it is with a projection: first a new viewpoint from the unconscious grows underneath and then at a certain moment the other is shed, so to speak, like an old husk, and that is the moment when one is able to, and even should, realize the projection. Why these projections are outgrown, why individuals and even whole nations outgrow them, and why scientific ages outgrow projections and develop new viewpoints, we cannot explain. We can only state the fact that after a certain time there comes up an unconscious need which sometimes can be foreseen through watching the dreams and which after a time breaks into the conscious situation.

Every viewpoint of reality, whether religious or scientific, is a system of ordering and relating to things. But probably just because it is a system for ordering the surrounding chaos, both the inner and the outer chaos which our ego complex confronts, the ordering process has limitations; which probably explains why after some time order is felt as a prison. One might even say that every scientific hypothesis is an instrument for enlarging consciousness which after a time limits further expansion. An example: the construction of every event in three-dimensional space was a very useful instrument at the beginnings of mechanics and geometry. The hypothesis then was that space had three dimensions and everything should be constructed geometrically in these three dimensions. This afforded a very useful viewpoint, a cage, so to speak, in which a number of macrocosmic events could be described in a convincing way. But when one approaches subatomic phenomena, the theory proves insufficient and one becomes uneasy; the facts one observes do not fit into the scheme anymore. If we could admit that the three dimensions form a working hypothesis but that in this or that field it does not work anymore, we could drop it and use another scheme. That would be all right, but, strangely enough, the human mind has a tendency to cling at all costs to an old scheme, even to the extent of twisting facts. People get emotionally attached to their working hypothesis as though it were an eternal truth, and then naturally this becomes a prison which hampers the development of consciousness, as much as it once before helped it along. This is so with most archetypal ideas used as a working hypothesis. If we overstress them and cling emotionally to them, they become prisons, and when they do is the moment when the breaking apart of the cage which they form is experienced as a widening of consciousness and an opening up of new possibilities of life. This is a kind of basic process present in every step forward, in every increase of consciousness. This is why it is described as one of the first and most basic events in many cosmogonic myths.

Another problem which arises together with the need for renewal of consciousness lies in the fact that in the collective unconscious all archetypes are contaminated with each other. In studying any archetype deeply enough, dragging up all its connections, you will find that you can pull out the whole collective unconscious! I am always reminded of the Chinese, who speak of a certain kind of grass whose roots spread so far that you never get it all up. The Chinese say that if you pull up a root of this grass, the whole lawn comes with it! It is the same with the archetypes, for if you pull at one of them long enough, the whole collective unconscious follows! That is why in psychology one cannot and must not approach these contents with the thinking function alone. For a psychological interpretation we need the feeling function, which considers the feeling tone of an archetypal image as well as its logical connections with other images. The tree, for example, has a symbol, a very special feeling connotation. It conveys something to you emotionally which is not identical with the sun, the great Earth Mother, the Source, and so on. As soon as you look at it with feeling, you realize that though these symbols are contaminated or connected, each one has a different feeling tone. You could, for instance, say that the earth is a mother, a death symbol is connected with the source, and so on, but Mother Earth and Mother Tree or the Tree of Life feel different. Logically you can identify them with each other, but with feeling you cannot, and that is what annoys scientists so much and why so many call us psychoanalysts unscientific. But, on the contrary, it is in order to be accurate and *not* to swim around in the unconscious that we have to use feeling. We are scientific when we use it, and we are not scientific if we do not use it, because without feeling we start swimming intellectually, calling every thing everything. At this point, we reach the limit beyond which one's thinking function alone is insufficient and an intellectual person must become conscious of his feelings. Owing to the nature of the archetypal contents of the unconscious, we cannot approach them with only the thinking function.

In most scientists the feeling function is inferior. The inferior function is a kind of hit-or-miss function; whatever the fourth function is, it has this quality of being either very good or below the mark. So I would say that a thinking type should pull up his feeling the way it is and try to trust it, but keep a certain critical attitude toward it by saying, "Am I projecting?" because he is more liable to project, it being his fourth function. But he should not say that because it is the fourth function it is certainly distorted. It might just as well hit the spot! Do not think the inferior function is inferior in the sense that it is lousy, for it is really very good, but primitive and unadapted. It functions autonomously and vigorously and in primitive ways and not in culturally differentiated ways, but that does not mean that a thinking type who trusts his feeling misses the point or distorts it; he may have just the right feeling, but he must remember that it is naive and functions primitively and therefore can commit very gross errors.

By touching upon the feeling function as representing the fourth function of most scientists, we have come upon our next motif in the discussion of creation myths: *the subdivision of the universe into four factors.* After the great division of heaven and earth, in between which earthly reality has appeared at the surface, very often there follows a fourfold division of this reality.

The motif of the double creator, the division and separation of the primordial parents, has to do with the polarization between consciousness and the unconscious. But there are also motifs which concern three or four creators which we will now focus upon. They are connected to Jung's typology, some knowledge of which I must take for granted.

The Blackfoot Indians, for instance, tell us that Chief Creator, the Second Creator, and a woman were drifting over the great waters in a canoe, discussing how to bring the earth above the water. They sent out four animals. Three failed, but the muskrat brought up a little bit of mud which was used to create the world.

In a Maidu myth, Earth Initiate creates the world, and he, too, has some earth fished up by an animal, the tortoise. He grasps it in his hands and rolls it about till he has a lump as big as a little stone, which he puts on his raft. From time to time he looks at it, but it does not get bigger until he looks at it the fourth time. Suddenly, it becomes as big as the world. It is very often said that three times an animal tries to fish up the earth but does not succeed until the fourth time; or three times he looks at the lump of clay and it does not grow, but when he looks at it the fourth time it suddenly transforms itself. Here you have fourfoldness in the form of a time division, and the fourth is decisively different from the three previous events.

One meets this same time division in fairy tales from all over the world; there are nearly always three rhythms and then a different decisive fourth event. In a famous Russian story the hero goes out to find Maria with the Golden Plaits, who sleeps in the Kingdom under the Sun. One day he meets a great sorceress, Baba Yaga, and asks her the way and stays the night. She cannot tell him the way but sends him to her sister, and after her he goes to another witch. The story in this case is even told rhythmically in exactly the same way. The third witch shows him the way, and he finds, as a fourth, Maria the Golden.

There are also many fairy tales in which the girl is looking for her husband, or the man is looking for his beloved. He goes first to the Sun, then to the Moon, and afterward to the stars to ask the way; or first to the Sun, then to the Moon, and then to the Night Wind.

In Christianized versions, the hero very often goes to a wise old man, a hermit, who sends him to another hermit, and the last one tells him where to go. Generally, investigators of myths speak of three rhythms, but really, if you look more closely, you see that three times it is the same thing and then with the fourth time comes the change. In Indian creation myths there is the same constellation.

Among the Blackfoot Indians, again, there is a creation myth in which the Sun created heaven and earth, but nobody knows how the Sun came into existence. The Moon had a child and the Sun had a child. The Moon's child is called Old Man and the Sun's child is Napi. The Sun's child is called the "Apistotoki God." These four figures begin to create the world. They are given four things—sand, stone, water, and the hide of a fisher—with which they complete the creation. Afterward there is a flood and they can save only the four things. Finally they create again four things, an old man, a dog, a man, and a woman. After a second flood there are only these four left on earth, and they create the rest of the world. So in these cosmogonies the motif of four constantly recurs.

The Southern Arapaho also have a myth in which
the earth was first created by God but with nothing
on it, and the creator of the earth said he needed servants to model and shape it. So he created Sun and
Moon, and man and woman—again four. Here they
are the servants of the Creator.

The Winnebago, a subdivision of the Sioux, have
the following creation myth. The Great Spirit felt
lonely. He took a part from his body, from the region
of the heart, and a little bit of earth and formed the
first man and then three more men. Then he created a
woman who is the earth, the grandmother of all Indians. The four men are the four winds, and they again
are the main helpers. Here there are really five, but
the fifth is something different, it is the passive earth,
while the four men become the helpers of the creative
spirit in shaping the earth. Another Winnebago variation says: What our Father said when he came to consciousness we do not know, but he began to cry. (I
already gave you this part of the myth.) Then he
formed the earth and sent four men, four brothers,
and put them in the four places of the universe to support mankind. There is another variation where it
says the Earth Maker made four beings who looked
like him and sent them to help mankind, first to create, then to help them.[62]

The Wichita tribes have a highest God called Man
Never Known on Earth. He is the type of God who,
after the creation, retires and never takes further part.
This Man Never Known on Earth created different

Star Gods and the four Gods of the four countries of the world. The Indian who tells the tale says that in the roof of a Wichita tent or house (they lived in cone-shaped grass huts) there are four poles: East, West, South, and North, which represent the four Gods of the four countries of the world. In the middle is a pole which points to heaven, to the Man Never Known on Earth. So here again is the one unknown, who represents the preconscious totality, the whole thing, and then in subdivision the four Gods of the four countries of the earth. The house is still built in this same way.

In other myths—there is unfortunately no mention of the tribe but only of the Prairie and Plateau tribes in general—the highest God creates the stars of Northeast, Northwest, Southwest, and Southeast and says to them, "You four shall carry heaven as long as it exists, this will be your main task, but I will also give you the power to create and teach human beings."

Among the Aztecs one finds the fourfold creation in many forms. For instance, they teach that there were four creations of men, each destroyed by a flood until the Gods created the world which exists now: four world periods, as well as four original Gods who created the world. The fifth is called Four Movements and is the day of the Fifth, the present world period. Then there is the myth of the four original Gods who decided in the year "One Rabbit" to create four ways of reaching the middle of the earth in order to lift up heaven. To do this they created four men whose four names are given. When they had created these four helpers, the Gods Tetzcatlipoca and Quetzalcoatl turn into two trees and retire.

In a variation of the Winnebago myth is the same story of four male beings, brothers, who were created and placed at the four corners of the world.[63] But that did not suffice, because the world continued to spin around like mad and the creator could not stop it. So he created the four corners of the world. This again was a failure, and so the creator pondered for a long time. Then with his own hands he made four beings, water spirits, and placed them under the earth; they are called Island Anchorers. Finally he scattered a female being over the whole earth, and that is the fifth! By female being is meant stones and rocks. After all this, the creator looked at what he had created and saw that the earth had at last become quiet; it was anchored, with the four water spirits holding it from underneath and a female weight, in the form of stone and rock, upon it.

In mythology the step from one basic number to another can be achieved in different manners. You can count two procedures, either by splitting the one unit or by adding another unit to make the two. But as soon as there are two, there is again a problem, for you can proceed to three in two ways, either by adding another unit or by reconstructing the first unit by cutting it into two, which would make three. The same thing with the three: if you have a triangle, you can add a fourth, or you can say that the three are really a unit, so if the unit of the three is added to the three, that gives the fourth. The same thing holds for four: there are four units and you can proceed by adding a unit, which might give a pentagram, or there are the four and you can reconstruct the original unit, which then gives the quinta-essentia of the alchemists. When you add the next number as a reconstruction of the original unit, it is not really the next number but only the *one* of the preceding number. Mythologically, it is simply the one of the four and is not felt to be the fifth. If you read alchemical texts, it is the quinta-essentia, the quintessence, which is really the one of the four, while the fifth is looked on as the number of nature, of deficiency, of natural imperfections and bodily existence; some speculations about number symbolism say this is the *natura naturata,* the imperfectness of just-so nature. But the other type of five is the quintessence, the greatest perfection—just the opposite of the *natura naturata.*

So in number symbolism it always depends on which type of number you have. For instance, in our theological speculation there is the problem of the three in the Trinity of Father, Son, and Holy Ghost. But Joachim of Flora talked of the common substance of Father, Son, and Holy Ghost, and some of his sayings were condemned by the Church for secretly introducing a Quaternity, since he hypostatized the common substance of the three as if it were something independent. Actually he only looked at the one of the three, which is different from adding a unit, but naturally the one leads into the other and he was understood to be adding a fourth and accordingly condemned. When you count, you could say that the original one forms a continuum, so every number can be understood as representing the oneness of the foregoing in a new form. The two are really two aspects of the one, the three are really three aspects of the original one. Four is only the four aspects of the one having become manifest, and so on. So there is a kind of continuum association underneath the original unit, the original *one.*

As I understand it, in this Aztec myth therefore the fifth world would not really be a fifth, but a borderline five phenomenon. One sees the same thing in China. We in the West have four basic elements, while in China there are five or six. But when you look at it, they are always in the same order, so they are not really different from our four elements, except that the oneness of the fourth, the original unit, is separately emphasized. That is why, if you count superficially, you say the Chinese have five, and not four. But if you look at Chinese drawings, you see that it is not a contradiction to the quaternity but the other type of counting.

When there is a sacred number, the next number is always a trespasser. With us it is thirteen. Twelve is completeness because three times four is particularly complete. Thirteen is a trespassing number, so it is either very lucky or very unlucky. It trespasses on the natural feeling of totality and grouping. Numbers, in their original meaning, always have a group quality. For instance—and this is a very deep story, though it sounds naive—Jung made an experiment with some tribal people in Africa: he showed them three matches and asked how many there were. The answer was three. He then made another set of two matches and asked how many there were. The answer was two. He

then took one of the matches from the three-group
and transferred it to the two-group and again asked
how many that made and got the answer two-two
matches and a three match. Pointing to the other
group, he asked how many there were and got the
answer two-three matches. So the original grouping
had imparted a three quality to its group, which it
kept even when one was transferred, while the others
belonged to the original two-group.

This transferring of quality has to do with how the
unconscious counts. For example, primitive shep-
herds can count their cattle without really being able
to count, for in words they can only count up to seven
or ten, but in a minute they can correctly count the
sixty-three sheep they have. There is a kind of unconscious awareness of the number as a group and a capacity to see it directly through the unconscious without being able to count discursively, as we do. Such
number awareness would correspond to awareness
for the completeness of a group. This is a very mysterious business; I can now only call your attention to
it, but there is a lot more to this problem which we
have not yet solved.

I want to give a few more references to the fourfold
divisions of creation. In Hindu tradition it sometimes
is said of the original being, Purusha, that one-fourth
of him is all creatures and three-fourths are the world
of the immortals in heaven. He is the totality, but subdivided into one-fourth and three-fourths. There is
also a tendency toward fourfold division in China,
where the Miau tribes still worship P'an Ku, the original being, together with the three sovereigns. Here

again is an original group of four, and again the differentiation of three and four. They are not simply four; three are sovereigns and the one is the original being. We have again the original oneness, added to the three afterward.

In Germanic mythology one finds the idea that the world is created from the primeval giant Ymir. The Gods took his skull and spread it over the earth and over it made the sky. The skull was held up by four dwarfs standing at the four corners of the earth. In later poems, therefore, heaven is not called heaven, but is very often called the burden of the dwarfs, or the burden of the four dwarfs.

In certain African myths, there is an original God who goes down to earth, where he finds three other beings whom he had not created. He had created everything but these three: thunder, the Ndorobo, and the elephant. It is not quite clear what the Ndorobo is, but it is a kind of secondary creator God and from its swollen knee the first human beings come into existence. Here again is the rhythm of one and three, but the original group then brings everything into existence in four.

The Bena-Lulua say that the supreme creator was Fidi Mukullu. He did not create the world directly, but had four sons whom he sent down to earth to create the world.

In Egypt there are the original waters of Nun, the first water in which the creative spirit of the God Atum dwelt invisibly. Out of it came either four apes or four frogs, or eight apes and eight frogs, and they worship the sun coming out of the waters. In this case there is either a group of four or eight beings who worship the first appearance of the light.

The fourfold act of creation is found in a much more differentiated form in certain Gnostic myths, for instance in the teaching of Valentinus, who is now better known to us through the *Codex Jung*.[64] According to Valentinus the first being, whom he calls Auto-pater, the Father of Himself, or the Self-Father, that is, the self-created totality, in the beginning embraced the whole universe. He was unconscious in himself, never aging, eternally young, and a hermaphroditic being. He contained in himself Ennoia, Thought, also called Sige, Silence. They united and brought forth Man (Anthropos) and Aletheia (Truth). Again from the first couple there is first created a group of four Gods: God and his female inner partner, Man (but do not think of Man now as mankind, for the Anthropos is the divine elder brother of mankind, to speak Indian language—I mean the idea of Man as a divine being), and Aletheia, Truth, which in Greek is a female word. So now there are two couples, which he calls the first, never-aging spiritual Tetras, which means a group of four. These then create four others, namely Anthropos, Ecclesia, Logos, and Zoe. Anthropos, the spiritual shape of man; Ecclesia, the female personification of human mankind, the spiritual church you could say; Logos, manifested and outspoken thought, and Zoe, life. These again produced another fourfold group, which is the Holy Ghost, and so on, but I will spare you all this. There are innumerable different Godheads to which I will return later in the chapter on the problem of the chain reactions—the many, many Gods which are created. The important thing is that in some of the systems of Valentinus there are fourfold beginnings, and even afterward the process continues in fourfoldness, probably having been influenced by Pythagorean philosophy (the Pythagoreans worshiped the Tetras as the holiest of all numbers).

Probably dependent on Valentinus is the gnosis of a man called Markos, founder of another Gnostic sect. Markos says that in the beginning was the first being who had no father, of whom one cannot think, who had no substance, and who was neither male nor female, which cannot be understood. He opened his mouth and produced the Word, which was the same as himself, the Son, the Logos (you see here the Christian influence) and the first word he spoke was *Arche*—which in Greek means *beginning:* A as number 1; R as number 2; CH as number 3, and E as number 4. He spoke only words which consisted of four letters, and by speaking these creative words he created the universe.

If you look at the number symbolism of creation myths, you must by no means think that two and four, then eight, are the only relevant numbers (though I have only picked out myths where those numbers are specially relevant, and have skipped a considerable number where there are three creators). For instance, two creators are drifting in a boat and the tortoise comes as a helper, as the third. A group of three Gods create the world in South American myths, and in Aztec myths there is very often a group of three in the form of a father figure, a mother figure, and a son. The creative triad is not quite so frequent, as far as I can tell, as the tetrad, but it is also a very frequent number in creation myths.[65]

The difference between three Gods creating the world and those twofold and fourfold divisions is the following: whenever the emphasis lies on creative action, on creative activity, you can just as well have three or six or nine. There are, one could say, triadic groupings of creative potencies. Whenever the emphasis of the tale is on establishing an orientation, or an order, there are four creators: the four pillars of the world, the four directions of heaven, four helpers of the Godhead, etc. So we can see that "three groups" emphasize the creative flow of action, while "four groups" emphasize the establishment of an order, which fits in with our idea of the conscious structure. We can say that the number four, from our practical experience, always points to a totality and to a total conscious orientation, while the number three points to a dynamic *flow* of action. You could also say that the three is a creative flow and four is the result of the flow when it becomes still, visible, and ordered.

The temptation, naturally, for a Jungian psychologist is to say that here we have the four functions of consciousness. I think this is turning the problem the wrong way around. We should say that here we have the archetypal pattern upon which our idea of the four functions of consciousness is built. In other words, the archetypal fourfoldness of the reality of the world, of every mythological establishment of order, is the more basic and the more embracing symbol, and our idea of the four functions of consciousness is one aspect of it. The fourfoldness of the orientation of reality is the more general concept, and our four function theory is a derivation. We have to turn it this way and must not project backward by saying that those four servants, and so on, are the four functions.

Abortive Attempts at Creation

10

By abortive attempts at creation I mean the following. Very often the God tries to create human beings and does not succeed. What he does create are like Titans, gigantic, or idiotic, or unable to move properly. In any case, it is not a successful business, and so he has to destroy them and try again. Sometimes there are even several abortive attempts until the Godhead, or the creator, the demiurge, succeeds in producing something which can remain. But sometimes these abortive attempts survive, and then they either form evil demons or Gods of a superior and positively superhuman kind. To translate it into the language of our civilization, the results are either demons or angels, as if the God sometimes produces something which is a bit too good and then tries something which is a bit too bad, and only succeeds in creating man as a middle being, as he unfortunately, or happily, now is.

In the myth of the separation of father and mother which I quoted at the end of the last chapter, there were the deaf mutes and the fools who did not help the God to tear heaven and earth asunder; they were too lazy and inefficient. After he had found the other animals to help him, the deaf mutes and fools or idiots disappeared into the sea. Though it is not said expressly, they become the creatures of the sea, the fish and the eels and so on. In part, therefore, the first inefficient beings are simply identical with lower forms of animal life, especially those which live in the sea. This comes strangely near to our theories of evolution.

In the Samoan creation myth, the supreme God Tangaloa creates the world by throwing down or fishing up a rock from the waters, and this rock is also called Ika Maui, the original fish of Maui, which becomes what we now know as North Island in New Zealand. This rock covered itself with vegetative life and certain holy plants, and within the decaying mass of these plants certain worms came into existence from which human beings finally arose. The aristocracy of this island later got very disgusted at the idea of having originated from worms, so they said that they were created *directly* by the supreme Godhead and only the inferior plebians were the result of worms evolving into human beings.

In the Germanic creation myth, as it is told in the Edda, men were not created first. Before the Gods there were the giants, then came the Gods, who created the dwarfs, and only after having created innumerable dwarfs, who in the Edda are all mentioned with very strange names, did they create mankind. There are different dwarfs. The original ones are called Wolf Dwarfs, Guardian Dwarfs, Morning and Midday and Midnight and Evening, New Light and Low Light, Mist Producer, Night Producer, Stretcher, Licking One, the Killer, the Son of the Killing One.

Earth Dwarfs who are called the Clever Thief, the Snapping One, the One Who Quickly Gets into Quarrels, the One Who Hits, the One Who Can Shoot Arrows, the One Who Is Always Ready to Quarrel, the Shrewd One and the Violent One, the Quick One, the One Who Has a Quick Wit, the Fox, the One with the Healthy Face, the One Who Has Quick Ideas, the One Who Finds Easily, and the One Who Always Acts on the Spur of the Moment.

There is another division which is called the Mist Producers, the Son of Dead Leaf, the Fire. They live in the earth and in the original cavities of the hills. One is called Thief of the Hills, others are the Finder of Hills, the One Who Finds Rewards, the One Who Finds Praise, the Former, the Builder, the Burner, the One Who Colors in Brown, the One Who Cools, the One Who Clarifies, the One Who Makes Dropping Noises, another who makes Knocking Noises, the One Who Produces Sparks, the One Who Produces the Iron Smith, and many others.

These dwarfs seem to me very interesting. What are those abortive creatures? What are the giants? What are the dwarfs? Are they abortive attempts to produce a man? I think the names of the German dwarfs are most revealing. They mostly represent single impulses, single semiconscious or conscious impulses. For instance, the One Who Has a Quick Wit—to have a quick wit means that something suddenly comes to your mind and you give the right answer. You know how often, if somebody attacks you, you just stand there hurt, and then at midnight you suddenly think: I should have said . . . ! It would have been so witty!

But the quick wit did not come when you wanted it. A lot of other dwarfs have the names of crafts. Ultimately, the invention of crafts and the capacity for crafts depends on the inspirations of the unconscious. Others have the names of quick, impulsive gestures, like Quarreling Before One Reflects—just jumping up and quarreling and then: Oh, God, I should have thought before I hit back, etc. The One Who Hits Quickly, and Quick Stealing, that means the one who not only hits quickly, following an affect, but sees something and pockets it—that is also a good idea, a quick momentary impulse.

All these represent sudden momentary invasions of unconscious impulses of either an affective emotional nature or a more intelligent nature. They represent something which one could sum up in German by the word *Einfall*. *Einfall* is very difficult to translate into English. It is something which drops into one's head; it falls in. *Fall* = fall, and *ein* = in, in-fall. It is a beautiful word for something that suddenly pops up in consciousness, comes in a flash from the unconscious. These invasions are not yet human, they are not human consciousness, they are the first flickerings of something that when it then becomes continuous we call consciousness; they are like lights flickering up here and there, but are not a continuous lamp burning. They are the preforms, the *not-yet* forms of human consciousness.

In Greece, there is the same kind of abortive creation of humanity in the form of the Titans. The Titans, the oldest beings, were created before man by Mother Earth. They were enemies of the Olympian

Gods, and according to certain mythological versions, after they were burnt up by Zeus with his lightning, human beings were created from their ashes. That is why we have Titanic impulses within us still, which make us revolutionary and a dubious kind of species. Here, in contrast to the dwarfs, the Titans resemble more the giants of Germanic mythology, overpowering emotional affects. It is very appropriate that one is small and the other big, because affect makes everything very big. As soon as you get into an affect, you tend to exaggerate. We have a saying, for instance, "to make an elephant out of a louse," if somebody makes a big emotional fuss over some unimportant detail. Now, if someone makes an elephant out of a louse, it means that he has been hit by this louse on a personal complex, and a terrific affect has been let loose. This magnifying quality of affect is not only negative, it is also positive in the sense that an affect can literally give us "grandeur," greatness. You see this, for instance, in the heroism some people show in war. When carried away by nationalism, or by the affect of fighting, they sometimes perform heroic deeds of which, in a normal mental reflective state, they would be incapable. It is the affect which makes them great. We therefore have such expressions as *holy rage* and so on. A holy rage is something! The Holy War, fighting a holy war with a holy rage, with a holy affect! Other great creative performances also are very often carried through with the help of terrific affect.

Jung tells of an interesting dream he himself had when he wanted to write *Psychological Types*. He had collected the material for the book over many, many years and had it all piled up, and then he came to that crucial moment where he had to write the book. How was he to pull all that material together and write what he had to say about it? You know that this is one of the most difficult steps in creative work. He wanted to write it in a rational, refined form, so as to convince rationalists of what he had to say. He tried and it did not work very well. And then he had the following dream: he saw in a port an enormous ship laden with goods which should now be pulled into port. Attached to the ship on a cord was a very elegant white horse, absolutely incapable of pulling in the ship, which was much too heavy! At this moment there came suddenly through the crowd an enormous red-headed giant who pushed everybody aside, took an ax and killed the white horse, and took the rope and with one pull pulled the whole ship into port. After that, Jung got up at three o'clock every morning and just wrote the whole thing down in one *élan*, carried by an enormous affect of enthusiasm, the only possibility for bringing such complicated material together. It had to be hammered together with an affect! The white horse was connected with his plan to write a refined, formal treatise, but that was not adequate to deal with the mass of material which he had to land in consciousness. That shows how giants are not only destructive titanic powers, but can be very constructive.

Jung's dream illustrates something which one finds in innumerable medieval legends where the most beautiful churches, monuments, and cathedrals were built by giants outwitted by a saint who made them build the entire edifice. A saint has not the physical strength to pile up the stones of a cathedral! He needs a giant to help him. So if the giant is tamed, if he is under control, then he is a most useful helper in every creative work. If you have a giant to do the job for you, that's wonderful! It is only a question of having him under control! The giants and Titans—such preforms of human beings—are only destructive in mythology because they are not under control, because they represent chaotic impulses from the unconscious which are not yet controlled by that continuous civilized form of consciousness for which the symbol of man stands, perhaps wrongly, but he does.

I have mentioned how the deaf mutes, some Samoan and New Zealand stories, the dwarfs and giants in Germanic mythology, and in Greece the Titans from whose ashes man was made give man a Titanic quality which gives rise to his inordinate desires and revolutionary impulses. In the North American Indian myths there exists a similarly dual idea about the creation of man.

It can be seen from the biblical tradition in the Book of Enoch that when dealing with giants, one is also dealing with inflation. In the Book of Enoch it is said that some angels fell in love with human women and had sexual intercourse with them, as a result of which the women later gave birth to demoniacal giants who, little by little, destroyed the world. These giants, however, also introduced all art and science to man. We are therefore given to understand that a too-fast development in consciousness in man has catastrophic consequences. Jung interprets this passage from the Book of Enoch in his book *Answer to Job* as an overhasty invasion from the unconscious. The unconscious (angels are the messengers of the beyond and therefore represent the unconscious) has, to some degree, burst into the human world too hastily. As a result, mankind's expansion of consciousness has been too rapid. It is only when a continual creative broadening of consciousness takes place by degrees within the tradition of a culture that there is a chance that it will not prove to be destructive.

We are living in such a destructive situation today. One can say that with the enormous expansion of our consciousness and knowledge (the arts which were brought to man by the angels), for example in modern nuclear physics and in science and technology in general, which have gone ahead at such a tremendous speed, the rest of humanity has not been able to keep pace and continuity has been interrupted. We have not been able to keep up morally, neither with our feelings nor with our minds. Certain fields of science suffer from delusions of grandeur—for example, when one reads studies in which scientists boast that ten to fifteen years from now they will be able to genetically put a human being together as they choose, and other similar articles.

Now I would like to return to the motif of these mute abortive creatures, for they represent yet another creative problem. I would like to revert your attention to the deaf and dumb beings who later turned into fish. And also to the place in the *Popol Vuh* where the Gods created human beings who were not able to speak, but because the Gods wished to be praised, they made a further attempt to create a new human creature and this time they succeeded.

In a creation myth of the Joshua Indians there were two creators, the one called Cholawasi and the other, his companion, without name in this version. Cholawasi and his companion created the world together. When they walked about it, they found, with horror, the traces of a human being. Desperately they tried to find out what it was, but could not, and then Cholawasi tried to destroy these traces by five floods. He exclaimed with terror, "This will bring confusion," and since then there has always been confusion in the world. Cholawasi then began to create the animals. He also tried to form men, twice without success. Then his companion smoked for three days, and during this time a house appeared, and out of it came a beautiful woman. The companion married this beautiful woman whom he had constellated by smoking, and they had sixteen children, from whom came all the different Indian tribes.

Here you see two failures of creation, and then the shadowy companion, by smoking instead of actively creating, indirectly constellated a situation where the human being could come into existence. But, at the same time, there was already, somewhere, another human being about whom the two Gods could find out nothing, and he is the cause of confusion.

In Eskimo tradition there is also the idea of a first failure in the creation of human beings. In one myth it is said that the first earth which came into existence had neither seas nor mountains, but was completely flat. The God above did not like the human beings who were on it, and he therefore destroyed the earth. It burst, and the human beings fell into the ravine and became the Ingnerssiut. The Ingnerssiut are evil demons. Water covered everything, and when the earth reappeared it was completely covered with ice. This slowly disappeared, and then two human beings fell down from heaven, and they populated the earth. Everywhere the ice is now still fading away. Here the first human beings seem to be a failure: they are no good, and the world in which they live is no good, so the Godhead destroys them and they become demons. You will see later that this is a very frequent archetypal idea: that the former human beings, the failures, have become demons or hidden ghostly powers.

There is a North American Indian myth where the human beings looked too similar to the creator; they were big and heavy and could only move very slowly. So, when a flood came, they all died. Then everything was dead, and the earth was fished up again, after which the God decided to create human beings again. He did so, but again noticed that they were too similar to him and therefore too powerful. He got frightened and destroyed them all and then created a man who looked like the present-day human being, and he said, "Why does it happen that I still do not feel quite at ease about it?" Then he created a woman and put her beside the man, and the man said, "Well, you knew that I was not yet satisfied, something was still lacking, but now we can walk together over the earth."

Also Adam, according to certain Midrashim, was

heavy and clumsy and had no pneuma in him for a long time and could only crawl like a worm. Here, in a completely different setup, is the same motif that the first attempts at creation produced something clumsy and without life and spirit. You will also remember the very first creation myth I told, in which Father Raven in Heaven created a human being who looked something like himself but who started at once to dig in the earth with his hands. In complete restlessness he shoveled on and on with a kind of hot temperament, and Father Raven did not like him and threw him away into the abyss. This creature, they say, became Tornaq, the evil spirit. From him come all evil spirits. It is also in Eskimo tradition that the first man is created in heaven but is a quick, bad-tempered, impatient kind of being who is thrown away and becomes a demon and the basis for all other demons who exist later.

In another rather similar story—also Eskimo—it is said that in the beginning there was not much difference between human beings and animals. The animals could become human beings and vice versa; the human beings walked on their hands, they crept about on all fours, and only later did they learn to walk upright. So, with this kind of clumsy human being there is also sometimes associated the closeness to animal life, as you find in this example. One sees the same thing in the myths of the Incas. For instance, one story runs that there were two creators. The first was called Con, and he created normal human beings, but then Pachacamac, who was also the son of the sun and whose name is creator, chased away Con and transformed the human beings Con had created into cats with black faces. A footnote to this report says that in other versions he transformed them into apes, and then he created male and female human beings as they look now and gave them all things, and that is why these human beings elected Pachacamac to be their God. There you have two generations, the first is created by one creator, Con, and they become either apes or cats with black faces, and only afterward the second creator comes who creates human beings, definitely those who exist now.

The archetypal idea that the creation of all beings, especially of human beings, has failed, survives in Greek philosophy, in the system of Empedocles. According to him, the first being was the spherical God Sphairos, who is held together by the principle of Eros. When Eros prevails, the world is one unit, but when the principle of Neikos prevails (Neikos means "quarrel"), the world falls apart. There are always these two warring principles, Neikos and Eros, the one fighting to reconstitute the original oneness and the other to make it fall apart. And then, Empedocles says, all the limbs of the God were whirled about and then met, as if by chance, and so there were at first completely monstrous creations.[66] In the beginning animals and plants were not at all complete; there were only separate parts. In the second stage these parts melted together in the most monstrous formations, and only in the third stage did certain bodies come into existence. Not until the fourth did they become really beautiful formations. First out of the earth came many heads without necks, arms walked about quite lonely without shoulders, and eyes roamed about lonely without a forehead (a real schizophrenic vista of the world). Sour elements attracted the sour, and warm elements poured themselves upon the warm, and there was a terrible chaos in which chance events happened until everything came into a more or less reasonable formation.

This is more or less a survey of the material, to give an idea of what I mean by abortive attempts at creation. As you see, they do not so much refer to the cosmic world, to the earth and plants and trees, but mostly cluster around the creation of man. This is where there are so many failures, as if the creation of man was a specially difficult chapter for God in his work of creation, and he had to try several times before he achieved, approximately, what he had in mind. There is also a relatively widespread thought that the results of these abortive attempts were not destroyed but survived either as animals or as black-faced cats and apes, or they survive as demons of some kind, as in the Eskimo versions, and as, for instance, in Greek mythology where the Titans and the dwarfs are demonic powers which still survive beside later created human beings.

That was also such a failure, or rather a failure in continuation, for it was not a creation. Sometimes these failures in human beings are too close to the animals, too inferior, they are clumsy, they cannot talk, they creep about on all fours, and are in that way no good. Sometimes they are just the opposite and are too good, and the God gets frightened and thinks the thing is too powerful and must be cut down a little bit because otherwise there would be too much rivalry for comfort. For instance, the Greek Titans launched a general attack upon the Olympian Gods; the famous Titanomachia had to be thrown down by Zeus with his lightning and since then, overcome and conquered, they live under the earth but still produce earthquakes and all sorts of mischief. So there, too, this first failure in creation is in a way too powerful and therefore dangerous for the divine order; it is what the Greeks call *hybris,* or hubris, megalomanic presumption.

We can see all these pre-stages in the creative process of the individual as well. The giant formations and the Titans would correspond to the terrific affect and excitements and sometimes also the inflated moods one gets when a progress of consciousness or something creative is constellated. We often experience that when we have a good idea, a creative plan; one is emotionally too much filled by it and carried away by terrific enthusiasm, which makes one overvalue the plan. Generally, also, one overvalues oneself and gets inflated, and then when one bends down to the laborious effort of realizing one's creative impulses, the result looks pretty poor in comparison with the original inner vision. Thus we can say that every creation is an impoverishment and a failure, compared with the glory and glamour of the first intuition about it. If you talk to artists, they are very rarely satisfied with their production; at best, they say that now they can put down brush or pen and think that what they have produced is more or less all right, but that is the maximum of satisfaction they generally get. There is usually a kind of lingering sadness, because compared with the inner vision the realization is always second rate and not so good. Even if you try on a very small and humble scale to paint, for instance, what you saw in a dream, look what a miserable result you have on your paper, compared with what you saw inside yourself.

People in a precreative stage are thus often inflated; they are identical with their inner conception and filled with its glory and beauty and its load of energy. But generally when the work is finished, instead of being happy they feel a bit deflated and sad. Women very frequently cry after a birth, as if they were unhappy about the child they have borne. The same is true of spiritual birth. One cries from a mixture of exhaustion and deflation. This has also to do with the tremendous load of energy with which one is filled by a creative impulse. It is also one reason why some people never get down to do something creative, especially men of the puer aeternus type, also women of the puella aeterna type. They never step down to do something creative because they feel vaguely, or foresee intuitively, that if they produce the thing they have in mind, it will be much less good than what they conceive inwardly. They do not want to go through this process of creative deflation but prefer to remain all their lifetime would-be artists, or would-be geniuses, on a very great scale rather than the producer of a humble product on a very much lower scale. Of such people a biographer could say, "Till he was forty there were no symptoms of genius—there weren't any later either."

Together with the *élan vital* of creativity very often, naturally, comes hubris, in the Greek sense of the word, Titanic hubris: the overestimation of one's power and a megalomanic inflated attitude. On a minor scale it is inevitable, even necessary, to have these moods, because otherwise one would not be able to make the extra effort of creating something; one needs to be carried by the enthusiasm of the big goal; otherwise one would give up and prefer to lead a comfortable life. One must never forget that man's greatest passion, greater than any other, is probably laziness, and to overcome the passion of laziness one needs a lot of energy, characterized by the giant and Titan forms.

The dwarflike figures have more to do with tiny little weak impulses of a more playful and even sometimes of a rather funny or scurrilous character. Most creative people, as you probably know, have a tendency to playfulness; they produce, even in their spare time, funny little ideas and all sorts of creative playfulness.

The names of those German dwarfs intimate what dwarfs are: Quick Witted Idea to Do Something, for example. Usually the words are connected with a quick reaction, that tiny little good idea one has sometimes, which completely depends on the unconscious. For instance, somebody invites you and you don't want to accept the invitation; you depend completely on the unconscious to serve you with a good lie, a good excuse! Sometimes one is terribly proud if the right answer comes! One says, "Wasn't that wonderful! It just came to me to say that!" And you are out of all your trouble! Another time you blush and say yes and no, and at the other end of the telephone the person knows that you are lying—the unconscious just does not want to deliver a good idea! Or somebody attacks you and you want to give a witty answer and you just have none and behave clumsily and then, at midnight, you wake up and know what you should have said! If you get it at the right minute, that is a dwarf—that kind of sudden *Einfall* from the unconscious which, in a playful way, just comes into your mind quickly, at the right moment, and naturally you must be quick in expressing it and getting it, otherwise it is lost.

The dwarfs are everything that has to do with a good idea, even on a minor scale. If you visit a farmhouse in the country you will see a lot of tiny, very good tricks: how the man gets his electricity to the stables, how he prevents the water from seeping into another place, etc. Farmers, and most simple people, do not get specialists to help with the difficulties which nature always produces, but they invent their own little devices, which work quite well. They may be worried by humidity in the stables, or something or other, and then one day they have a good idea as to what can be done, and generally on their own, because everything would cost too much money otherwise. Naturally there are more and less gifted people in this respect. For instance, near my holiday house I have a neighbor who is just fantastic in this respect, and always has the right idea, so all the neighbors always say to ask so-and-so. He is an extraverted intuitive, and whenever one is in trouble, one just asks him, and he comes with his fat belly and restless eyes and kind of sniffs about and says, "Oh, you could do this!" Generally it is a very good idea. I know that all the other peasants do the same thing and turn to him if they want a good idea about getting water running somewhere or other, or a tap made, and so on. The helpful ideas need not be on a great scale; they can be just little practical solutions for a problem.

That is more or less the dwarf. The person who has such hunches will have a much more comfortable life and usually can save himself a lot of work and trouble—which is why one usually does invent things! Many stories tell us that the dwarfs do the work for us. Someone who is in good relationship with dwarfs, or *Heinzelmännchen*, or fairies, has only to put out a bowl of milk at the door every evening, or something like that, and the dwarfs will do the work for him. This is literally true, for by those nice little tricks you can save a tremendous amount of worry and work.

The great difficulty with dwarfs, namely those good ideas and impulses of the unconscious, is that they are small and therefore easily overlooked. If you watch yourself, especially if you are a rationalist, you will see that very often you have a good idea but then think it is nonsense and go on with your rational planning; only afterward do you discover that that would have been a good idea, but unfortunately you set it aside or overlooked it. You repressed it and did not lovingly pick it up, and so you are annoyed, remembering that you thought of it and then didn't do it. The dwarf gave you the good idea, but because he was small and didn't press his point, you didn't pick it up. That annoys dwarfs tremendously. If one makes a habit of not picking up one's dwarf's suggestions, one is in a very bad situation. They are like tiny little voices, little fleeting ideas, or pictures which come into one's mind, and one generally has a strong tendency to think of them as being unimportant. Quite in contrast to the emotional overcharge of the giants and Titans, the dwarfs are very inconspicuous, and it needs a certain trained eye to pick up the ideas. As you know, dwarfs, in common with most ghosts, usually have pointed caps of some kind. Even nowadays in periodicals such as *Punch* the ghosts are dressed in a sheet and pointed cap. The pointed cap probably has to do with the fact that they represent unconscious impulses which have a certain dynamic load of their own which points toward, or aims at, consciousness. It is like a plant when it comes out of the earth: a shoot is pointed to get through and shoot up into the open air. So these pointed caps in general refer to contents of the unconscious which have not to be dug up but which have a load of their own; they are pointing literally toward the threshold of consciousness. As soon as an unconscious being comes up with such a cap, a pileus, you can be quite sure that you don't need to make a great effort; only listen humbly, and it will tell you what it wants, because out of its own energy it is tending toward consciousness.

The deaf-mute brutes and those heavy creatures who creep around are closer to the giants in some ways. They have to do with the time when you have an idea and a kind of confused emotion inside and don't know how to express it. You mean something but you can't get it out—you don't know how to formulate it. Let's say you are in a course, and the lecturer asks a question, and there is something moving in you which is like an answer, but you can't get it into words; you feel it in your solar plexus but can't get it out; it does not take enough rational or pictorial shape for you to be able to do so. There are people who are more gifted in this way than others, and it is a tragedy if a human being is filled with tremendous, overpowering unconscious views and discoveries and has a relative incapacity for formulation. That can even be the reason for a schizophrenic split.

A borderline case of that kind is, for instance, the famous German mystic Jakob Boehme. He was overwhelmed by a vision in which he saw the Godhead and all the connections of the world, the whole system, but being a poor shoemaker and a peasant's son, he had no historical material in his field of knowledge and in his memory and no practice in formulation. Thus he spluttered out what he had to say in a most unreadable chaotic German, into which one can only work one's way after many, many years. He never explains a term and will use the same word sometimes in one way and sometimes in another. You have to find your way through his work by comparing, by making synopses, by rereading, and then you slowly get at the important and interesting ideas he is trying to produce.

I once saw such a dramatic need for expression in analyzing a woman of a very simple layer of the population. She had no education and had been only to a few classes in an elementary school. She was overwhelmed by an invasion of unconscious contents, mostly of a religious character, tremendous visions, and she first tried to convey them to me but gave that up and then had a psychotic episode. It only lasted a few days, but during that time she had a dream in which North American Indians were exposed in a public place; they had had a vision of a golden wheel, which had made them mute. A voice said that if they did not learn to talk about it and learn to overcome their speechlessness, they would be dragged around in public places and exposed to everybody. This she associated later to the fact that, in the asylum in which she had had to be put, she was shown around to all the doctors and students, which she resented tremendously. So you see, she knew that if she, or the primitive side of her, could not find a way to express itself, she would be shown around as a classic case of schizophrenia; she would be shown to the students in the clinics and exposed to all that clinical treatment if these Indians (who represent the primitive animus, the transmitter of the deeper layers of the unconscious) did not find a way to express themselves. She then started to write down her visions and work on them and soon became reasonable and normal and could be released from the clinic.

Jung even says that one can heal schizophrenics insofar as one is able to help them to give some form of expression to their inner world. This is why in nearly all clinics today patients are given the opportunity to paint, to make music, or have access to some other means of expression. So substantial progress has been made in this respect, and, in my opinion, with a little more understanding one could, if not heal, at least greatly improve the patient's condition.

According to Jung, one can distinguish between a "stupid" fantasy and a creative one, first of all, by its subtlety, secondly, by its consistency—that is, whether it is coherent or reveals cracks in its structure—and finally, by its historical continuity. Behind every creative innovation, there is always a very archaic archetype, which first needs to be modernized in its form.

Giving shape or form to what comes up from the unconscious is vitally important. I want to remind you what Jung says on education in *The Development of Personality*. In the chapter "The Gifted Child" he says that the gifted child from early youth onward is generally caught up in inner fantasies; very often he pretends, or appears outwardly, to be very stupid, idiotic, and absent-minded, but he does this to protect his inner fantasies against outer influences, so as to be able to carry them out. But then Jung goes on:

> Admittedly the mere existence of lively fantasies or peculiar interests is no proof of special gifts, as the same predominance of aimless fantasies and abnormal interests may also be found in the previous history of neurotics and psychotics.

If a child is so lost, his fantasies can just as well be the beginning of a later neurosis or psychosis. Jung continues:

> What does reveal the gift, however, is the *nature* of these fantasies. For this one must be able to distinguish an intelligent fantasy from a stupid one. A good criterion

of judgment is the originality, consistency, intensity, and subtlety of the fantasy structure, as well as the latent possibility of its realization. One must also consider how far the fantasy extends into the child's actual life, for instance in the form of hobbies systematically pursued and other interests. Another important indication is the degree and quality of his interest in general.[67]

You see from these four factors—originality, consistency, intensity, and subtlety—the difference between someone who has creative fantasies and someone who is only spinning neurotic nonsense. One could say that the continuity of devotion an individual is capable of giving his fantasy is very important and shows the difference between someone who is gifted with creative fantasy and somebody sucked into sterile unconscious material.

This has been pointed out by many scientists who have written about the problem of the creative impulse. For instance, the French mathematician Poincaré says that some very highly complicated mathematical formulas were revealed to him from the unconscious. But, he adds, if he had not worked for many, many months to the point of fatigue, and if he had not known what could consciously be known about mathematics beforehand, he could not have caught the inspiration.

One needs a kind of preparatory, devoted work in consciousness, which makes a fishing net with which you can then catch the fish which come up from the unconscious. You can't just sit there and hope that God will throw it into your lap. He sometimes does too, but that is rare. The importance is the strength of consciousness, the devotion and the continuity of devotion which transforms apes, cats, giants, and dwarfs into something human.

Dwarfs are only negative, mythologically speaking, if one has annoyed or hurt them, and even there much more frequently, if you annoy dwarfs and fairies, they disappear and don't help you anymore. For example, let us say that the fairies always finish a woman's knitting, or the peasant's stables are protected and his hay is always collected overnight. If he stops doing what the dwarfs want him to do, or giving them milk, or if they ask for a favor and he does not listen, then they disappear and don't help him anymore, so he has lost his helpful spirits. Sometimes they do take revenge, if you really annoy them, for then a flood comes, or all your cows get sick, or something like that. But in general they are very good-natured, and it needs really a lot to make dwarfs negative, in contrast to giants, who need a lot of soothing to get them to behave halfway decently.

If there is a prevalent church attitude that dwarfs are nonsense and superstition, and ought not to exist, that, naturally, does hurt them tremendously. I said only eighty-five percent are positive. There are admittedly mischievous dwarfs, negative not because they are annoyed, but because they like to be mischievous. They are rarely destructive, but they love to be mischievous. I think that they represent dissociative childish impulses which have no creative character, what the schoolteacher has to fight all the time.

While I was studying I earned my living by private tutoring, by giving lessons to children who could not keep up with Latin in school. I once had a girl whose parents invited me for the holidays on condition that I would make her learn a page of Latin words every morning. Well, that was nothing! I thought that would be done in no time. But that girl succeeded in taking five hours over it and not enjoying those five hours. She would take her book and read the first line and repeat it and then would say, "I wonder what Tom is doing?" That was her brother. She would look out the window. I would call her back and she would start again, and then she would look up and say, "By the way . . ." and I would say, "No, not by the way, keep at it!" As a result it took five hours. She was a highly intelligent girl; she just could not concentrate. She had a nice life with several brothers and was very spoiled. It needed nearly killing her to get her to work! These are the childish deviating impulses. Naturally they can be destructive if they distract one from one's main goal. Now, this is typical for young people; they cannot chase away such impulses as a more adult consciousness can. If I am concentrated on doing something, then I just cut out such impulses. I have rather to educate myself to listen a bit, because there is sometimes a good dwarf among them! So one can say, in general, when dwarfs and poltergeists and so on distract one too much, it has to do with a not-yet-concentrated consciousness, with childishness. It has to do with the destructive aspect of infantilism, with an infantile outlook and attitude, a weak ego.

Schreber's case was a great tragedy in this respect. He was a schizophrenic who was capable of writing his own experiences in the form of an autobiography, and he said that whenever he wanted to do something useful or creative, the ghost voices said in his ear, "We have that already written down!" They would make it absolutely impossible for him to write.

We have to distinguish between what wells up from the unconscious: whether it has a destructive or constructive impulse, if it is an intelligent fantasy or something which distracts and has a deviating effect, something of a childish nature. That is discrimination and needs a differentiated feeling function.

A middle thing between being deaf and dumb and being clumsy is stammering, not that I wish to say that this is the only psychogenic reason for stammering. But with children and youths it is very often connected with terrific emotions that have piled up and which they cannot express. Stammering is still a great problem for many adults, but frequently it is outgrown at the time of puberty, or a little later, and in general it is outgrown when the stammerers learn to express themselves more along their own lines, and when their emotional life becomes more fluent. I knew two stammerers in my school who stopped stammering as soon as they could choose their profession. As soon as they started on the profession they had always wished to adopt, the stammering disappeared. I have seen others who have stopped stammering when they had their first positive love experience. This means that when some life flow is released which has been formerly dammed up, the stammering disappears, or is outgrown at the same time. One should always at least look to see whether there is not such a dammed-up emotional problem somewhere, for it is more a direct solution to release it than to make endless speech exercises. These do help too, but the main trouble is sometimes the dammed-up emotion. Stammerers have, one could say, an emotional knot in them; the coming and going of the autonomous emotional complex makes them stammer. The complex contains something unutterable, which has not yet found any mode of expression, so it comes out as an inhibition in speech. This can also affect people so that they cannot talk at all if emotionally upset.

Chains

 In this chapter I would like to take up the theme of the long chains of (a) generations, (b) particles, and (c) numbers. That may seem rather odd, but we will find a common analogy among the three.

First, the long chain of generations in creation myths. These can be generations of Gods, world powers, or ancestral beings. I have already cited some New Zealand material and other creation myths where there are long lists of names or figures before something comes into existence. In the following text I am not going to interpret the different steps, but I want to convey an impression of this type of cosmogony. It is a Samoan cosmogony.

The God Tangaloa lived in the far spaces. He created all things. He was alone, there was no heaven, no earth. He was alone and wandered about in space. There was no sea, and no earth, but where he stood there was a rock: Tangaloa-faa-tutupu-nuu. All things are created from this rock but all things were not yet created. Heaven was not yet created, but the rock grew there where the God stood.

Then Tangaloa said to the rock: Split yourself open. Out came Papa-tao-to and Papa-soso-lo, then Papa-lau-a-au, then Papa-ano-ano, then Papa-ele, then Papa-tu and then Papa-amu-amu and their children.

And Tangaloa stood there and looked to the West and spoke to the rock: and he hit the rock with his right

hand and it split again and out came the parents of all
the nations of the earth, and the sea came also. And the
sea covered Papa-soso-lo, and Papa-tao-to said to Papa-
soso-lo: Blessed are you, that you own the sea. . . .
Then Tangaloa turned to the right side and water
came out. And again Tangaloa spoke to the rock and
heaven was created. He spoke again to the rock and Tui-
tee-langi came forth. And then Ilu came forth, which
means immensity and Mamao, meaning space, came at
the same time in female form. And then came Niu-ao.
Tangaloa then spoke again to the rock and Luao, a boy,
came out. Tangaloa spoke again to the rock and Lua-
vai, a girl, came forth. Tangaloa put both of them on the
island of Saa-tua-langi.
    And again Tangaloa spoke and Oa-vali, a boy, was
born and then Ngao-ngao-le-tei, a girl. Then man came
forth, and then came the spirit (Anga-nga), then the
heart (loto), then the will (fingalo), and finally thought
(masalo).[68]

And that was the end of the creation of Tangaloa.
Such lists appear in many other Polynesian and New
Zealand cosmogonies. There are immense lists of
powers, Godheads, or primeval powers, and they
come out in such chains of names.
    The following is an excerpt from an Hawaiian cos-
mogony. First is an introductory song, which I am not
including, and then comes Po wale ho-i, which means
"still night everywhere reigning."

Hanua ka po—born in the night.
Born Kumulipo [the abyss] out of the night as something
    male.
Born Poele [the darkness] out of the night as something
    female.

Born the worms in crawling swarms.
Born the mites, the small worms which turn over the
   earth.
Born those who wind about in dirt, in moving rows.
Born the eggs in the sea without number, born their
   striped children.

Born in Hawae, the white sea egg, and Wana [a species of the sea egg in the size and shape of a turnip] with
their children Keiki, and Haukeuke [a small sea animal]
and Pioeoe [a species of mussel or small shellfish], then
Pipi [the spirulidae], Papua [oysters], and Olepe [still another type of shell], etc.
   And the males swelling in creative power and the female yielding in conception.
   Born all the plants in the sea.
   Born all the algae in the sea, and so on.

These are holy songs, which are always repeated in
the same way. The priest who sings knows these long,
long series of animals and creatures by heart, and it
would be a great sin or blasphemous to omit one line.
This is all a series of the holy generations which came
forth before the world was created, at the beginning
of creation. Only at the very end of this immensely
long series is the human being created, and from then
the song continues with just as long a list of the great
ancestors of the kings and the great noble families of
Hawaii.
   There is the same archetypal pattern in the creation
myths of the Japanese. I refer to the publication of
Post Wheeler, a conscientious author and a diplomat,
in his book *The Sacred Scriptures of the Japanese*. I
can recommend it as a very good publication. It is a

narrative in which all the different Japanese legends are coordinated, and there is the list of the Godheads who appear. I will not interpret this; I am including it only to give an impression of the material.

Of old times the Sky and the Earth were not yet set apart the one from the other, nor were the female and male principles separated. All was a mass, formless and egg-shaped, the extent whereof is not known, which held the life principle. Thereafter the purer tenuous essence, ascending gradually, formed the Sky, the heavier portion sank and became the Earth. The lighter element merged readily, but the heavier was united with difficulty. Thus the Sky was formed first, the Earth next, and later Kami were produced in the space between them [Kami are divine beings].

When the Sky and the Earth began, there was a some-thing in the very midst of the emptiness whose shape cannot be described. At the first a thing like a white cloud appeared, which floated between Sky and Earth, and from it three Kami came into being in the High-Sky-Plain. [These three Kami, appearing earliest, were born without progenitors and later hid their bodies. They were MID-SKY-MASTER, HIGH-PRODUCER, and DIVINE-PRODUCER. And then High-Producer produced the Kami SKY-DIVINE-STANDER.

These Kami are also, according to the footnotes, ancestors of certain noble families in Japan. For instance Sky-Divine-Stander is the ancestor of the Governors of Kuga in Yamashiro. So you see they are Gods and ancestors of certain clans.

Now, while the soil of the Young Earth which made the Lands drifted about as floating oil, like a jellyfish sporting on the water surface, or a cloud floating over the sea without root or attachment, a something clear and bright like crystal sprouted up like a horn, like a reed shoot when it first emerges from the mud. This became transformed into Kami of human shape, and there appeared, springing out of the buds of the reed-shoot, two more Kami called PLEASANT-REED-SPROUT-PRINCE-ELDER and ETERNAL-SKY-STANDER. [Some say the latter preceded the former. Others also consider Mid-Sky-Master and Pleasant-Reed-Sprout-Prince-Elder to be Companion-Born-Kami.] These likewise were born without progenitors and later hid their bodies. The Three-Creator-Kami and these two are called the Sky-Kami. Pleasant-Reed-Sprout-Prince-Elder was a divine man.

Then come the SEVEN SKY GENERATIONS.

There next appeared, spontaneously, through the action of the Sky Principle, the following male Companion-Kami, who later hid their bodies: ETERNAL-EARTH-STANDER, EARTH-SOIL, and FRUITFUL-SHAPE-MOOR.

Eternal-Earth-Stander and Fruitful-Shape-Moor were Companion-born Kami. From the last was produced the Kami: SKY-EIGHT-DESCEND.

Next after these appeared the following mated Kami:

LORD-MUD-EARTH	LADY-MUD-EARTH
GERM-INTEGRATOR	LIFE-INTEGRATOR
GREAT-PLACE-ELDER	GREAT-PLACE-ELDER-LADY
PERFECT-FACE	AWFUL-LADY
HE-WHO-INVITES	SHE-WHO-INVITES

As to these five mated pairs, some say that Germ-Integrator and Life-Integrator preceded Lord-Mud-Earth and Lady-Mud-Earth. Still others say that He-Who-Invites was produced later by the Kami Foam-Calm.

Lord-Mud-Earth and Lady-Mud-Earth, his younger sister (wife), together produced the Kami SKY-MEET.

Germ-Integrator and Life-Integrator, his younger sister (wife), together produced the Kami SKY-THREE-DESCEND.

Great-Place-Elder and Great-Place-Elder-Lady, his younger sister (wife) together produced the Kami SKY-EIGHT-HUNDRED-DAYS.

Perfect-Face and Awful-Lady, his younger sister (wife), together produced the Kami SKY-EIGHTY-MYRIAD-JEWEL.

The two Companion-born Kami and five generations of mated Kami are called the Seven-Generations-of-the-Deity-Age (Some, however, count these as beginning with Mid-Sky-Master.).

The next to appear were the two Kami SHAKE-JEWEL and TEN-THOUSAND-JEWEL.

The former produced the two Kami LUCK-JEWEL and SKY-EAGLE-STANDER, and the latter produced the single Kami SKY-HARD-RIVER.

Now, all the Sky-Kami (some say High-Producer) deigned to bid He-Who-Invites and She-Who-Invites to make and consolidate the drifting earth, saying, "There is the Fruitful-Reed-Plain-Land-of-Fresh-Rice-Ears-of-Thousand-Autumns. Go and set it in order." So, a Sky-Jewel-Spear whose staff was of coral having been granted them, the pair took stand upon the Floating-Sky-Bridge (or, as some say, in the midst of the Sky-Mist).

At some later time, while He-Who-Invites slept, this bridge fell down, and it is now the great stony cape northwest of the village of Guke, in Yosa, Tango Province. It was named, at its upper part, Wondrous Beach. . . .[69]

Then they produce a God called LEECH and a God called BIRD-ROCK-CAMPHOR-TREE-BOAT, and then they

create all the different islands, the MY-SHAME-ISLAND,
DOUBLE-NAME-ISLAND, and so on, infinite numbers of
them. These lists go through almost the whole book,
and it is a slow, slow, slow descent from the most
heavenly deities, to ancestral deities, to geographical
deities of the different scattered islands of the Japanese empire, and finally to those of human beings. It
is a long, long line of descent.

In the beginning there is Chaos, then separation of
earth and sky, the appearance of primordial deities,
the appearance of lesser deities, the appearance of the
creative deity pair, the formation of the first land by
the creative pair, the first house, the first marriage,
cohabitation, trial, birth. Then comes the earth, the
birth of lands, the birth of elemental deities, the deities of food, trees, mountains, rivers, the birth of the
fire deity, the first death, the first murder. Then comes
the underworld, the first divorce, the creation of phal-
lic deities, the creation of the three ruling deities: the
Sun Deity, the Moon Deity, the Rebellious Deity.
Then comes the earth, the distribution above the All
Rule, the withdrawal of the earlier creator, the murder of the fruit deity. Then comes the struggle between the different deities, and so on.

It ends with the beginning of what we call history.
On the earth appears the first earthly emperor, so the
final result is the beginning of Japanese history, with
its still very legendary first emperor.

These creation myths—I have only briefly sketched
their structure—are very typical for primitive and
semi-primitive civilizations which have never disinte-
grated. The Japanese civilization is certainly not what

we would call a primitive civilization, but it is a civilization which has never been cut off from its original primitive roots, but has kept its continuity. Primitives and civilizations which have kept their continuity tend to have such cosmogonies in which there are innumerable lists of divine and semi-divine and royal ancestral beings. The catalogue of the theogony of Hesiod in Greece is a parallel example and is probably more familiar than this kind of material. In the many, many chains of deities, in this manifoldness, one sees quite clearly that there is a kind of secret, final tendency at work; it all ends up with human history, or with the birth of man, so in spite of looking chaotic there is a secret development in it. For instance, in this Japanese procedure one sees quite clearly that the first deities are completely vague and mistlike, and in each step to the next deity the figure becomes more definite, more specific. First it becomes a specific ancestor of a specific family, and then perhaps a specific island, and then single objects, like a fir tree, and so on. So that you could say that the evolution goes from an all-embracing vagueness to the creation of more and more definite units.

Before we consider what this means psychologically, I would like to add to this the material on particles and numbers. You will see that it is connected and that combined we can understand the whole problem better and from a richer angle.

To introduce the material in chronological order, I first would have to quote the texts on particles, from which the concept of the atom has arisen, then the texts concerned with numbers, and then as presented in the philosophy of the Pythagoreans and of Democritos, and then the Gnostic material. However, I intend first to bring the Gnostic material because it is closer to the primitive and the Japanese material. It is as if in the rational Greek philosophy certain prescientific intuitive concepts had developed with a kind of scientific rational flavor, and in Gnostic speculations these were historically reconnected with more primitive ideas, as though these concepts, to a certain extent, had regressed into a more pictorial, primitive way of expression.

In the system of the Gnostic Valentinus,[70] the first figure is the Autopater, the father of himself, the self-begotten or self-generated father, unconsciously resting within himself, eternal, hermaphroditic, never aging, and embracing the whole universe, not embraced by anything himself. Within him he contains the Ennoia, Thought, which others also called Silence or Grace, and all the other treasures he contains in her. But then Thought, Ennoia, wanted to unite with Autopater, whom she married—it is a completely internal marriage, because it is his inner thought which he marries within himself. They together produced Aletheia (Truth) and Anthropos (Man).

Now, these concepts, Aletheia and Anthropos, are conceived in a completely archetypal form. It is *the* man, the *eternal man,* as a divine image, and Aletheia is a feminine being, a kind of divine personification of Truth. Then Aletheia also wanted to marry, and so she united with her father, Autopater, in an eternal union. They produced a spiritual quaternio, which was a repetition of the first quaternio. The first qua-

ternio was Autopater, Ennoia, Anthropos, and Aletheia; now there is another with Anthropos, Ecclesia,
Logos, and Zoe—again Man, and the Church, but the
Church as a Goddess, a feminine personification, and
Logos, and Zoe, Life, another feminine personification. This is a quaternio of two male and two female
figures. Then the Autopater and Anthropos and Ecclesia produced twelve other Gods; six are male Gods,
who are called Parakletos (the Holy Ghost), Patrikos
(the spirit of the father), Metrikos (the spirit of the
mother), Aeinous (the eternal spirit), Theletos (the
completion, which is the Light), Ekklesiastikos (the
spirit of the Church); and six feminine powers who
are called Pistis (faith), Elpis (hope), Agape (love),
Synesis (understanding), Makaria (bliss), and Sophia
(wisdom).

Then comes a further group of divine powers,
which increase, eight more being added. In the Valen-
tinian systems it goes on and on with such groups of
divine powers, called Aeons, meaning eternal divine
powers. Our notion of the archetypal image is really
the best possible translation of the Greek concept.
There are similar ideas in many other Gnostic systems
which depend on Valentinus and are partly influenced
by him, but some have conceived Aeons not as personified divine powers carrying specific theological
names but partly as numbers and partly as letters of
the alphabet. The number-letter speculations, on
which most magic even nowadays is still based, comes
in here.

The striking fact is that before any creation takes
place, one finds this motif of chains and chains of gen-

erations of such divine archetypal powers, one gener-
ating the other, until finally we come down to the creation of reality as it is now. I use the word "down"
deliberately because the feeling one gets when one
reads those texts is that the most all-powerful and
eternal, and at the same time indefinite, powers are
condensing, like a chemical substance which is precipitated, slowly condensing into concrete reality, becoming by this more multiple on the one hand, and
more distinct and less eternal on the other, less powerful in becoming more distinct and at the same time
more manifold. First there is one, then a group of
four, then twelve, then a group of twenty-four, and so
on. It is a multiplication act which goes on ad infini-
tum and in certain systems expands to thirty-six
Aeons and sometimes even to numbers as high as six
hundred and more, expanding to an ever-increasing
number. Although certain abstract elements are involved, for the names of these Aeons are definitely
theological and religious concepts, and also what we
would nowadays call scientific concepts (namely the
idea of numbers), you see that the prevalent pattern is
still the same as in those very primitive myths I cited
before, with the idea of the divine powers slowly condensing downward and multiplying to become the
basic elements of reality.

Probably based on the same archetypal pattern are
certain representatives of classical Greek philosophy,
especially the atomistic theories. The creators of the
concept of the atom are Leukippos and his even more
famous pupil, Democritos. Leukippos is difficult to
reconstruct as a personality because we have no origi-

nal fragments of his writings, or practically none, and in later reports we only read that "Leukippos and Democritos say. . . ." We cannot distinguish if there was any difference between their theories, or which is which, so we have to take them as a single unit. But in general one attributes the whole theory more to Democritos.[71]

Democritos's idea was that reality consisted of different particles, which he called atoms, indivisible units, the basic units of reality. He was the first materialist in the sense that he asserted that the soul too consists of material particles which are round. Other material particles were like pyramids and others were square, or had different shapes, which accounts for the different elements. Those particles had hooks in their corners with which they connected to each other. They made chains of these connections, and that is how the different material phenomena, the different material particles, came into existence. Since the fire-soul particle is round, the soul can spread through the whole body and through everything, because the round thing without hooks can roll between other particles, which is why the soul pervades the whole body.

You see here a very primitive form of the modern concept of the atom, but a terrifically important step, really, in the history of the Western mind. These basic bodies, or atoms, can only be realized by thought—I mean we cannot prove their existence and you cannot see them in reality.

Democritos also assumed that reality consisted of an infinite number of different worlds, all built in the same way and of the same structure. With this is connected, and nobody knows how, another theory of his, namely that whirling around in this cloud of atoms in which we walk about there are certain images. He said that the atmosphere in which we live is full of invisible images, not completely eternal but very long-lived, much longer than a human life. Positive and negative images fly about among the atoms and in sleep penetrate our bodies, which is how dreams come into existence. They possess us when they are negative and have demonic effects, and when they are positive they have favorable effects upon our personalities. Evil people, we would say black magicians, can emanate evil images and send them to somebody they hate, who then will be disturbed by them in sleep. In the autumn we are especially likely to be depressed because the storms and wind and rain stir those images more than at other times of the year and then we breathe in a lot more of them.

What remains unclear is how Democritos related these images to the atoms. In one way his schema is at first completely materialistic, even the soul is a concrete atom, but then he has also those *eidola* (Greek; in Latin *simulcra*), which fly about among the atoms. Unfortunately, because the teaching of Democritos is only handed down to us in single passages and quotations, we do not know how he related the two, and whether he thinks the images, too, are in some way material. But the whole of reality is an enormously confused *mixtum compositum* of atoms and their combinations, including the soul atoms and images with which he definitely identifies the good and evil spirits of folklore. He says that the good and evil spirits, the demons and minor Gods, in folklore are really only images which whirl around. They are not eternal but can last two, three, or four hundred years before they decay or change. There is an infinite number of them in reality, just as there is an infinite number of worlds.

We have another fragment which says that Democritos asserted that even stones have souls (this explains why they form crystals and so on), but whether those souls are meant to be fire atoms or images is not clear. When the elements of the soul have the correct admixture, then the soul produces the right kind of thought; when disturbed, it produces the wrong kind. But the images touch us from outside, they flow toward us from the outside and enter us at certain moments. Thinking is partly the right or wrong combination of such images.

I have sketched this atomic theory because if you look at it more closely from a psychological angle you will see that Aeons, numbers, and letters are not basically different from this type of particle and image; they are but a variation of the same archetypal concept of having a multiplicity of basic indivisible eternal elements which in their various combinations create reality. We have no definite report about Democritos, but he seems to have thought that these basic elements are given from all eternity and have not generated each other, as have the Aeons.

Another idea of such a multiplicity of basic elements is to be found in the Pythagorean speculations, though there they are not atoms, material particles, or images, but numbers. The natural numbers one, two, three, four . . . (i.e., the series of natural numbers) were for the Pythagoreans ungenerated, ever-existing, divine formative powers which produced and ordered the whole universe. We actually have to correct this statement that the Pythagoreans regarded numbers as being the basis of the universe, for they were already wise enough to realize that reality in itself cannot be described, that we shall never know what it is in itself, but that everything one becomes aware of as reality is realized by a number.

One fragment of the famous Pythagorean Philolaos, for instance, says that everything which can be recognized as real is numbers because it is impossible in our thinking to become aware of anything without number. The number has two specific forms of appearance, odd and even, and a third is a mixture of both and from these derive all forms of existing things. Nobody could ever say anything about any outer reality, nor establish any relation between things, or between himself and things if there were not the number, and the number is what enables the soul to become aware of outer reality. It is therefore also what lends physical existence to all things. One cannot only see the true nature of number and its power in the world of Gods, but also in all works and talk of men, and in the realm of all their technical activities and in music. The nature of numbers admits of no error and allows only harmony. Terror and jealousy do not exist in the realm of numbers.[72] You see, he is deviating into strange psychological facts.

An anonymous older Pythagorean fragment (re-

ported by Aristotle) asserts that the Pythagoreans first
concerned themselves with mathematics because they
were convinced that the principles of all real things
are numbers, because numbers are symbols for everything which exists and happens, more than fire, earth,
and water, which others thought were the basic elements of the world. They also realized that every relationship and every law, for instance of musical harmony, is based on numbers; even the whole of nature
seems to them to be based on numbers as the basic
principles of nature and the basic elements of the
cosmos.

Now, what is the common denominator of it all?
To find out more about this, we first have to go back
to the primitive cosmogonies I quoted before. There
we saw that at first there were divine powers, which
slowly became less important and less divine and increasingly acquired the characteristics of ancestral
souls of certain clans. This is the case in the Hawaiian
and Japanese cosmogonies, where certain of these
lesser Gods, when they had already diminished in
glory and developed downward toward the earth, became the ancestral souls of certain clans.

This is a typical feature of cosmogonic texts. The
Enuma Elish, for instance, also ends with a long list
of primordial kings. The same phenomenon also is
found in Egypt where the King, wherever he moves in
a procession, is always followed by his last fourteen
Kas, that is, his ancestral souls. When the King
moved, for instance, in the great procession of the Sed
festival, behind him were carried fourteen poles with
the statues of his fourteen Kas. The popular belief was

that he had a greater number of Kas behind him, but the last fourteen were more distinct and one was more aware of them. If you look up the birth of Jesus in the Bible—and I believe there is an historical connection with this Egyptian material—he has his list of ancestors who are definitely grouped in groups of fourteen; so he too has his groups of fourteen Kas behind him.

These divine, semidivine, and then royal ancestral catalogues seem to be of great importance. Perhaps we should tackle the problem from here and ask what these fourteen Kas mean, the ancestral catalogues which we find everywhere in the sacred scriptures and in certain cosmogonic myths. The first hypothesis one could make is that they must have to do with what we call complexes. We know that a human being has an ego complex, of which he is normally aware and with which he normally identifies, and that he is surrounded by a "cloud" of what we call autonomous complexes. For us the personality, if not analyzed, would be about as is shown in the diagram.

The ego complex would be the one luminosity a person is aware of, and then there are all the other complexes which as a whole form a kind of cluster, the relatively closed system of the total personality. During analysis one gets slowly acquainted with the

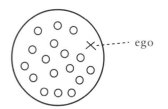

ego surrounded
by other separate
complexes

different complexes, which gradually get into an associated connection with the ego. Some are completely
integrated and some become only to a limited extent
connected with the ego complex. That means that if I
work enough on a complex it melts with the ego complex and then it has practically disappeared in the
sense that it does not evidence itself anymore as an
autonomous complex.

There are others of which one is not unconscious,
one knows of them, but all the same they still develop
autonomous effects. Someone can say, "Oh, I know I
have a positive mother complex and that is why I
have such-and-such reactions!" That person is partially aware of his positive mother complex, but there
will still be projections in reality, emotional reactions
toward certain facts which will catch him again and
again and where only after the event he will say, "Ah,
that was my mother complex again." So such a complex is what we would call semiconscious; one is conscious of some aspects of it and of others not. It is
still, to a great extent, autonomous; it is only partially
integrated.

The aim of analytical work is to try to get the ego
into a state of being as aware as possible of the total
economy of complexes, because that is the only pro-

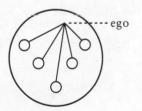

ego with connected
complexes

tection against sudden dissociating effects. If you are relatively aware of the total family of complexes with which you must live in your inner house, you can, so to speak, stay in a certain quiet position because nothing really completely unexpected can happen. The awareness of them is therefore of essential importance; it is the only relative protection against constant emotional inner dissociation. With it you then discover that this whole economy of the household is ruled by another center, namely the Self. This means that it is not the ego which has to rule or order all those complexes; it cannot. There is a secret regulation of the whole system which emanates from the main unconscious complex of the personality, the Self. So, if the ego can find a bridge, a relatively solid connection to the Self, indirectly it is also aware of all its other complexes, because it has reached that center from which the whole economy of the personality is ordered and guided. It is therefore a desideratum that one should be in accord and in harmony with one's unconscious structure, with an inherited unconscious total structure, to an absolute maximum, in order to have maximum efficiency of consciousness, of Mana, of intensity of the personality. And when you see these images, or processions, where the Egyptian king walks ahead and behind him come all the priests carrying his Kas, you see more what is meant; he is, so to speak, not acting as an individual and out of his arbitrary ego opinions, but is the carrier of the whole tradition which he has behind and supporting him, and that gives him the power and authority he needs to rule his country.

Having one's ancestral souls behind and supporting one, instead of being cut off from them, is of absolutely essential importance. Jung has expressed it in a nutshell in his essay "The Gifted Child." We read:

> . . . it seems to me especially important for any broad-based culture to have a regard for history in the widest sense of the word. Important as it is to pay attention to what is practical and useful, and to consider the future, that backward glance at the past is just as important. Culture means continuity, not a tearing up of roots through "progress." . . . Just as the developing embryo recapitulates, in a sense, our phylogenetic history, so the child-psyche relives "the lesson of earlier humanity," as Nietzsche called it. The child lives in a pre-rational and above all in a pre-scientific world, the world of the men who existed before us. Our roots lie in that world and every child grows from those roots. Maturity bears him away from his roots and immaturity binds him to them. Knowledge [and this is the essential sentence for us] of the universal origins builds the bridge between the lost and abandoned world of the past and the still largely inconceivable world of the future. How should we lay hold of the future, how should we assimilate it, unless we are in possession of the human experience which the past has bequeathed to us? Dispossessed of this, we are without root and without perspective, defenceless dupes of whatever novelties the future may bring. A purely technical and practical education is no safeguard against delusion and has nothing to oppose to the counterfeit. It lacks the culture whose innermost law is the continuity of history, the long procession man's more than individual consciousness. This continuity which reconciles all opposites also heals the conflicts that threaten the gifted child.[73]

You see here, though treated from a completely different angle, why it is so important to be connected with historical continuity, that is, from the inside, with one's ancestral soul, to be connected with the archetypal foundations of the psyche. It is the only protection against being carried away by delusions of novelty. How destructive this is we see, for instance, if a primitive tribe is cut off from its ancestral continuity by some kind of external spiritual influence, for these tribes then generally decay and lose within the shortest time all their will and power to live. They have lost their continuity, their historical past, and their human dignity; they are no longer supported by all their Kas walking behind them and supporting the actual modern individual. The reading and learning by heart of such long catalogues of ancestral kings and Gods therefore has probably to do with the fact that it is a sacred ritual action by which man connects himself with the continuity of the past. It is the countermagic against dissociation.

In the Chinese text *The Secret of the Golden Flower* it is said that meditation reaches a stage where consciousness is dissolved.[74] This state, for which the meditating person in this Chinese yoga practice has been watching, is a kind of conscious dissociation. The picture which accompanies this text is that of a man sitting in the lotus position, and from his head rises one buddha after the other, so that he has a whole crowd of buddhas, each buddha again creating two more, and so on. There is an infinite multiplication of different buddhas, all sitting in the lotus position. After this state of consciously reached dissociation, the next step is to reintegrate all these buddhas by becoming aware of the so-called rotation of the light.

Jung in his comment on this part of the book speaks about the necessity of becoming aware of all one's soul particles and different autonomous complexes in order to prevent dissociation. What happens in this Chinese meditation exercise is a kind of consciously induced dissociation, just as we do it, for example, in the meditation we call active imagination, for there too we talk to all our different autonomous complexes. We make them appear, we let them come into existence, and then we start a conscious discussion, an *Auseinandersetzung* with them. If one does not do this consciously, as a meditative practice, then it happens involuntarily under the effect of certain shocks, and then it has the opposite effect of these meditations, namely it dissociates and destroys the whole personality. Then—to put it in plain words—there is a schizophrenic dissociation, a "falling apart" of the personality. In an advanced state of schizophrenia you can actually see how the human being has dissolved into a cloud, a cluster, of autonomous complexes, which is no longer organized. Schizophrenics complain that different voices overwhelm them and that their ego is drowned among them.

I remember a schizophrenic girl who had been interned for a long time and who, when her relatives visited her, gave the impression of not recognizing anybody, so that they gave up the visits as hopeless. But later, when cured, she remembered everything that had happened, even to the extent of knowing the blouse her mother wore and what she had said during the visit. She had been aware of every detail, but she said that all the devils and demons had prevented her from showing any recognition. She used another simile and said that it was as if she had been under the sea and could see the others but could not wave her hand, could not show that she saw them. There you see how the ego complex is overpowered by the confusion of the other complexes and is no longer strong enough even to rule the body or to manifest in any way. It is still there but in too weak a position; it is just one among many others.

Then there is the famous case of Schreber, who gave a very interesting survey of his schizophrenia, but said that he was constantly disturbed by his demons and voices. For instance, as I mentioned before, if he wanted to write something down, the spirits would say that it was already done and he would then drop the pencil and be unable to write anything. They constantly interfered, which is what schizophrenics in the beginning stages generally complain of. They say they may want to go to the kitchen and put on the soup, but some demon says something and they cannot do it. One maid told me that she wanted to make a pilgrimage to Einsiedeln, but when she arrived at the door of the church the demons' voices and their shouts forbade her to enter and became so loud that it was like a cloud of devils and she had to return home without accomplishing her pilgrimage. The autonomous complexes overpower the ego complex in a chaotic way.

These tragic dissociations show clearly why the

primitive is so terribly keen on having his ancestral
souls, his Kas, marching in order behind his ego complex. That the Egyptian king walks ahead of his fourteen Kas is the symbol of his integrated personality.
That is probably why it is also in the ancestral genealogy of Christ as well; it is an allusion to his royal personality. He is again a symbol of an integrated personality who has the whole development of the past,
so to speak, behind him, as if the whole past pointed
to his reality.

In van der Leeuw's *Religion in Essence and Manifestation* you will find still another aspect of this.[75]
Van der Leeuw has collected an enormous amount of
material to show that a dead person, according to the
belief of many different nations, changes in character.
That means that a father, an aunt, a mother, a mem-
ber of the family who has died, does not remain Uncle
John or Aunt Mary after death and spook around in
this form, but tends slowly to change character, becoming a more numinous and more powerful figure.
Some slowly become evil demons and others become
positive numina, protective spirits. They lose their individual characteristics more and more and become
more general and powerful factors. In this way, the
image of the dead ancestors mixes, as one can see
clearly from the material van der Leeuw has collected,
with the archetype. We would say, in our language,
that the dead father slowly becomes something like a
father archetype in the psychic system of the surviving
son. The connection with the personal Mr. Smith or
Johnson fades, and the memory of his individual personality fades. Instead the son feels that a protecting

father archetype, or a negative father archetype, is behind him.

Certain Neoplatonic philosophers had the same idea. They said that after death the surviving souls of people combined with numina, that is, with divine beings. Apuleius, for instance, following Plutarchus, said that people who have attended to their psyche, have nursed and looked after their psychic condition in their lifetime through meditation and religious exercises, after death have a specially powerfully numen and survive as such. This is the same idea of a mixture of what we would call archetypal figures and ancestral souls.

This also may have a physiological basis. The problem of how patterns of behavior are inherited in animal life (and ours will in this respect naturally not be different) is still a very big one, but it seems to be linked with the genes in some way. Konrad Lorenz has been able to make a very meaningful experiment in this respect. He found two types of ducks which were far enough apart to have definitely different patterns of behavior, for instance, a different wooing dance for mating, but still closely enough akin to permit cross-breeding. He mated the two types, and it turned out that the product not only physically had a mixture of the characteristics of both races, but also mixed the wooing dance! One type of duck would immerse its head in the water twice and waggle its tail four times, while the other did this three times. The cross-bred duck combined the two patterns. The pattern of behavior as a whole does not seem to be inherited through one gene, but elements of it recombine in the new individual in a new form, for instance in the different type of wooing dance. We could therefore say that if the Lorenz experiment should prove to be valid in a wider sense (one single experiment is naturally not enough to solve all the problems), it would mean that our archetypal patterns of behavior too consist of different ancestral fragments which come together again in a new pattern of behavior. So there would be an actual element of inheritance and continuity also within these psychic patterns, which would justify still more the importance of those ancestral catalogues. It is as if those primitive ancestor genealogies were intuitive insights into the laws of such a continuity.

If we puzzle nowadays how the elements of the pattern of behavior relate to the genes, we are still stuck at the same problem as Democritos, namely how do the images, the simulacra, relate to the atoms? This relationship is still the great problem for us. You see now why I have introduced, in such a strange way, the divine numbers and the letters of the alphabet. The basic elements of mental processes would be numbers, the letters of the alphabet, the Democritos simulacra, or what we call archetypal representations on one side, and the physical inheritance problem on the other side. The two run parallel, but we do not yet know exactly how they link. But certainly the importance of these genealogies and chains of Gods has to do with the great importance of being connected with one's basic instincts and not being carried away through new mutations in our mental life.

There is one more element which I want to mention

briefly. In the Hawaiian and Japanese cosmogonies I mentioned, either rocks or islands were created at a certain point. Certain Gods who came after a long chain of other Gods were identical with certain islands of the archipelago. Naturally, in countries where they have such an insular formation of the terrain, this is an obvious means of projecting the archetypes. But you find it also among peoples who have no island structure in their domain, and in those cases the Gods at a certain point in evolution become mountains, rivers, or other outstanding geographical points. So we can say that the common denominator is a geographically marked point, whether it is a single old tree, or a hill, or a mountain, or a rock, or an island. The particulars naturally depend upon the country from which the people come.

On such outstanding geographical points the God lands when he concretizes by coming down from the mist in the sky. He becomes identical with certain geographical features and therefore there is, in many systems of primitive religion and thought, a whole psychic geography. You can generally see the outstanding mountain near such a tribe; it is a place of relationship to God, that is where the great men receive their dreams, their revelations, where the medicine men go and fast and from where they bring back their contacts. We also have the mountains Sinai and Tabor in our religion. There is generally also a place where the dark God, or the God of evil, is projected; it is either a dark cleft, a dark creek, an abyss, or the crater of a volcano, anything which may be a suitable place where you can project the uncanny, the dark, evil thing, a place where one does not go at night, and so on. Certain places have a suggestive character. If someone goes about planning to commit a murder, the fantasy of carrying it out might get the murderer best when he comes to a certain dark place in the wood. Jung, for instance, always cited the murder of Erzherzog Johann, who was murdered in a dark creek, and the murderer rode behind him knowing from the very morning that he was going to kill him on this ride. When he came to this dark passage he cried out, "That swine should not live any longer," and speared him from behind. It was that place which catalyzed his decision to commit the murder. It is also interesting, in criminology, that at certain dark places again and again rape and murder are committed, certain places in certain woods near towns. Really, one feels as if evil ghosts were luring people there and that an individual who is already on the verge of committing a crime will have his intention catalyzed in this place.

So there is still a psychological geography, and it is still as if certain constellations of the landscape constellate our inner psychic moods as well. They are fitting places for certain deeds and fantasies and ideas. In primitive mythology you see that to an even greater extent. If you read the names on the map of the territory of a primitive tribe, you actually have a map of their collective unconscious: the place where the positive God manifests himself, where evil breaks out, where children are conceived. If you look at the symbolism of the names, the whole collective unconscious is identical with the geographical terrain in which the tribe lives. This shows that the outer surroundings of a living being serve to catalyze the projection of certain unconscious contents. We are born with all those inherited archetypal patterns of representations, and when we get into the appropriate situation or landscape this acts like a stimulus and the archetypal content projects itself into the place. That is probably why there is in so many primitive cosmogonies this strange connection of the Gods becoming rocks, islands, and hills, or places where two rivers cross. There the God "lands" in reality.

With modern people, when something is approaching conscious realization via projection, or directly, generally the dreams show that something has come down to earth somewhere. I remember that I once had a dream which amused me no end. I dreamt that the archangel Michael had landed in Switzerland on a hill near Bern, but that the government got so frightened that it made a military cordon all around him. Bern is the capital; that means the center of the psyche, a symbol of the center, and there an important content had landed, but conventional consciousness was very frightened of this realization. This preceded by about three weeks a very important mental realization, which then came into consciousness. At the time of the dream my consciousness was quite at rest and not frightened of archangels or anything of the kind. But that was the annunciation that now an archetypal content would approach the field of awarenesss; this divine figure landing on an outstanding geographical point preceded a realization.

Again, whenever people have to make a very important decision, a tremendous step on which one could say their whole future depended, they get such dreams as the assembly of the ancestors or the assembly of the dead. I remember once, when I had to make an important decision affecting my whole life, I dreamt, the night after I had made the decision, that all the dead people in heaven, who were playing Halma (a kind of game with pawns), stopped playing and went to the windows of heaven and looked down, as if they would all participate in the decision. Though they are unconcerned as to what those live lice down on earth are doing, for they are in their eternal bliss and play Halma, yet when a human being makes a crucial decision they stop playing and look out of the windows.

I have seen many other dreams of this kind. They generally occur when the individual really has to concentrate all his potential personality in order to take the next step, a decisive step upon which the whole individuation process depends. Such steps are so terrifying that the weak ego cannot make them; this is why such concentrating processes occur and show in the dreams, because the ego cannot concentrate its powers. It is a spontaneous event, as if the whole vital makeup of the personality would concentrate on it. Naturally, such a dream, or such an experience, gives one a terrific feeling of certainty, of firmness, of courage; one has the feeling that the whole past is behind one, supporting one, and then one can do risky things which one would not have the courage to do in a normal mental condition. That is why whenever primitives have to make an important decision, they first dance to identify with their ancestors, and by wearing their masks and becoming their ancestral spirits and merging with them, they acquire the strength to take a difficult step in life.

So the motif of the Gods slowly condensing down into the ancestral ghosts on the one side, and the motif of dead people slowly rising again onto the level of archetypal powers on the other, are really to be seen in connection. It all means the reestablishing of the ancestral archetypal basis of the personality, becoming aware, or conscious of it as a necessary support for the flimsy, short-lived existence of an individual ego. There is the same experience behind all the different popular beliefs in the ghosts of the dead roaming about in groups, as for instance in the Germanic belief in the wild hunt of Wotan, where the ghosts ride through the woods carrying their heads under their arms. They are generally benevolent to those who treat them well and evil towards those who hurt them.

The first night that I slept in my holiday house in the country after building it, I dreamt that an enormous procession of peasants in medieval Sunday clothes arrived—and they were actual ghosts. They visited me, and I thought of how I had wanted to be alone there and that I would not open the door, but then I saw that it was also a wedding, with a peasant-like bridegroom and his bride, so I thought I would have to do something and rushed to the cellar to get some wine and then woke up. Jung interpreted this as the accumulation, the concentration of the ancestral souls, positively approving of the step I had taken. In a later dream, some months afterward, even the apes came; first ghosts, peasants again who wore the masks of ghosts, visited me and after a while these turned into beautiful silvery-gray apes who enjoyed themselves around the house. It was a very agreeable experience. I woke up with a feeling of delight and happiness, having watched from the window how the apes danced around the house, jumping from branch to branch with elegant movements. This would mean, practically, not only the integration of the ancestral soul but even of the animal ancestors. Naturally, if you live in a country house where there is no electric light, and where you can practically not wash and can only cook on a fire, the ape in you feels infinitely happier than if you imprison it in a town flat, with all its electric gadgets, for there the ape is pretty unhappy. So, subjectively interpreted, the animal soul, the ape, felt alive through this way of life; he recovered, and that is naturally felt by the individual as a support, for he is supported by his ancestral roots, even by the animal spirits. Thus, in many primitive rituals they not only identify with their mythological ancestors in their dances but even with their ancestral animals and become and act out the role of those animals. A primitive tribe is in constant danger of losing its connection with the animal life within and even on that level must constantly reconnect with it.

In many peasant communities people still believe that the dead go around in the country and bless and visit certain people who have second sight; they can see and talk to the dead. I had not been more than about a fortnight in my house when a peasant woman from the neighborhood visited me and, with a very anxious expression, gave me a long sermon on the fact that the souls of the dead live and go around and that one should treat them decently so that they can protect the house and prevent it from being set afire or burglarized, etc. She obviously assumed that I was a city rationalist and that she should introduce me to the habits of the surroundings. When I assured her that I was a hundred percent convinced of this anyhow, she looked at me rather amazed, and really a little bit disappointed, because the whole point of her sermon had gone off, and then I realized that she herself had doubted what she had told me and after a while felt rather agreeably reassured. In about six months she was dead, unexpectedly, after an operation. She had had appendicitis, and following that something went wrong. Her concern had been also a premonition of death, and therefore she was in such a passion to convince me, or rather herself, of the survival of those ancestral souls roaming about in the woods. She was very pleased when I assured her that I had absolutely no difficulty in believing what she told me. So you see how much, even in our society, this is still completely alive, if only people have enough confidence to tell you, for they do not always open up about it.

The motif of the genealogies of the past—Gods and ancestors—has in my belief still another implication which is not in contradiction to what I gave you before, but rather relates to it. In his paper "Synchronicity: An Acausal Connecting Principle," Jung speaks of a factor which he calls absolute knowledge. What I am now talking about ventures onto very unexplored territory, so please take it as it is; it is one of the borderline fields of our knowledge, where we more or less still grope in the dark.

As you know, when synchronistic phenomena occur, one cannot avoid concluding that somewhere "things are known," things which outwardly seem to coincide by chance, but which coincide in a meaningful way. If, for instance, you use the *I Ching*, it looks as if "it," the unconscious constellation, knew about facts which have not even yet occurred. Most divinatory methods are based on this, and if we accept the hypothesis of meaningful coincidence being a form in which an archetype manifests, then we have to assume that with this archetype a certain luminosity or half-consciousness is constellated. In the chapter in which Jung speaks about the forerunners of his ideas about synchronicity, he quotes the famous Agrippa von Nettesheim, who speaks of the fact that in oracles and ecstasy and in the phenomenon of prophecy, the human being can foretell the future. Jung goes on to say in "The Structure and Dynamics of the Psyche":

> Agrippa is thus suggesting that there is an inborn "knowledge" or "perception" in living organisms, an idea which recurs in our own day in Hans Driesch. Whether we like it or not, we find ourselves in this embarrassing position as soon as we begin seriously to reflect on the teleological processes in biology or to investigate the compensatory function of the unconscious, not to speak of trying to explain the phenomenon of synchronicity. Final causes, twist them how we will, postulate a *foreknowledge of some kind*.[76]

To put it more simply, you can say that whenever a process has a final aspect, is moving toward a goal, it postulates that this goal is known ahead of time, at least vaguely. So every final explanation of factors presupposes the existence of some kind of foreknowledge.

> It is certainly not a knowledge that could be connected with the ego, and hence not a conscious knowledge as we know it, but rather a self-subsistent "unconscious" knowledge which I would prefer to call "absolute knowledge." [That is the important point that I am driving at.] It is not cognition but, as Leibniz so excellently calls it, a "perceiving" which consists—or to be more cautious, seems to consist—of images, of subjectless "simulacra." These postulated images are presumably the same as my archetypes, which can be shown to be formal factors in spontaneous fantasy products. Expressed in modern language, the microcosm which contains "the images of all creation" would be the collective unconscious.[77]

So the importance for the primitive to keep his connection with the ancestral elements is also because it is the only way by which he can reach this absolute knowledge of the collective unconscious. If you cut yourself off from the instinctive basis of your personality, you also cut yourself off from all possibility of this "absolute knowledge," which means that your possibility of recognizing reality is reduced to what you know through your ego personality. You deprive yourself of connection with this absolute knowledge and of all possibilities of foreknowing the future, of knowing somewhere through the unconscious about what is going to happen and how things are going to happen.

Now, especially for primitive people who have to live in conditions where unexpected events constantly happen and who are exposed very much to nature, the divinatory knowledge, the tapping of the absolute knowledge, is essential. You cannot know, rationally, when you go on a rhinoceros path that in ten minutes the rhinoceros will meet you. That is impossible from any conscious calculation, but you can know it through the absolute knowledge, because it will be synchronistic to the whole constellation of your life. You can even know when you get up in the morning that today you will have an encounter with a rhinoceros—*it* knows it; *you* cannot know it!

Therefore, tapping the source of the absolute knowledge, constellated in the collective unconscious, is of vital importance for the primitive, and we may say that it is of just as vital importance for us. We, too, are constantly in situations where our rational weighing of facts is insufficient. We are still exposed to an enormous number of unexpected events, and if we have methods or possibilities of tapping the so-called absolute knowledge of the collective unconscious in us, we are naturally in a much better position than if we lose this knowledge. I therefore believe that this terrific stress put by so many religious systems and mythological systems upon the ancestral continuity is also partly justified by the necessity of keeping the connection with the absolute knowledge of the unconscious.

In this chapter also belongs the role of numbers. We

know that eighty percent, if not more, of all mantic or divinatory methods are based on natural numbers. You can, for instance, make a divination by reading the name of a person: you replace every letter of the name with the appropriate number. This Kabbalistic tradition is still sometimes in use nowadays. From the number combination you make your divination. The Chinese *I Ching* is based on a number divination. Throwing bones, as among the Africans, and similar practices are based on number divination. The natural number plays the essential role in most of them. Jung says in the same paper:

> There is something peculiar, one might even say mysterious, about numbers. They have never been entirely robbed of their numinous aura. If, as a textbook of mathematics tells us, a group of objects is deprived of every single one of its properties or characteristics, there still remains, at the end, its *number,* which seems to indicate that number is something irreducible. (I am not concerned here with the logic of this mathematical argument, but only with its psychology!) The sequence of natural numbers turns out to be, unexpectedly, more than a mere stringing together of identical units: it contains the whole of mathematics and everything yet to be discovered in this field. Number, therefore, is in one sense an unpredictable entity. Although I would not care to undertake to say anything illuminating about the inner relation between two such apparently incommensurable things as number and synchronicity, I cannot refrain from pointing out that not only were they always brought into connection with one another, but that both possess numinosity and mystery as their common characteristics. Number has invariably been used to charac-

terize some numinous object, and all numbers from one
to nine are "sacred." . . . The most elementary quality
about an object is whether it is one or many. Number
helps more than anything else to bring order into the
chaos of appearances. It is the predestined instrument
for creating order, or for apprehending an already existing, but still unknown, regular arrangement or "or-
deredness."[78]

This would mean, in simpler words, that the collective unconscious consists of *simulacra, eidola* in the
Democritan sense, or images, which are not logically
connected. These images include a certain order or or-
deredness, an order of their own. Number is the most
simple, the most primitive instrument of setting order.
The first thing I do when I want to bring something
into order is to count the objects; afterward there is
more differentiation—I define the objects or their po-
sitions, but that is already more complicated. If you
want to have order with your sheep, you count them,
then you might also separate the males from the fe-
males, and put some into stables and others not, but
the most primitive way is to count them—if you want
to dominate them mentally. Number is therefore the
most primitive instrument of bringing an unconscious
awareness of order into consciousness; from it you
can best tap the unconscious constellation. This is
probably why it is used in most mantic methods.
There is a lot more which is very mysterious, but this
is where Jung stopped, hinting very strongly that
there is an infinite amount more in this field to be
found out. All this is connected with the problem of
the genealogies in cosmognoic myths because in cer-

tain gnostic and Neoplatonic cosmogonies, the archetypal chains are replaced by numbers. Creation comes
about, as it were, by two developing out of the one,
and three developing out of the two, etc. Or con-
versely, the natural numerical series reflects the law of
organization behind every act of creation.

Creation Renewed and Reversed

In the Revelation of Saint John, after the immense destruction of the world, we find the following passage:

> And I saw a new heaven and a new earth: for the first heaven and the first earth were passed away; and there was no more sea.

And I, John, saw the holy city, new Jerusalem, coming down from God out of heaven, prepared as a bride adorned for her husband.

And I heard a great voice out of heaven saying, "Behold, the tabernacle of God is with men, and he will dwell with them, and be their God."

And God shall wipe away all tears from their eyes; and there shall be no more death, neither sorrow, nor crying, neither shall there be any more pain: for the former things are passed away.

And he that sat upon the throne said, "Behold, I make all things new."

And he said unto me, "It is done. I am Alpha and Omega, the beginning and the end. I will give unto him that is a thirst of the fountain of the water of life freely." (Rev. 21:1–6)

The idea that after an apocalyptic catastrophe the world will be re-created, or some creative cosmic processes will be renewed, is not only to be found in the Bible but also, for instance, in Germanic mythology, where after the Götterdämmerung, the dawn of the Gods, and the enormous final fight between the old Germanic Gods and the demons of the abyss and hell, in which most of the Gods will be killed, a new world will suddenly blossom out of the depths. In the grass, the new Gods will find the golden tablets of the wisdom of the past, and Baldur and some of the other resurrected Gods will live in this new world. There is also the idea in different Hindu mythological systems, where it is even more expanded, that the cosmos will always be created in a *kalpa* (aeon), destroyed at the end of it, re-created in the next period, and then destroyed again, in enormous periods of time. The Germanic and Hindu concepts point to a cyclic process, namely that there is a constant rhythm of successive creation and destruction. Not much will be really changed; the beginning is always wonderful, and toward the end this world slowly decays, evil and the forces of decadence slowly prevailing until the final catastrophe, and then everything emerges again in the vernal beauty of a new possibility for life.

In contrast to this, as has always been pointed out by Christian theologians, the new creation in our civilization is a more unique event. It is not imagined that in this *kaine ktisis,* the new creation after the Last Judgment, there will be a re-beginning of everything as it was before and that after some time the devil will again do some mischief and the whole thing will start again for ever and ever. The idea is rather that the new creation is something basically, or substantially,

different from the old one. The basic difference is that
this new creation is identified with the heavenly Jerusalem, the heavenly city, which, as we know from
other passages of the Revelation, is definitely thought
of as a mandala. At the same time it is likened to a
woman "adorned for her husband" and is an essentially more spiritual reality than the material reality in
which we live. Also, if we behave well enough to be
admitted, we shall live in this heavenly Jerusalem, not
with our old bodies but with the so-called "glorified
body."

This idea bothered medieval people a lot, for they
wondered, if there was a resurrection of the body,
whether, if one had a wooden leg or some other dis-
ability, one would be resurrected with the wretched
crippled body again. The theological answer is that
we shall have a glorified body, which in a vague way
will not be quite identical with our material body, and
in the same vague and unclear way the heavenly Jerusalem also will not be the same as the deficient sphere
of reality in which we have to live now. The same idea
applies to both, to the single body of the individual
and to creation as a whole. In official Christian doctrine this renewal of creation will take place at a
definite moment in the future. The re-creation of our
individual bodies as glorified bodies also is projected
into a future state of the world, which is thought of
as being a definite event to come.

There is a very interesting variation of this in alchemy. The alchemists, even in the earliest texts we
know, which means those going back to the first century A.D. and even to the first century B.C., had the

idea that the alchemical work in the retort and the making of the philosopher's stone is a repetition of the creation, and at the same time a fabrication of the glorified body. In other words, the idea of the philosopher's stone of the alchemists is identical with the idea of the glorified body. This offers an archetypal approach to some Eastern ideas, because in different Eastern yoga practices and meditation the goal is to produce within oneself the so-called diamond body, which is an immortal nucleus of the personality.

There existed long ago in Tibetan, Indian, and partly also in Chinese Buddhism the idea that the religious practice of meditation serves the goal of producing within the still-living and mortal body the diamond body into which you move, so to speak. Already in this lifetime you use your diamond body more and more as a dwelling place, so that at the moment of death, like a skin which falls off from a fruit, this mortal body falls away and the glorified body—or in Eastern language, the diamond body—is already there. The glorified body, a sort of immortal substance as carrier of the individual personality, is already produced by religious practice during one's lifetime. This same idea, which is strange to official Christian teaching, does come up vigorously in alchemical philosophy. The alchemists, too, strove from the beginning to produce such a glorified or diamond body, and Christian alchemists from the beginning identified it with the glorified body. In order to build up this glorified body, called the philosopher's stone, you must repeat the whole process of creation.

One of the oldest alchemical treatises is "The Phi-

losopher and High Priest Komarios Teaches Cleopatra the Divine and Holy Art of the Philosophical
Stone."[79] *Komarios* probably comes from the Syrian
word *Komar* and means priest. There is also an alchemical substance, a mystical substance, called *komaris*, which is looked at as being the *prima materia*,
the basic matter of the whole process. So perhaps the
word alludes to this basic material. This would not be
a contradiction, for probably the word *komaris* derives from the idea of the priest's secret, the matter
which is the priest's secret. At that time in Egypt and
Syria, and everywhere where alchemy was practiced,
it was still the secret kept by the High Priest and was
generally not divulged to ordinary people. Originally
in Egypt the different classes of priests had a monop-
oly on certain techniques. For instance, embalming,
enameling, and so on, were all trade secrets of certain
classes of priests, a practice which survived for some
time also in the alchemical tradition, for alchemy
comes mainly from Hellenized Egyptian sources. The
text begins:

> This treatise is the golden and silver writing which the
> priest and philosopher Komarios told the wise Cleo-
> patra about the creation. He teaches Cleopatra the
> mystical philosophy sitting on a throne and touching
> the secret philosophy. He has the mystical gnosis
> which he can teach to those who know and he
> showed it even in his hands, namely the All Monad,*
> which he exercises through the four elements.

---

*The word is actually *monas*. This refers to one of the oldest alchemical texts which we still have, and one has the idea that it really is concerned with the secret of creation; the writer Komarios is really, in the
whole writing, pointing to the one monad.

This is a very strange statement, but, as we will see later in the text, the idea is that there are the four elements—Earth, Water, Fire, and Air—and that the process is a kind of circulation through the four elements until one produces from them a subtle body which contains all four elements in one. This points to a completely central and basic idea of the various alchemical traditions throughout the ages, namely that the totality of the world is divided into four elements. When you unify them again by a circulatory process, instead of four you get the basic one from which originally these four came. They are reduced again to their *prima materia,* to their one element and you then have the All-Monad, the all-embracing, the all-pervading monad, and/or, as the Latin alchemists called it much later, the *quinta essentia,* the quintessence which is really not a fifth but, as it were, the extract and condensed product of all the four other elements.

The text goes on:

> The earth coagulates above the waters and the waters are above the mountains. Take, O Cleopatra, the earth which is above the water and produce from it a spiritual body to serve, or for, the spirit of the alum (alumen). This will be then similar concerning its warmth like the fire, and resemble, concerning its dryness to the air, and the waters which are above the mountains are similar to the air, as far as their coldness is concerned and the waters are similar to the moisture. . . .

Then comes a lacuna in the text which we cannot reconstruct. The idea here is that you mix not only the four elements but at the same time also the four qualities. In late antiquity (coming from Greek natural science), there is the idea that there are four elements and four qualities, sometimes eight qualities, which unite. For instance, the earth is dry and cold; water shares its coldness, but is moist and cold; air shares the warmth of the fire, but is of a different consistency. Thus they have all sorts of mixtures of eight or four qualities.

> Behold out of one pearl, and another one, O Cleopatra, all pharmakon, all tincture, is produced. Cleopatra then took this writing of Komarios and began to comment on it about the cutting into four of the beautiful philosophy, i.e., about the basic substance of all natures. She taught and found the form [the Greek word is *ideam*] of all the operations and their differences and thus we found that the philosophy in everything separates the basic substance of nature into four, so that we have first the Nigredo or Blackness, second the Albedo, third the Citrinitas or Yellowing, and fourth the Rubedo or Reddening of the substance. We can also subdivide those basic elements into a similar half element, or half step, and so we get between the Nigredo and the Albedo the mummification and the washing of the form; between the Albedo and the yellowing the melting of the gold, and between the yellowing and the redness there is the division into two of the whole product. The final goal of this whole treatment is a vessel which has breasts and is the becoming one of all parts.

It needs a great amount of background knowledge to understand, at least in part, what the writer is driving at. What we see is two things: an identity of philosophy and nature, and that means that the subdivision of nature into four is identical with the subdivision of the "philosophy" into four parts. Philosophy (in this case meaning the alchemical theory, or the theoretical approach of the alchemists) is responsible for the fact that everything in nature is divided into four. Then the author, speaking through Cleopatra, jumps from that to the fact that there are four stages of matter, namely black, white, yellow, and red, the famous theory which survived till the very end of alchemy, that is, until the seventeenth century. These theories have really lasted for seventeen hundred years, unchanged. Between them then she includes half processes. So we have again a mandala: not the four elements only, but nigredo, albedo, citrinitas, and rubedo, the four stages, and in between them the mummification, the melting of the gold, the subdivision into two, and (then it is not clear, for the author jumps to the remark that the goal is a vessel with breasts) the becoming one of all parts. So, instead of going on to the fourth and the re-beginning, there is a sudden movement to the center. Here again is an amusing document on the problem of the three and four. Cleopatra really begins with wanting to put in four steps, goes only to the third and then, in going toward the fourth, instead of saying that between the rubedo and the nigredo there is a fourth step, she jumps into the center. Suddenly the goal of the whole thing is to make a vessel with breasts.

The vessel with breasts is an interesting kind of alchemical vessel which probably was invented in Egypt; it is a vessel similar to what was later called the pelican. In the original manuscript there are drawings of the vessel, so that we know exactly what the vessel with breasts looks like. It works on the system of a coffee percolator. There is the fire underneath; the substance is sublimated and gets condensed and precipitated as moisture from the two sides, as milk from the woman's breast, which explains the name. There is another type of this vessel which, instead of releasing the liquid (as in type 1) and continuing the alchemical process, lets it back, which suggests the pelican. It is a vessel for circulation, in which the substance is constantly cooked and precipitated back for further purification or clarification.

The vessel was said to be the invention of Maria Prophetissa, the sister of Moses, an entirely legendary figure. She is also found as a prophetess in certain Gnostic writings. We still use the *bain Marie* in the kitchen—it is a container stood within a bath of boiling water. So you see, when you heat up a can of

SKY

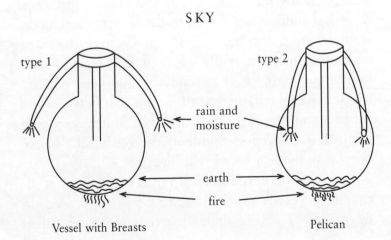

Vessel with Breasts   Pelican

asparagus, for instance, you still use Maria Prophetissa's great invention, without knowing it!

In alchemy this vessel was looked at as being a representation of the whole universe. It was thought (as
certain astronomers still think) that the universe was
a closed system; the vessel was a replica of the universe in shape: below the earth and above the sky,
which explains the references to the clouds condensing and the rain falling. This whole process in the retort is a kind of cosmic process—according to what
was then thought of as the cosmos; so under the earth
is the fire, like hell underneath the earth's surface, and
above is the air and the sky. This vessel became a mystical concept in alchemy. You can read a whole chapter about it in Jung's *Psychology and Alchemy;* there
he collects an enormous number of alchemical quotations about the nature of the vessel, from which it becomes very clear that in alchemy it was not thought
of as a banal retort, as we would think of it, but was
a mystical concept.[80] This mystical concept boils
down to the fact that for the alchemists the vessel represented something like the possibility of a unitary
psychic concept of reality, acquired, or built, either by
what they called "the philosophy," which for them
was a material thing, or, in many other texts, "the
soul," as you will find in Jung's chapter on the vessel.
It is really a symbol of the human psyche as a whole, a
microcosm, a vessel within which all the macrocosmic
processes are caught and at the same time grasped
and conceived. In the whole of alchemy, since the
mental processes are completely projected into the

material operations, there is no difference between the actual retort and what we would call the psyche.

The next part of this text, the oldest alchemical text which we have *in extenso,* says:

> You, too, O Friends, if you want to approach this marvellous art of alchemy must proceed in the same way. Now look at the plants, where they come from, they come down from the mountains or grow up from the earth. Then see how one approaches them, namely one must collect them at the right moment and on the appropriate day, and see how the air serves them and the earth surrounds them so that they are not killed. Because they are all of one substance.

Here Cleopatra compares the central process with the growth of a plant. Psychologically, there is a connection. First she has circled around between four or nearly eight—seven and a half—stages and then jumped to the central problem of the vessel. Now she comes to the idea of a growing plant, by collecting material from air, water, and earth—from everywhere. So we see that the growing plant is a simile for the same thing, for that mystical center upon which the alchemists had all their attention concentrated. She now used the simile: just as a plant uses mineral stuffs, water, and air—all the elements—and condenses them into a new being, namely the plant, so our art produces one substance which is drawn from all the surrounding substances.

Then Ostanes and his friends answer Cleopatra. You see, Komarios and Cleopatra are speaking to a whole assembly of alchemists.

In you [meaning Cleopatra] is hidden the terrific and wonderful secret. Please explain better about the elements; how what is above comes down, and what is below rises, and how the middle approaches the uppermost and the lowest, and how they all become one in the center, and tell us also what all those elements are, and how the blessed waters come down and look at the dead in the underworld who are fettered there and unhappy and look how the elixir of life enters them and how they are woken up so that they come out of their beds. And when the waters enter the top part of their beds then the light comes and the cloud carries them up, the cloud comes from the sea and the water comes up and the philosophers can see what is visible and are filled with great happiness.

The first remark is interesting because the assembly of philosophers say to the teacher, Cleopatra, that in her, that is in this female alchemist, the terrific secret is hidden. The projection is clearly that the secret of creation and the secret of restoring it is hidden within a feminine figure, in this case in the wise Cleopatra. If you remember, in many of the creation myths I cited, in the beginning there was a pregnant female figure which contained the whole world. This motif appeared *in extenso* in the Iroquois myth where the whole of creation was contained in the womb of the woman who fell down from heaven. Here again in alchemy is the same idea, that within a mystical feminine figure the whole secret of the art of creation is first contained, but it has a more spiritual nuance, in that it is the *knowledge* of the secret. The heavenly Jerusalem was also said to be prepared "as a bride adorned for her husband" so there too the secret of the new creation was likened to a female figure moving towards the act of the *coniunctio*. In the Apocalypse, this "bride adorned for her husband" was identified with the famous woman who has the crown of the twelve stars on her head and who gives birth to a new Savior.

Then the text skips to the fact that all elements, the uppermost, the lowest, and so on, are united in the middle: all the elements are brought together in the center, and this is the secret. Then the text skips again to a new idea, that simultaneously with this condensation of all the scattered elements, with this terrific act of condensation, the water of life penetrates in the underworld where the dead lie and resurrects them. So the condensation coincides with a resurrection of the dead, and here we come to the motif of the glorified body.

> And Cleopatra said to them: the waters enter and awake the bodies and the weakened spirits in them since they must suffer in the underworld for a long time and then they sprout out of the underworld and come up and clothe themselves in beautiful colors like the flowers in Spring and Spring itself rejoices in the beauty which it gives to them. To you who understand me, I will say, when you lift up the plants and the elements and the stones from their original places, they *look* beautiful but are not, but after having been tested with the fire then they acquire the beautiful color and much more beautiful glory, namely the hidden glory which has the longed for beauty, and that comes when the matter is changed by the fire into a divine substance.

The idea is that you take the original bodies, whether stones or plants, matter in its original form—

which might look beautiful but is not—and burn it down. That means you test it in the fire. Then you produce something which contains a hidden spiritual glory and which this text even calls divine. So what you produce by condensing the different materials is a divine body. It has changed into the divine nature.

> Our holy art is just like a child which, as an embryo, is nourished in its mother's womb and slowly grows. First the waves of the sea hurt the corpse and the waves of the underworld destroy it in its tomb, but when you open the tomb that which was formerly a corpse, but lives, now comes out like a child out of the mother's womb. And when the philosophers see the beauty they become very happy and, just as a loving mother nourishes her newborn child, so they try to nourish their corpse which has now become a child, not with milk but with water, for the whole art [meaning alchemy] is an image of a child, because it gets the form of a child and in all these points it is complete and that is the secret sealed mystery.

Here there is an interesting motif, namely the destruction of the corpse in the tomb. From that somehow, in a secret way, comes the resurrection of a child out of the tomb, and this child is the art of alchemy and is a mystery which is brought forth by the efforts of the philosophers. This old text, *Komarios to Cleopatra,* contains all the most basic ideas which are found in the later alchemical texts. Again and again the philosopher's stone was also thought of as being a divine child born out of the art of alchemy, using the simile of death and resurrection. The nigredo, the state of blackness, is always likened to the state of death, when the corpse is destroyed in the tomb; the albedo is the washing off of death and of the stench of the grave; and then a child is born which is either the infant Mercurius or a divine child, or the philosopher's stone, and at the same time is simply also the renewal of the alchemical philosophy.

I am omitting a part of the text here and continue with chapter 13:

> See the paradoxical mystery, O Brethren, the completely unknown truth which I tell you. Watch that you nourish your own earth and that you nourish your own germs so that you will reap beautiful fruit. Listen and think about what I say: Take from the four elements the uppermost male and the lowest, the white and reddish one, in similar equilibrium, male and female, so that they can be united, and just as a bird broods with warmth and completes its eggs with warmth, you, too, must melt the two and put them in sunburnt places and roast them on a mild fire with virgin's milk and smoke. And when they have become one [i.e., when soul and spirit have become one] and are one, then project them into the body of the silver and then you will have a gold which all the treasure houses of kings do not have.

You must remember that alchemical thinking never proceeds in a straight line; it is circulatory and always circles around one central motif. Here that same central motif, which was first likened to making the vessel and to the plants, or imitating the growth of the plant, is now likened to a *coniunctio* of male and female and to the idea of the bird which broods on an egg, so that soul and spirit become one, an inner unification of the soul and the spirit which then acquires the body of the silver and thus becomes a gold which

is not found in the treasure houses of kings. It is therefore a unification of a soul, a spirit and a body, called
the body of silver, a female body, and those three together make a fourth, namely gold. Obviously, as is
added, the gold is not to be found in the treasure
houses of kings, which means that it is not ordinary
gold, not the metal which we see and which was well
known in those times, but a mystical gold. The alchemists tried to make a substance which they called gold
but which had nothing to do with the metal. They
meant by that something divine, incorruptible, which
cannot be burnt up again by fire, an immortal body,
so to speak. This gold, which in later texts is usually
called the philosophical gold, is the immortal body
which comes forth through the union of opposites
and which is no longer subjected to the decay of this
world.

> This is the mystery of the philosophers and they have
> sworn an oath never to reveal it or to profane it be-
> cause it is divine. It is divine because it is united with
> the Godhead and brings every substance to divine
> completion and it is a mystery in which the spirit in-
> carnates, the dead receive a soul and receive the spirit
> and then overcome each other. There is also a dark
> spirit full of nonsense and discouragement which first
> rules over the bodies so that they cannot become
> white and receive the color of the creator. They are
> weakened by this dark pneuma. But when the stench
> of this dark spirit has disappeared, then the corpse is
> filled with light, and soul and spirit and body rejoice.
> And then the soul calls out to the enlightened body:
> "Wake up from the underworld, get up from the
> tomb, get up from the darkness, clothe yourself in

spiritualisation and deification because the voice of
the resurrection has reached you and the elixir of life
has entered into you." The spirit then again rejoices
to be in the body and the soul and also rejoices to be
wherein she lives and she embraces her husband in
joy because the darkness has disappeared and everything is filled with light and can no longer be separated from the light, and the soul rejoices in her house
[meaning the body] because it was first dark, but now
she finds it full of light and she becomes one with it
because it [the house or body] is now divine and she
dwells in it. She has clothed herself with divine light
and they have become one. The darkness has gone
away and they have become all one in love, body, soul
and spirit. They are all one and in this the mystery is
hidden, and in the fact that they came together and
united with each other the mystery is completed, now
the house is sealed and the statue full of light and
divinity is erected. The fire has made them one and
changed, and it has come out of the maternal womb.

I have given this text *in extenso* because here you
see very clearly how the whole description of the alchemical process switches into religious hymnic language, praising an experience of resurrection after
death and entering immortality. This portrays better
than many of the later texts the ultimate goal of the
whole endeavor of the alchemists, namely to produce
the glorified bodies by their own art, in this life, and
not to wait for it to happen at the end of days. It is
clear that the alchemist represents the introverted undercurrent of official Christian doctrine, because the
official doctrine was more influenced, especially in
earlier times, by extraverts and remained projected
into form, in the sense that we can do nothing our-

selves but must decay in our graves and then will be resurrected by God at the end of days. The introverted tendency tried to support the work of God, so to say, by meditative activity, and build up and produce or realize this fact, which the extraverts expected to happen outside somewhere in time, as an inner mystical event. In a certain way, therefore, except for this typological contrast, alchemy has never been anti-Christian; it is just an undercurrent which gave the whole Christian representation a more inner psychic and mystical aspect, which brings it nearer to the doctrines of the Far East. Such neglected factors as the glorified body, therefore, here became their central concern.

I now want to cite a few more alchemical texts. This next text probably comes from the twelfth or thirteenth century, so it reflects a jump of "only" eleven hundred years from the one I have just quoted. You will be amazed to find how conservative the alchemists are and how similar the ideas still are.

It is a text entitled *Aurora Consurgens* that has been ascribed to Saint Thomas Aquinas. Until now this ascription has only been laughed at and never taken seriously, but I have made an attempt to discuss the ascription. As, however, this is not the point here, we will simply look at it as it is, as a medieval alchemical text.

In the first chapters the author describes in ecstatic form how a woman comes down from heaven and toward him, whom he calls Sophia, the Wisdom of God, and who, according to his idea, is also the mystical knowledge of alchemy. In the chapter before, the eleventh, he describes the philosopher's stone as being identical with the heavenly Jerusalem. So here is the same idea as in Revelation, the idea that the heavenly Jerusalem, a kind of female divine figure personified as the *Sapienta Dei,* is identical with alchemy and her product; it is the heavenly Jerusalem and the philosopher's stone. The author then continues to describe the philosopher's stone as identical with the heavenly Jerusalem in a parable called "The Parable of Heaven and Earth and the Arrangement of the Elements," which is a collection of quotations from Genesis and other parts of the Bible, all referring to the creation. The point I am still driving at is to show that the alchemical opus is a repetition of our creation myths.

> He that is of the earth, of the earth he speaketh, he that cometh from heaven is above all. How here also is the earth represented as the principle of the elements, but the heavens stand for the three higher (principles), wherefore a little ought to be said of earth and heaven, for earth is the principle and mother of the other elements, as the Prophet beareth witness: In the beginning, O Lord, thou didst found the earth, and the heavens are the works of thy hands, that is, water, air, and fire. For from the earth are the elements separated by dying, and to it do they return by quickening, for what a thing is composed of, into that must it be resolved, as the holy word testifieth: Man is ashes and to their ashes shall he return. Such ashes did the philosophers ordain to be mixed with the permanent water, which is the ferment of gold, and their gold is the body, that is the earth, which Aristotle called the coagulent, since it coagulateth water. It is the earth of the Promised Land, wherein Hermes commanded his son to sow gold, that living

rains might ascend from it, and water which warmeth it, as Senior* saith: And when they desire to extract this divine water, which is fire, they warm it with their fire, which is water, which they have measured unto the end and have hidden on account of the unwisdom of fools. And of this have all the philosophers sworn, that they would nowhere set it forth clearly in writing, but they have left it to the glorious God, to reveal it to whom he will and withhold it from whom he will, for in him is great cunning and the secrecy of the wise. And when the heat of that fire reaches the earth itself, the earth is dissolved and becomes a boiling, that is an evaporated water, and afterward reverteth to its own former earthly form. Therefore by water is the earth moved and the heavens poured out upon it, and flows as if with honey throughout all the world and tells its glory. For this glory is known only to him who hath understanding, how of the earth the heavens were made, and therefore the earth remaineth forever and the heavens are founded upon it, as the Prophet beareth witness: For thou hast founded the earth upon its own bases, it shall not be moved for ever and ever. The deep is its clothing, above it shall stand water, air, fire, and the birds of the air shall dwell therein, watering it from the upper elements, that it may be filled with the fruit of their works, because in the center of the earth the seven planets took root, and left their virtue there, wherefore in the earth is water germinating divers kinds of colors and fruits and producing bread and wine that cheereth the heart of man, and also bringing forth grass for cattle and herb for the service of men. This earth, I say, made the moon in its season, then the sun

---

*Senior—or El Shaykh in Arabic—was a famous Arabian author whose real name was Muhammad ibn Umail; in Latin texts his name was always translated as Senior, as they did not know his Arabic name.

arose, very early in the morning the first day of the
week, after the darkness, which thou hast appointed
therein before the sunrise, and it is (night). For in it
shall all the beasts of the wood go about, for thou has
set them a bound which they shall not pass until the
whitening, but in their order (the days) go on even
until the reddening, for all things serve the earth, and
the days of its years are threescore and ten years passing over it, because it upholdeth all things by the
word of its godhead, as in the *Turba philosophorum*
[a famous alchemical classic] it is written: The earth,
since it is heavy, beareth all things, for it is the foundation of the whole heaven, because it appeared dry
at the separation of the elements. Therefore in the
Red Sea there was a way without hindrance, since this
great and wide sea smote the rock and the (metallic)
waters flowed forth. Then the rivers disappeared in
dry land, which make the city of God joyful; when
this mortal shall put on immortality, and the corrup-
tion of the living shall put on incorruption, then
needed shall that word come to pass which is written,
Death is swallowed up in victory. O death, where is
thy victory? Where thy sin abounded, there (now)
grace doth more abound. For as in Adam all die, so
also in Christ all (men) shall be made alive. For by a
man indeed came death, and by (Jesus) himself the
resurrection of the dead. For the first Adam and his
sons took their beginning from the corruptible elements, and therefore it was needful that the composed
should be corrupted, but the second Adam, who is
called the philosophic man, from pure elements entered into eternity. Therefore what is composed of
simple and pure essence, remaineth for ever. As Senior
saith: There is One thing that never dieth, for it con-
tinueth by perpetual increase, when the body shall be
glorified in the final resurrection of the dead, wherefore the Creed beareth witness to the resurrection of

the flesh and eternal life after death. Then saith the second Adam to the first and to his sons: Come, ye blessed of my Father, possess you the eternal kingdom prepared for you from the beginning of the Work, and eat my bread and drink the wine which I have mingled for you [instead of "from the beginning of creation" he puts in "from the beginning of the opus," by this literally saying that the alchemical opus and creation are identical], for all things are made ready for you. He that hath ears to hear, let him hear what the spirit of the doctrine saith to the sons of the discipline concerning the earthly and the heavenly Adam, which the philosophers treat of in these words: When thou hast water from earth, air from water, fire from air, earth from fire, then thou shalt fully and perfectly possess [our] art [etc.]).[81]

Here you see again in a nutshell the same idea, that you produce one thing from the four elements in an opus which repeats the complete process of creation and that this at the same time is the bringing forth or building up of the second inner Adam, against, or replacing, the old corruptible Adam. And there is this beautiful speech by the second Adam, in whom all people resurrect, addressing the sons of the first corrupt Adam, who is destroyed. In this speech there is also the idea of producing an immortal body by producing through an inward process the final resurrection of the dead within the philosopher's stone. For this author the philosopher's stone was identical with an inner psychic experience of what he called Christ, and what we would call psychologically an experience of the Self, which naturally a medieval mystic would call Christ. But it is the inner Christ whom he experiences and who is at the same time his own immortality, for the resurrection takes place within Christ, and for an alchemist, through this, within the philosopher's stone.

There is only one more chapter in the *Aurora* and that is the "Seventh Parable of the Conversation of the Lover with the Beloved," which is a paraphrase of the Song of Solomon and is a love song of the *coniunctio*. So you see that within, or after, this resurrection, exactly in the same pattern as the old text of Komarios, after the production of the immortal body, comes the unification of all the substances in a *coniunctio*. But what in the Apocalypse (where the heavenly Jerusalem is also a bride adorned for her husband) is only hinted at in one word, is here expanded by the alchemists into a whole process.

Through the fact that the ideas and work of certain medieval alchemical authors became imbued with Christian mystical experience, the alchemical work became more clearly and more expressly a religious inner experience, and there you already have the beginnings of a nonchemical idea of alchemy. I am personally convinced that whoever the author of this text was, he certainly was no longer a chemist who operated with a retort, but he used the chemical language to describe a personal inner mystical experience. Through the increasing development of the chemical aspect of alchemy, and through the discovery that atomic weight plays a role in the mixture of elements and other such factors, chemistry slowly evolved out of alchemy, and its spiritual doctrine became accordingly thin and more rational. In Jung's *Psychology and Alchemy* there is an eighteenth-century text which betrays this intellectualization and thinning of the original experience. As Jung says, the text is by no means old and bears all the traces of the decadent period. It runs:

> Take common rainwater, a good quantity, at least ten quarts, preserve it well sealed in glass vessels for at least ten days, then it will deposit matter and feces on the bottom. Pour off the clear liquid and place in a wooden vessel that is fashioned round like a ball, cut it in the middle and fill the vessel a third full, and set it in the sun about midday in a secret or secluded spot. When this has been done, take a drop of the consecrated red wine and let it fall into the water, and you will instantly perceive a fog and thick darkness on top of the water, such as also was at the first creation. [You see, now it is only a simile; it is not an identity.] Then put in two drops, and you will see the light coming forth from the darkness; whereupon little by little put in every half of each quarter hour first three, then four, then five, then six drops, and then no more, and you will see with your own eyes one thing after another appearing by and by on top of the water, how God created all things in six days, and how it all came to pass, and such secrets as are not to be spoken aloud and I also have not power to reveal. Let your eyes judge of it; for thus was the world created. Let all stand as it is, and in half an hour after it began it will disappear.
>
> By this you will see clearly the secrets of God, that are at present hidden from you as from a child. You will understand what Moses has written concerning the creation; you will see what manner of body Adam and Eve had before and after the Fall, what the serpent was, what the tree, and what manner of fruits

> they ate; where and what Paradise is, and in what
> bodies the righteous shall be resurrected; not in this
> body that we have received from Adam, but in that
> which we attain through the Holy Ghost, namely in
> such a body as our Saviour brought from heaven.[82]

Compared with the ecstatic mystical experience
which is described in the *Aurora Consurgens,* this
man has simply mixed certain chemical matters and
compared them as an allegory or a simile with the
creation. Because it is no longer a mystery, he makes
a great fuss about its being a secret—just because it is
not one anymore. For him, obviously, this is just playing with substances and fantasying and likening the
processes in the retort to the act of creation. So what
was an original archaic identity, a real experience of
the earlier genuine alchemists, has become a dry intellectual allegory in the decaying period of the art.

Clearly what got lost and disappeared underground
in this eighteenth-century text was what we would
call the emotional, psychological, mystical experience. Jung says in a comment in *Mysterium Coniunctionis*[83] on another late alchemical text by Gerardus
Dorneus that what the alchemist did in this late period was really active imagination with chemical substances. Already in this eighteenth-century text the
chemical experiment is just used as a basis for that.
Naturally, you can use dancing or painting or poetry,
or anything you like, to do active imagination as we
understand it, and those people did it with chemical
substances.

You can therefore say that from the eighteenth century on, the essential archetypal content, or the al-

chemical philosophy, went underground, and it is the great achievement of Jung that he unearthed it again and made it understandable to us as an unconscious psychic phenomenon. Before, there was only the either/or: either it is materially true and chemically true, which it obviously is not, or it is an intellectual allegory for a content of faith. Now we can see that it is neither chemically true nor an intellectual simile for some content of our creed, but that it is a reference to an original genuine experience of an archetypal psychic unconscious constellation and that as such it has a reality of its own. Alchemy in this sense really is a religious undercurrent of Christianity and approaches the Eastern viewpoint, where they knew long ago that the resurrection was an inner factor, an inner experience, and that the production of the diamond body, or the immortal body, is operated, made, or produced by transformation of one's own psyche. Parallel to Eastern meditation is Jung's discovery of the technique of active imagination by which, if one uses it properly, one can still produce the opus of alchemy in another dimension.

I mention this because, as you see in the texts, there is such a striking parallel between the alchemical opus, the production of the philosopher's stone and the diamond body, and the creation myths we had before. Naturally, some of the alchemists knew this and even pointed out the similarity of the two processes, showing that they understood the alchemical opus as a kind of inner psychic repetition of the cosmogony outside. What in all earlier civilizations was a teaching concerning the outer creation of the cosmos has

354 Creation Renewed and Reversed

with the help of alchemical philosophy now slowly come back and reentered the individual, whence it unconsciously originated. It has finally been even understood as a process of the growth of consciousness within the individual human being and, after the event, we can call all those creation myths projections onto the outer world of this originally inner psychic process.

There is one more important fact to point out. In the repeated creation within the individual, which is consciously brought forth as an effort toward more total consciousness, the process of creation, as described in Genesis for instance, is *reversed*. Here, unfortunately, you have to believe me, because I cannot now roll out all the relevant documentary evidence. In the alchemical process, what generally comes first within the nigredo are wild animals—lions, dragons, bears, wolves, and so on; the animal kingdom. After that there are generally similes of plant life, the making of the philosopher's stone being compared to planting a tree with golden fruit and watering it; there is the whole process of a tree growing within the retort and within the human being. The final goal is a metal or stone symbol, a crystal, or a mineral, what we would now call a symbol of inorganic matter.

You see how this strangely reverses our idea of evolution. We think that from inorganic matter first plant life came into existence, then the animal, and then the human being; but in the alchemical process there is a complete reversal of our idea of biological evolution. First we meet the animals, then the plants, and finally the inorganic gold. We can therefore understand the alchemical opus as a reversal on a psychic level of the outer biological evolution. It is as if what happens as an expanding process on the physical level were reversed on the psychic level and internalized in the reversed order.

We can only say that analysis usually more or less follows the same pattern as the alchemical opus. If we analyze a human individual, we first meet the wild appetites, autonomous complexes, sex and power drives, which are generally symbolized by lions, mating dogs, and such images. We meet the whole roaring wilderness in the human being. After that come symbols of plant life, which already show a certain unification and growth of the personality, mirroring a certain steadiness of the relationship between the unconscious and consciousness and no longer being driven along by one's appetites and desires. Later come the mandala and philosopher's stone symbolism; they show a solidification of the inner experience and a steadying of the connection between the ego and the Self, and with that, of the whole personality.

Thus, in a way, the alchemical process (in projection) and the individuation process as Jung understands it, are both reversed creations and contain all the symbolism of the creation myths in this reversed order. Just as we often had at the very beginning of creation the mating of the female and the male God and a pregnancy, so this motif of the *coniunctio* comes in the alchemical opus at the very end of the process, where a unified state is established. If we had time, we could now go back and look at all the symbols of the preconscious totality, and we would discover that they are all also contained in the images of the goal.

In one alchemical text this is especially clear, in the philosophy of Gerardus Dorneus. He was a pupil of Paracelsus. Dorneus describes the alchemical opus according to old medieval traditions which still survived in his age: the human being consists of body, psyche, and spirit (or the rational soul). In the act of meditation one has first to separate psyche and spirit from the body. That is what every monk does in a monastery; it means getting detached from one's physical drives and appetites, from sex domination and from all shadowy elements which are connected with the body. After that, you separate psyche and spirit and clarify what the spirit is, what the psyche is, and what the body is. Having done that, and that belongs only to the analytical part of the alchemical work, he describes how you reunite spirit and psyche. This he describes very much as in terms of *coniunctio* texts, but then he goes one step further, a unique step which you find in no mystical text of the Middle Ages: he feels sorry for this body which has been cast out, and says that it cannot simply be thrown into the rubbish heap, but that it too must be redeemed into the inner unification, into the already existing *unio mentalis.*

Through a process of meditation the body has to be reunited with the rest, and that he describes as the *unio corporalis.* It is the producing of the immortal body within the mortal body, the production of a *corpus glorificationis,* by which you, as it were, redeem the basic element of your physical makeup. Then comes the interesting step. You think—well, that is

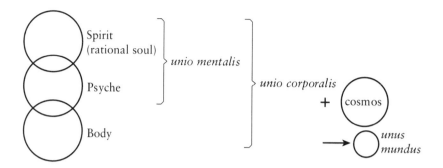

now O.K.! First you have cut it all apart, then you have thrown out the bad things, as you take a car apart and then build it up again after having cleaned every particle of it, so now you can sit back and be happy, now the whole human being has become one in the glorified body. No! Dorneus is a genius and he adds a further step, namely the union with the *unus mundus,* the one world, or the one cosmos. That means the unification of the individual at the end of the process comes not only within himself, but spirit, psyche, and body are united with the cosmos.

The *unus mundus* is a medieval theological concept which holds that when God created the world he naturally first made a plan, like a good architect, a model of the cosmos. He did that within the Wisdom of God—she is that *unus mundus,* the creative anima of God within which he casts the model of the world—or sometimes it is identified with the preexisting Logos, i.e., Christ before he was born on earth. This *unus mundus* is not the cosmos as it exists now, but an idea in God's psyche or mind, the plan which God proceeds to realize, as an architect follows his plan for the building of a house. When an individual has reached this stage of becoming conscious and one with himself, he does not unite with the actually existing cosmos, which, according to Christian doctrine, is corruptible and subject to death, but with the *unus mundus,* that mental model-world in the mind of God, or in the Wisdom of God. He becomes one, it is a coniunctio, he mates, he unites in a love act with the *Sapientia Dei,* who is identical with this *unus mundus* and identical with the experience of synchronistic events.

Synchronistic events hint to us at the fact that the archetypal constellations in the collective unconscious of a human individual can also appear in outer cosmic events. Naturally, if one experiences such synchronistic events and one thinks in a naive medieval way, one concludes that our psyche is, in a way, identical with cosmic reality. This is a causal way of explaining the fact, and Jung avoids it by his term synchronicity. Otherwise we would have to believe that the unconscious is an all-pervading thing, right to the borderlines of the cosmos. This cannot be proved, and from a scientific standpoint appears suspect. Jung therefore introduced the concept of synchronicity instead.

In medieval thinking, where they lacked the concept of synchronicity, they thought of a kind of magical union of the individual psyche with the whole cosmos. In order to separate it from the cosmos as we see it, Dorneus created the most ingenious idea that the union does not take place with actual reality but with this *unus mundus,* the reality in God's mind, or with the *Sapientia Dei,* the Wisdom of God, who in the Bible appears as a female personification.

The Wisdom of God is interpreted in modern Mariology as the preexistent model of the earthly Virgin Mary: Christ existed before his actual life on earth as the Logos, the Word, so Mary existed before. Her existence as the *Sapientia Dei* from all time would therefore be what we might call the psychic aspect of matter. From this you will probably see why Jung shouted with joy when Pope Pius XII declared the dogma of the Assumptio Maria! That was a real slap in the face for the materialistic world, because it means the recognition of the psychic aspect of matter. In fact, if one knows enough of the history of religion to understand, it was meant as a slap at the materialistic doctrine. Pope Pius himself understood the connection he was making here. For us it coincides with what Jung had long before already seen, namely that what we call psyche and what we call matter are really only two aspects of one living phenomenon which, if observed in an extraverted way and with extraverted methods from outside, give results which physicists describe, whereas if we describe it introspectively from the inside, we get the phenomenon which I tried to describe in this last chapter. It is a reversed creation, really just the mirror opposite of all the cosmological outer theories.

Notes

1. C. G. Jung, *Collected Works* (Princeton, N.J.: Princeton University Press, 1969), vol. 6, para. 783.

2. Ibid., paras. 741–42.

3. C. G. Jung, *Memories, Dreams, Reflections* (New York: Random House, 1963), pp. 255–56.

4. C. G. Jung, *Collected Works*, vol. 14, para. 766.

5. Margaret Sinclair Stevenson, *The Rites of the Twice-Born* (London, 1920), quoted in Mircea Eliade, *The Myth of the Eternal Return: or, Cosmos and History* (Princeton, N.J.: Princeton University Press, 1971), p. 19.

6. Ibid., p. 81.

7. Knud Rasmussen, *Die Gabe des Adlers* (Frankfurt am Main: Societäts-Verlag, 1937), p. 47.

8. Paul Radin, *Winnebago Culture as Described by Themselves* (Baltimore: Waverly Press, 1950), p. 9.

9. J. N. B. Hewitt, *Iroquoian Cosmogony*, vol. 21 (Washington, D.C.: Annual Reports of the Bureau of American Ethnology, 1903).

10. *Indianermärchen aus Nordamerika*, in the "Märchen der Weltliteratur" series (Jena: Diederichs Verlag, 1924), p. 93.

11. Eliade, *The Myth of the Eternal Return*, p. 6.

12. Mary C. Wheelwright, *Navajo Creation Myth* (Santa Fe, 1942), p. 39.

13. Frank Waters, *Book of the Hopi* (New York: Viking Press, 1963), pp. 9ff.

14. C. G. Jung, *Collected Works*, vol. 8, paras. 343ff.

15. Ibid., para. 420.

16. *Indianermärchen aus Nordamerika*, p. 76.

17. Manfred Lurker, *Götter und Symbole der alten Aegypten* (Bern: Scherz Verlag, 1974), pp. 37ff.

18. Günther Roeder, *Urkunden zur Religion des alten Aegypten* (Jena: Diederichs Verlag, 1923), p. 297.

19. *Indianermärchen aus Nordamerika*, p. 401.

20. Paul Radin, with commentaries by Karl Kerényi and C. G. Jung, *The Trickster* (New York: Schocken Books, 1972).

21. *Indianermärchen aus Nordamerika*, p. 406.

22. *Indianermärchen aus Südamerika*, in the "Märchen der Weltliteratur" series (Jena: Diederichs Verlag, 1921), p. 225.

23. Herman Baumann, *Schöpfung und Urzeit des Menschen im Mythus der afrikanischen Völker* (Berlin: Reimer, 1964) (Photomech. Nachdruck d. Ausg. v. 1936). A number of the African myths referred to in this chapter can be found in Baumann's book.

24. Ibid., p. 179.

25. Max Schmidt, *The Primitive Races of Mankind* (London: George G. Harrap, 1926).

26. Hans Leisegang, *Die Gnosis* (Leipzig: Kröner, 1924), pp. 116–25.

27. Ibid., chapter titled "Die Ophiten."

28. Wolfgang Pauli, "Naturwissenschaftliche und erkenntnistheoretische Aspekte der Ideen vom Unbewussten: Vortrag anlässlich des 80. Geburtstages von C. G. Jung." Reprinted in *Aufsätze und Vorträge über Physik und Erkenntnistheorie*, ed. Wilhelm Westphal (Braunschweig: Vieweg, 1961).

29. See Roeder, *Urkunden*, p. 166.

30. Mircea Eliade, *Die Schöpfungsmythen* (Darmstadt: Wissenschaftliche Buchgesellschaft, 1977), pp. 134ff.

31. Franz Vonessen, "Der Mythus vom Weltschleier," *Mythische Entwürfe* (Stuttgart: Klett, 1975).

32. Geo Widengren, *Der Manichäismus* (Darmstadt: Wissenschaftliche Buchgesellschaft, 1977), p. 175.

33. Mircea Eliade, *The Forge and the Crucible* (Chicago: University of Chicago Press, 1978), pp. 53ff.

34. Chuang Tzu, *Das wahre Buch vom südlichen Blütenland*, trans. Richard Wilhelm (Jena: Diedrichs Verlag, 1923), p. 60. English translation: Burton Watson, *Chuang Tzu Basic Writings* (New York and London: Columbia University Press, 1966), p. 95.

35. August Wünsche, *Schöpfung und Sündenfall des ersten Menschenpaares* (Leipzig: Eduard Pfeiffer, 1906), p. 7.

36. Cf. *The Upanishads,* trans. Max Müller (London: Oxford University Press, 1926), vol. 1, p. 238; vol. 2, pp. 73, 247.

37. Brian Branston, *Gods of the North* (London: Thames and Hudson), p. 41.

38. See Wünsche, *Schöpfung und Sündenfall,* pp. 8ff.

39. See Leisegang, *Die Gnosis,* p. 174.

40. C. G. Jung, *Collected Works,* vol. 9ii, para. 9.

41. See Tinbergen's *Study of Instincts,* where these problems are explained at great length. There is also Adolf Portmann's *Das Tier als Sozialwesen* (The Animal as a Social Being).

42. *Popol Vuh,* English version by Delia Goetz and Sylvanus G. Morley, from Spanish trans. by Adrian Recinos (London: William Hodge and Company, 1951), pp. 81ff.

43. Eliade, *Die Schöpfungsmythen,* p. 70.

44. *Indianermärchen aus Nordamerika,* p. 401. Paul Radin, *The Winnebago Tribe* (Lincoln: University of Nebraska Press, 1970), p. 302. Also, Paul Radin, *Winnebago Culture as Described by Themselves,* pp. 9, 37, 64ff.

45. Paul Radin, *The World of Primitive Man* (New York: Henry Schuman, 1953), p. 320.

46. *The Upanishads,* vol. 1, p. 240.

47. Paul Radin, *Winnebago Culture as Described by Themselves,* p. 9.

48. *The Upanishads,* vol. 2, p. 74.

49. Leisegang, *Die Gnosis,* pp. 60ff.

50. *Indianermärchen aus Nordamerika,* pp. 313ff.

51. Cf. *The Upanishads,* vol. 1, pp. 35 and esp. 238.

52. Sir George Grey, *Polynesian Mythology and Ancient Traditional History of the New Zealanders* (London: Routledge and Sons, 1906), pp. 1ff. Also, E. S. Craighill, *Handy Polynesian Mythology* (Kraus Reprint, 1985), pp. 14ff.

53. Karl Preisendanz, *)Papyri Graecae Magicae,* vol. 2 (Stuttgart: Teubner, 1973), pp. 110ff.

54. Mentioned by Professor V. Maag in lectures on Primitive Religion. I owe this information to Dr. K. Wipf.

55. C. G. Jung, *Collected Works,* vol. 5, paras. 237–40.

56. Leisegang, *Die Gnosis,* pp. 68ff and 79ff.

57. *The Upanishads,* p. 238.

58. Franz Lukas, "Das Ei als kosmogonische Vorstellung," in *Zeitschrift des Vereins für Volkskunde,* 1894.

59. *The I Ching,* Richard Wilhelm translation rendered into English by Cary F. Baynes (Princeton: Princeton University Press, Bollingen Series XIX, 1970), hexagram 61.

60. Sir Arthur Grimble, *A Pattern of Islands* (London: John Murray, 1953), pp. 168ff.

61. Grey, *Polynesian Mythology,* pp. 1ff.

62. *Indianermärchen aus Nordamerika,* p. 401.

63. Paul Radin, *Winnebago Culture as Described by Themselves.*

64. *Tractatus Tripartitus* (Bern: Francke, 1973), part 1.

65. For more on this subject, see Marie-Louise von Franz, *Number and Time,* trans. Andrea Dykes (Evanston, Ill.: Northwestern University Press, 1974).

66. Wilhelm Capelle, *Die Vorsokratiker* (Leipzig: Kröner, 1935), p. 189.

67. C. G. Jung, *Collected Works,* vol. 17, para. 237.

68. Grey, *Polynesian Mythology.*

69. Post Wheeler, *The Sacred Scriptures of the Japanese* (New York: Henry Schuman, 1952), pp. 3ff.

70. Leisegang, *Die Gnosis,* pp. 281ff, and James M. Robinson, *The Nag Hammadi Library,* ed. E. J. Brill (New York: Leiden, 1988), pp. 60ff.

71. Capelle, *Die Vorsokratiker,* p. 392.

72. Ibid., pp. 474 and 475ff.

73. C. G. Jung, *Collected Works,* vol. 17, para. 250.

74. *The Secret of the Golden Flower,* trans. Richard Wilhelm with a commentary by C. G. Jung (New York: Causeway Books, 1975), p. 63.

75. Gerardus van der Leeuw, *Religion in Essence and Manifestation* (London: George Allen & Unwin, 1938).

76. C. G. Jung, *Collected Works,* vol. 8, para. 931.

77. Ibid.

78. Ibid., para. 870.

79. Marcellin Berthelot, *Collection des anciens Alchemistes grecs,* vol. 1, trans. M. L. von Franz (Paris, 1887), p. 289.

80. C. G. Jung, *Collected Works,* vol. 12, para. 338.

81. This book appeared in German as the third volume of Jung's *Mysterium Coniunctionis* but separately in English: Marie-Louise von Franz, *Aurora Consurgens* (Princeton: Princeton University Press, Bollingen Series LXXVII, 1966), pp. 121–31.

82. C. G. Jung, *Collected Works,* vol. 12, para. 347.

83. Ibid., vol. 14, paras. 686ff.

Index

Reality
    conscious awareness and, 10
    forms of, 117–118
    fourth dimension, 117–118
    immediate, 117
    ordering, relating to, 245
    the Beyond and, 81
    transcendental, 117
Rebuilding symbols, 14
Reflection, 230–231
Renewal, 329–330
Repression, 129
Resistance, therapy and, 160
Rituals of initiation, creation
    myths and, 1
Rump, Dr. Ariane, 142

Sacred Scriptures of the Japanese,
    The (Wheeler), 291–292
Sand wasp, 178–179
Schizophrenia
    creation myths and, 13
    creativity and, 281–282
    dissociation and, 310–311
    ego building and, 174
    muteness and, 282
    recovering from, 174–175
Schmidt, Max, 103–104
Secret of the Golden Flower, The,
    309–310
Self, dreams and, 172–174
Sensory perceptions, 57–58
Separation
    conscious realization and, 240
    creation and, 233
    discrimination and, 243
    number symbolism and,
        254–255
    twofold division motif and,
        240–242
Sexuality, creation myths and,
    181–182
Smith motif, 138

Spinning, 135–137
Spiritualism, dogmatism and,
    71–72
Stone, growing motif, 99–100
Suffocation, psychogenetic,
    243–244
Superego, 170
Synchronistic events, 358
Synchronistic phenomena, 322

Tapas (brooding), 204–206, 224,
    230
Tawiskaron, 92
Thought motif, 202–204
Thoughts, 200–201
Threshold difficulties, 84–88
Titans, 265–266
Tortoise, 99
    as spirit of earth, 66
Transference, 151
Trickster, 95
Twin birth, 91–92
Twin particles, 119–120
Two creators
    coexistence of, 107
    enmity between, 100
    hidden creator and, 103–104
    motif, 105–107
    opposites and, 110
    twin motif and, 116–117

Unconscious, 5–6
    creativity and, 51
    fantasy activity and, 136
    fear of, 193
    impulses and, 151–152
    motifs and, 87–88
    reality of, 86–87
    relativity of time, space, spatial,
        temporal, 83–84
Unconscious creator, 34–35
Uruboros motif, 2–4

Valentinus, 201–202
Vessel with breasts, 335–337

C. G. JUNG FOUNDATION BOOKS

---

*Published in association with Daimon Verlag, Einsiedeln, Switzerland.